IMAGES
of America

CABOT

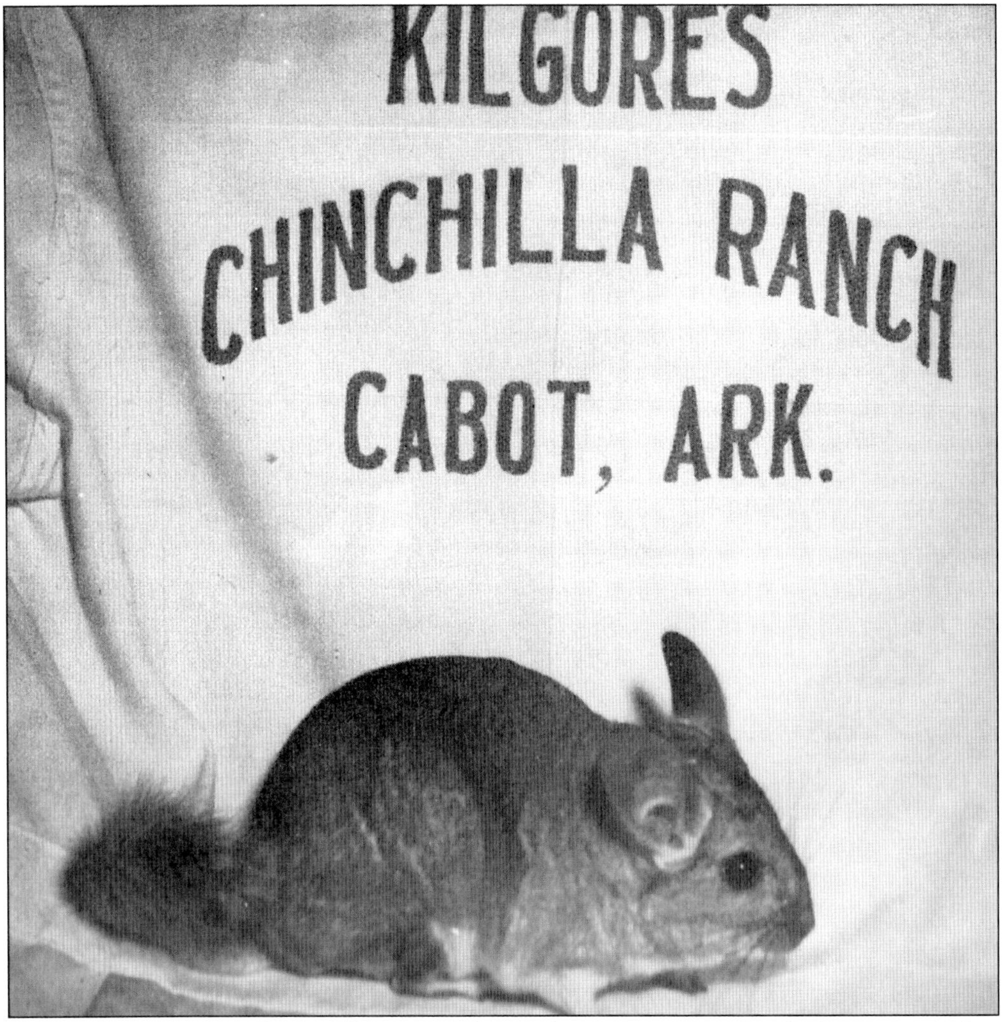

The chinchilla, a ground squirrel native to the Andes Mountains in South America, was first introduced into the United States in 1923. The first documented ranch was established in 1874 in Chile. By the mid-20th century, raising the furry rodent for their fur became a moneymaking venture for many in the United States. In the 1950s, Cabot was home to Kilgore's Chinchilla Ranch, whose owners claimed it as the state's first and largest. (Courtesy Museum of American History.)

On the Cover: When the court case of *Brown v. the Board of Education* of Topeka, Kansas, was handed down in 1954, schools across the United States began to lay the groundwork for the slow desegregation of public schools. Prior to the desegregation of Cabot Public Schools during the 1965–1966 school year, African American students were bused to McAlmont in nearby Pulaski County. During that year, six elementary students were enrolled. One of these first students, first-grader Curtis Smith, is seen here just to the right of his teacher, Alice Nipper. (Courtesy Jannice Ellis Horn.)

IMAGES
of America

CABOT

Mike Polston and
Debra Carrington Polston

ARCADIA
PUBLISHING

ISBN 978-0-7385-9102-5

Published by Arcadia Publishing
Charleston, South Carolina

Printed in the United States of America

Library of Congress Control Number: 2011936641

For all general information, please contact Arcadia Publishing:
Telephone 843-853-2070
Fax 843-853-0044
E-mail sales@arcadiapublishing.com
For customer service and orders:
Toll-Free 1-888-313-2665

Visit us on the Internet at www.arcadiapublishing.com

To our families for all their love and support in all our endeavors

Contents

ACKNOWLEDGMENTS

No one person can complete a project to document the history of a community. Any attempt to document the history of a community through photographs requires a considerable amount of assistance from community residents who, for years, have treasured such photographs. This project has been no different. Only the willingness of those people to share their photographs has made this project possible.

First and foremost, among those that we would like to thank is Bob Schelle. Over the years, Schelle has amassed a large collection of photographs of Cabot, collected from many local families. A large number of those photographs he collected are reproduced in this book. It is safe to say that without the use of his collection this book would never have been possible.

Another who made this project possible is Jannice Ellis Horn, who provided the image for the cover. Many photographs were used from a collection at the local Museum of American History, donated by Judy Lowman. Jack and Betty Carrington provided a number of images documenting the long legacy of Cabot High football. Jerry Sue Brewer Floyd also provided a number of early images. J.O. Isaac provided a number of important images documenting the restoration of Camp Nelson Confederate Cemetery. Special thanks go to Gene Ray, who provided images of longtime mayor Willie Ray. Also, a special thanks goes to Mike Calvert for technical support. All of these people, and many others unnamed, have made this project possible.

Unless otherwise noted, the photographs included in this book are from Bob Schelle.

INTRODUCTION

From humble beginnings in the 1870s, Cabot has become Lonoke County's largest city and one of the fastest growing cities in the entire state. Located along the railroad tracks, the city is home to a well-respected public school system that consists of the state's third largest district. As a bedroom community to Little Rock, the state capital, it continues to expand and as of 2011 has a population of over 25,000.

In the days before the founding of Cabot, the prominent town in the area was Austin, located about three miles east. The Butterfield Overland Express stage route ran through the area and at one time Austin was considered for the site of what would become Ouachita Baptist University. During the Civil War, a large camp of Confederate soldiers occupied the area for a few months in 1862. It was the construction of the railroad after the Civil War that resulted in the establishment of Cabot. Believed to have been named after a railroad employee, Cabot came into existence about 1873 as a railroad stop on the Cairo & Fulton Railroad. A post office was also established in that same year. By 1876, a statewide newspaper described the budding town "as a place of much promise, although in its swaddling clothes, and is ambitious to divide the trade with her elder sister, Austin." That division was short-lived. Austin, having been bypassed by the railroad, declined, while Cabot saw a burst of growth.

In less than 20 years, a respectable business district grew along the train tracks, and on November 9, 1891, the city was incorporated. At the beginning of the 20th century, the population topped 300. The city continued to experience steady growth in both business and residential areas. Much of that growth was based on the area farmers, who shipped their crops by rail and patronized the local businesses. By the 1920s, a city generator provided electricity to residents, and communication was enhanced by telephone service. Water, which in the early days had been supplied by private wells and a downtown cistern, was replaced by city water in the 1930s.

During the 1940s, many of the local men served in the armed forces while many of the women supported the war effort by working in the Arkansas Ordnance Plant, located in nearby Jacksonville. The plant brought many people to Cabot and, at its peak, employed over 14,000. By 1950, the city population had increased by almost 50 percent.

Improvements made to Highway 67, connecting to Little Rock, and the opening of the nearby Little Rock Air Force Base in 1955 contributed to rapid growth. By the late 1960s and early 1970s, Cabot was quickly becoming a bedroom community, with many residents commuting by car to work in Little Rock or at the air base. Within 15 years of the opening of the base, the population had more than doubled to almost 3,000. Just as it seemed that nothing could hamper the progress, tragedy hit the town.

In the early afternoon of March 29, 1976, a killer tornado tore a path through the downtown area. Before the storm lifted into the sky, millions of dollars of damage and five dead were left behind. Almost immediately, the town leaders, led by Mayor Willie Ray, began cleanup and plans for rebuilding the city. Soon, the debris was removed and construction was begun to replace what had been destroyed. In 1978, CabotFest, a citywide festival celebrating the city's recovery, was initiated.

Following the recovery from the tornado, the city began a steady growth that continues to this day. While the downtown business district recovered, many new businesses began to develop along the north and south ends of Highway 89. Much of this new growth was prompted by the completion of the nearby four-lane Highway 167. Since its completion, many additional businesses have opened close to it at exit 16 near Highway 321. A steady growth in population resulted in an increase from approximately 3,000 in 1970 to over 25,000 by 2010. The rapid growth makes Cabot the third fastest growing city per capita in the state. A quality public school system, which is the third largest in Arkansas, has also been a major factor in attracting additional citizens. In 2009, one online business publication described Cabot as Arkansas's "boomtown." There seems to be no end in sight to the city's growth and development.

One

EARLY CABOT

Since its founding as a railroad water stop in 1873, Cabot has become one of the fastest growing communities in the state of Arkansas. Within 10 years of its incorporation on November 9, 1891, a population of approximately 300 supported a substantial business district, which included six general stores, among others. During its first 50 years, many of the wooden store buildings were replaced by more fire-resistant brick structures. An impressive brick school building was also constructed in 1912 and remained in use until the early 1970s. During these early years, the town experienced economic ups and downs but through them all continued to grow and prosper. Coming out of World War I, the farming community was poised for major growth and development.

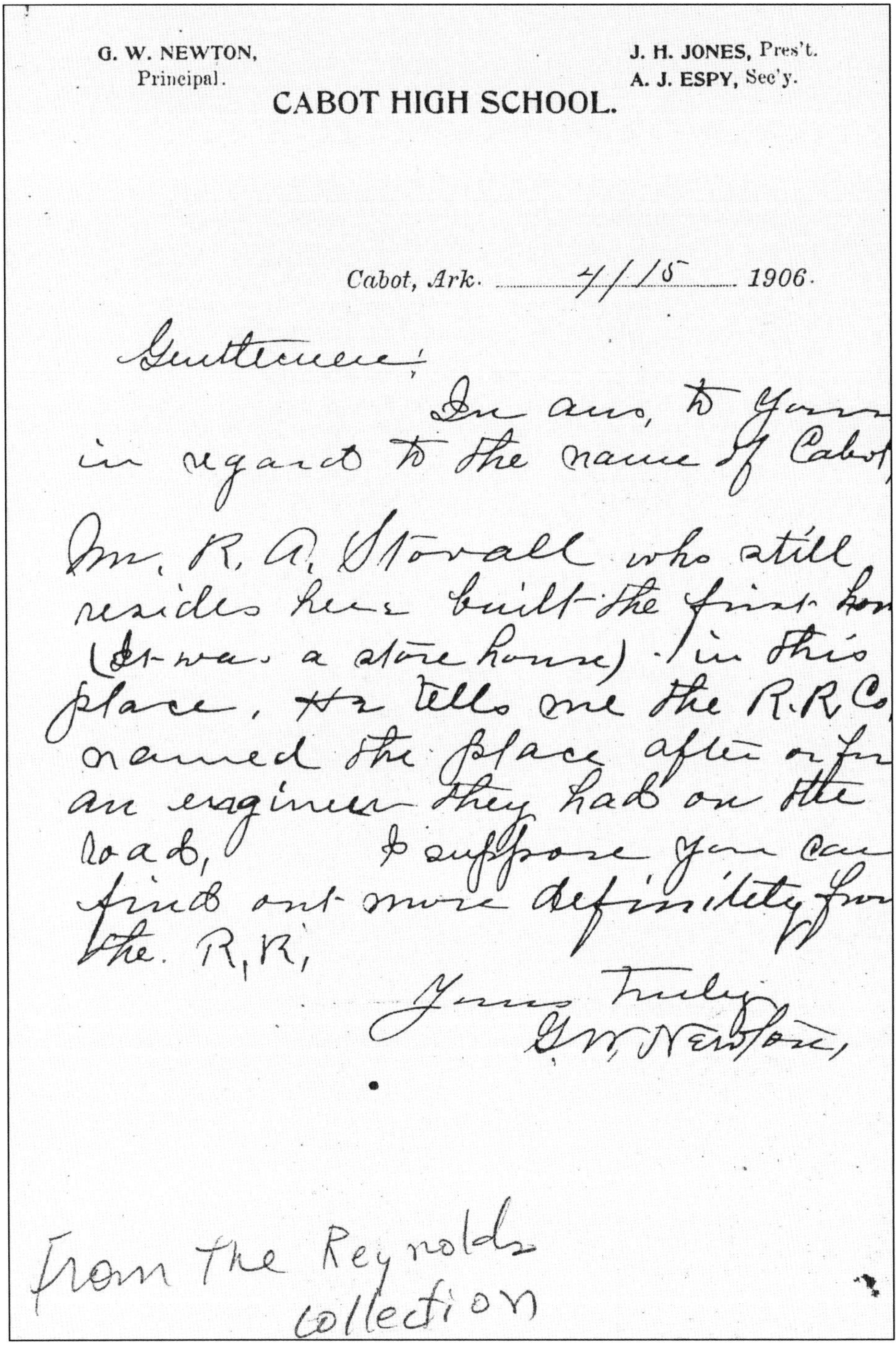

G. W. NEWTON,
Principal.

J. H. JONES, Pres't.
A. J. ESPY, Sec'y.

CABOT HIGH SCHOOL.

Cabot, Ark. 4/15 1906.

Gentlemen;

In ans. to your
in regard to the name of Cabot,

Mr. R. A. Stovall who still
resides here built the first house
(It was a store house) in this
place. He tells me the R.R. Co.
named the place after or for
an engineer they had on the
road. I suppose you can
find out more definitely from
the R.R.

Yours Truly,
G.W. Newton.

From the Reynolds
collection

Factual information as to the origin of the name Cabot is elusive. The most common story as related in this 1906 letter written by high school principal G.W. Newton is that the town was named after a railroad worker. As of yet, this letter, housed in the collection of the Arkansas History Commission, is the only documentary evidence to be found. (Courtesy Museum of Natural History.)

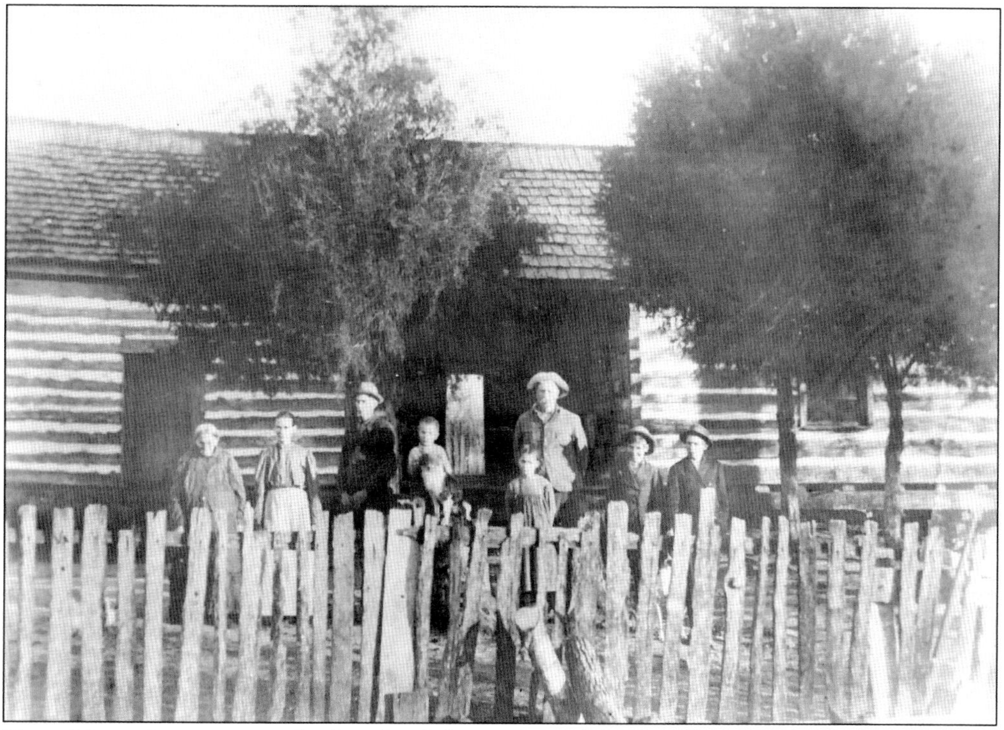

One of the earliest structures built in the Cabot area was this typical log cabin hand built by Sidney C. Pickard in the 1850s. Over the years, the home was enlarged. The Pickard family is shown here about 1910 with Mrs. Sidney C. Pickard, wife of the original builder, shown at the far left.

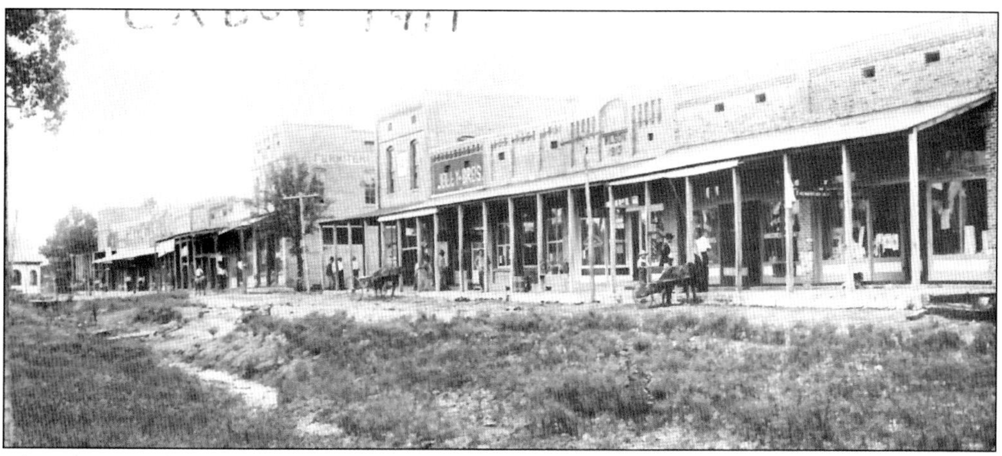

This photograph, taken some 22 years after the city was incorporated on November 9, 1891, is believed to be the oldest known photograph of the downtown area. When it was taken in 1913, less than 500 citizens lived there. Several of these buildings remain today, though covered by a modern facade.

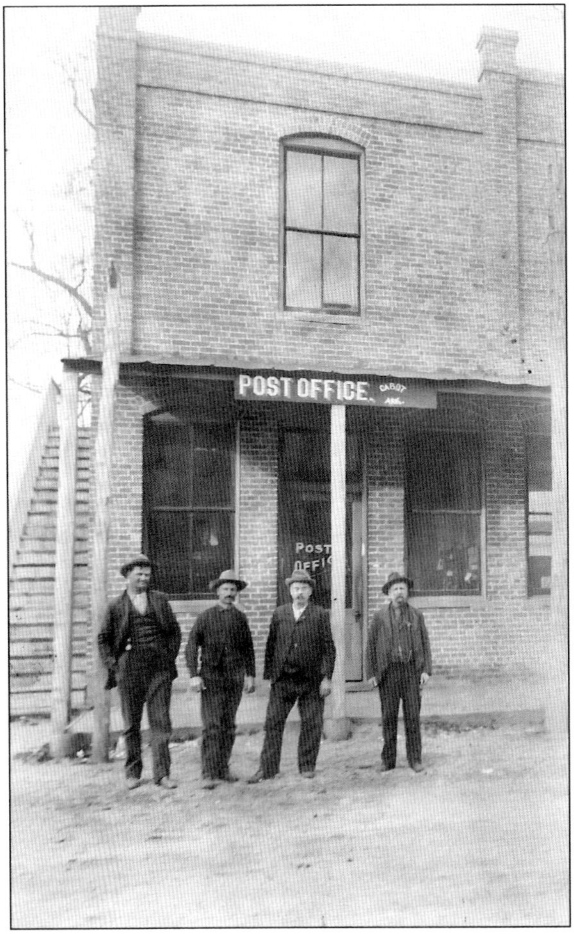

Most early town post offices were located in a local store or the postmaster's home. The Cabot Post Office was established in 1873. By the early 20th century, it was housed in a room on the backside of the Bank of Cabot.

An early-1900s promotional program by local businessmen, called Trade Days, was designed to attract potential customers to downtown stores. Tickets for a chance to win donated merchandise were distributed to all those attending the crowd-pleasing festivities.

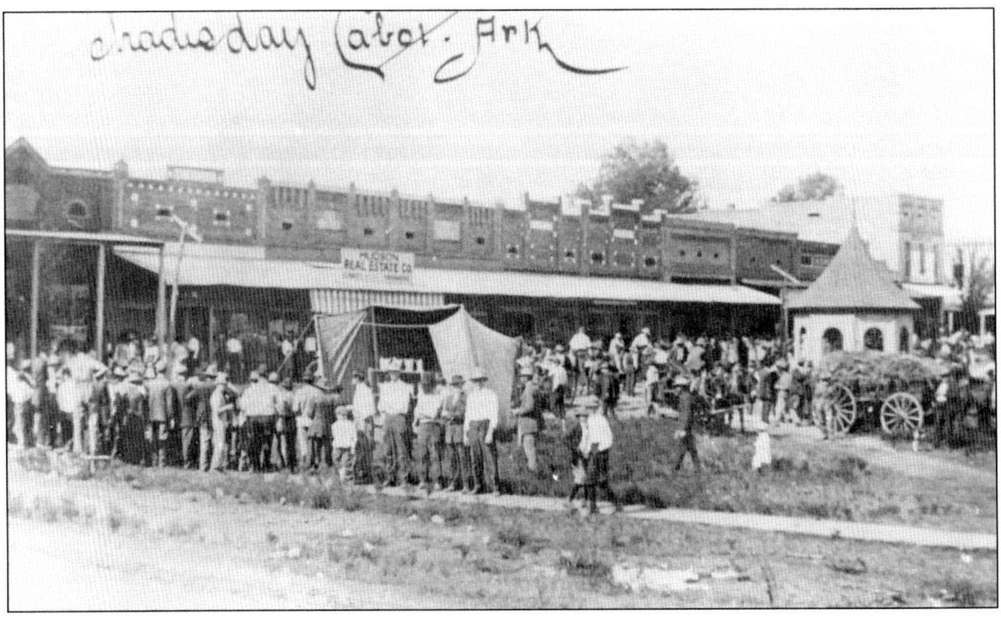

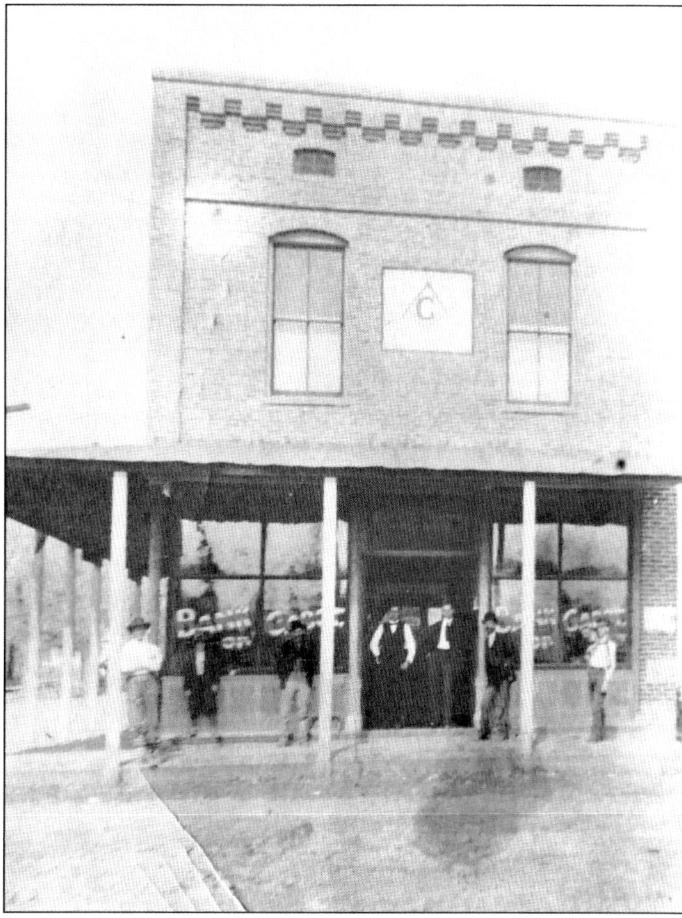

The first financial institution, the Bank of Cabot, opened in 1903 with a capital stock of $50,000. During its early years, it occupied this substantial brick building on First Street. The local Masons met on the second floor, and the post office occupied a room in the back. By the late 20th century, the bank's location had changed as well as the name—first to Community Bank and later Centennial Bank.

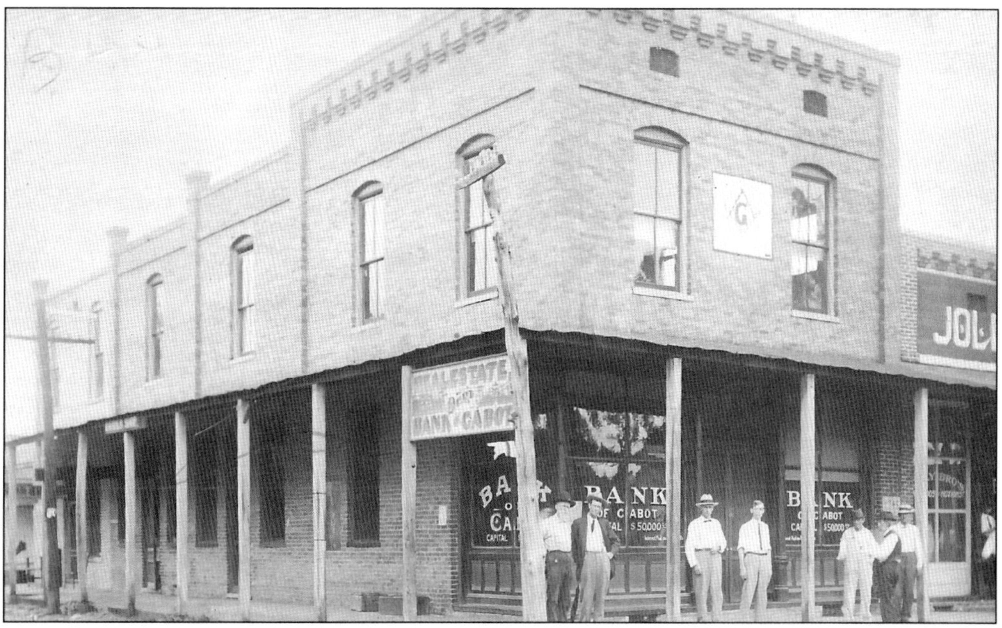

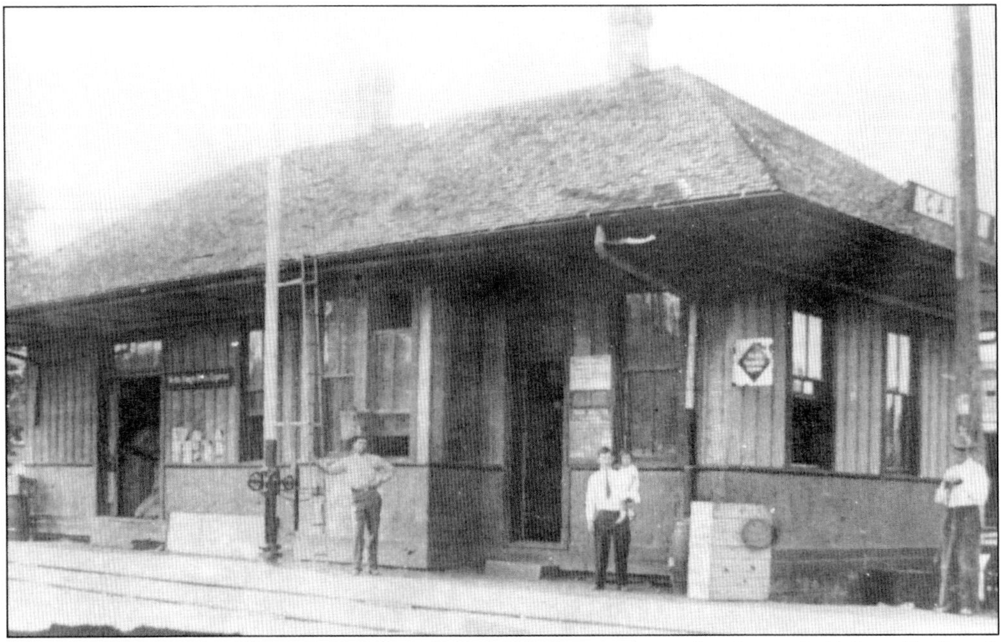

About 1873, the city of Cabot was founded as a fuel stop along the Cairo & Fulton Railroad. Sometime after its founding, a typical small frame depot was built alongside the tracks. By the 1930s, the station had been enlarged and modified into the structure shown here.

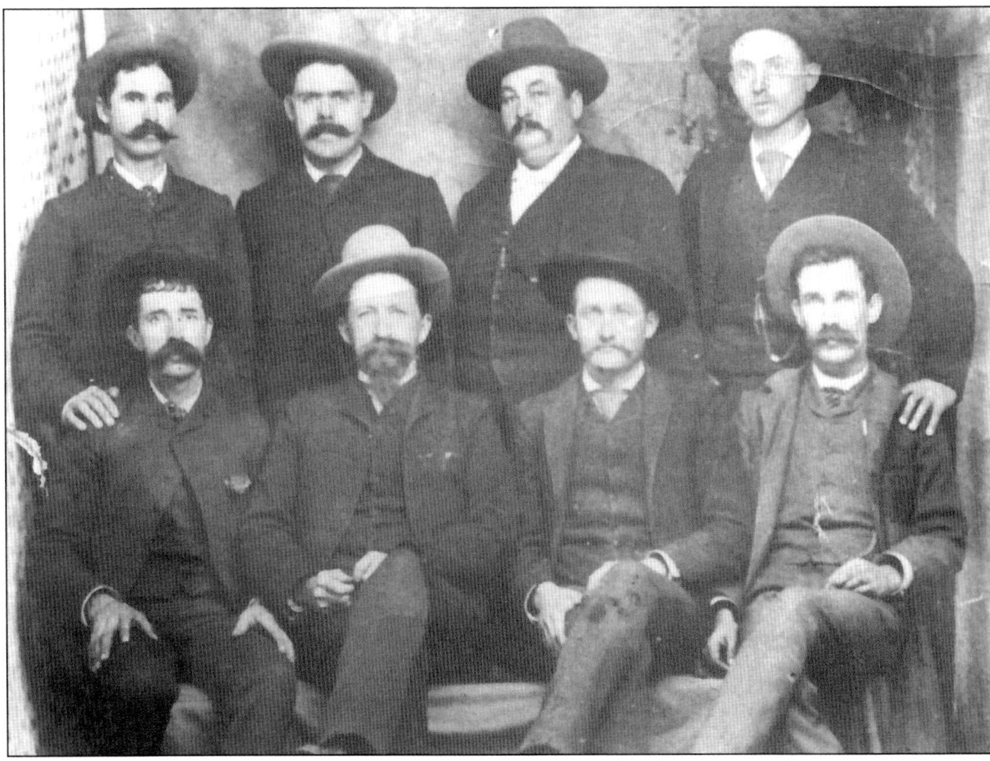

Since its founding, city operations have been carried out under the mayor and city council system. Shown here are unidentified members of an early city council.

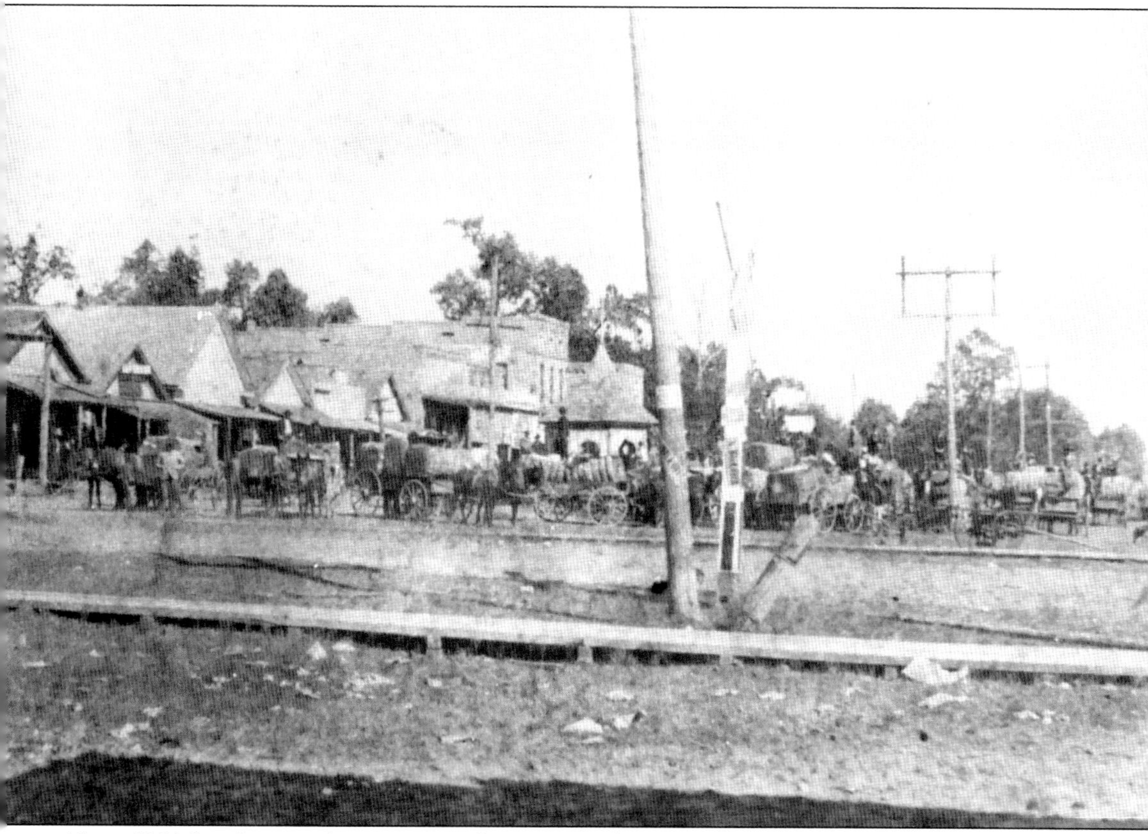

About 1904, local cotton farmers are in the process of lining up their loaded wagons, anticipating the arrival of the train to carry their year's work to world markets. Many of the wooden buildings, destroyed by fire, were replaced by more substantial brick structures. One of several boardwalks to enable pedestrians to navigate the muddy streets can be seen just in front of the wagons.

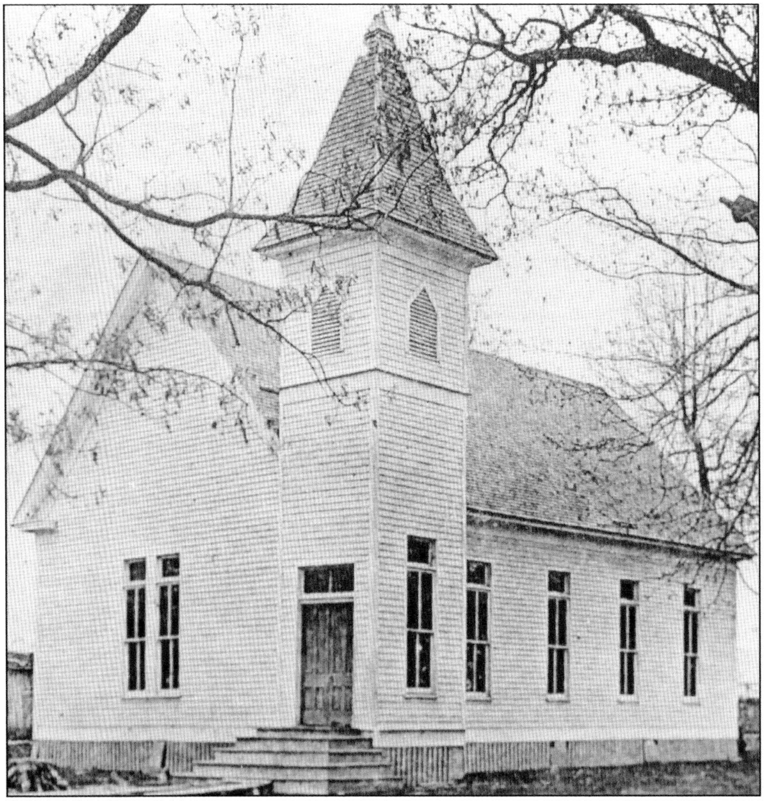

Modern-day Cabot is home to a number of churches. The first to be located within the city was First Baptist Church. Church members constructed this building, which was located at the site of the current structure, about 1885.

Around 1916, the Baptist congregation moved into this impressive brick building. In 1987, after almost 80 years of service, it was razed to make way for the construction of an education building.

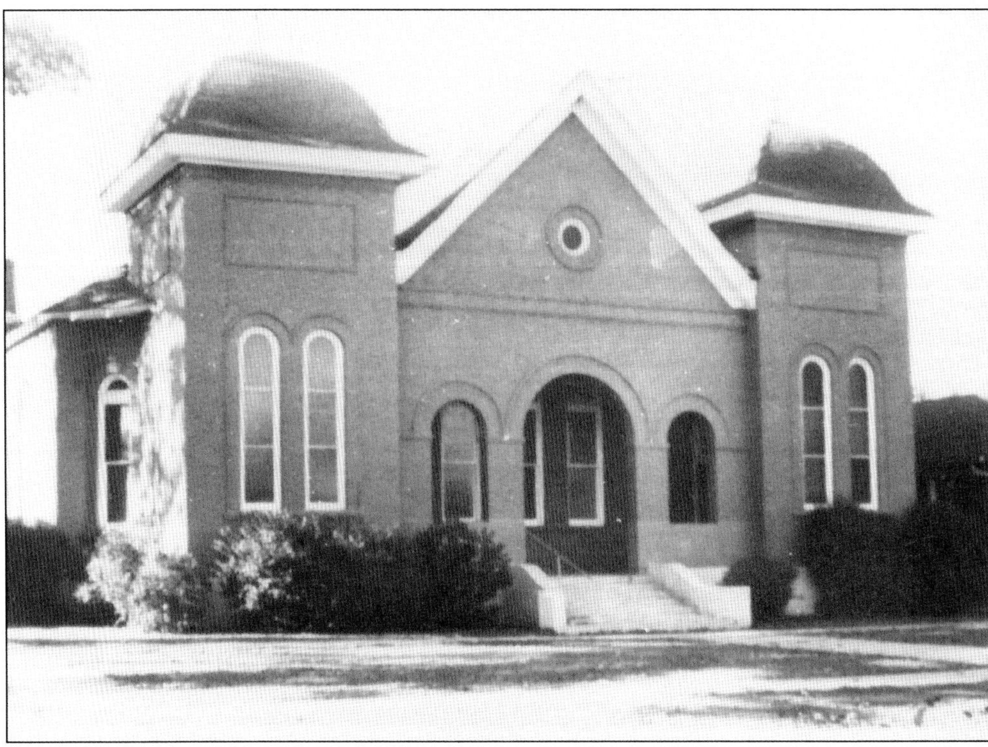

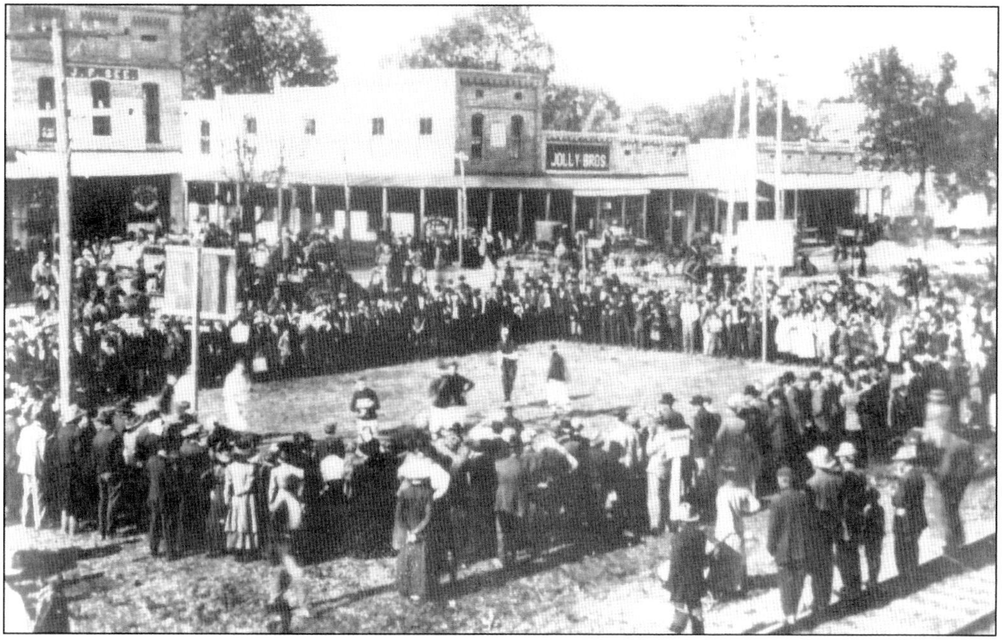

The downtown area has seen many activities over the years. In this early-1900s photograph, a large crowd has gathered to observe what some believe to be a basketball game, or perhaps a boxing match. In later days, the area became the center point for CabotFest activities.

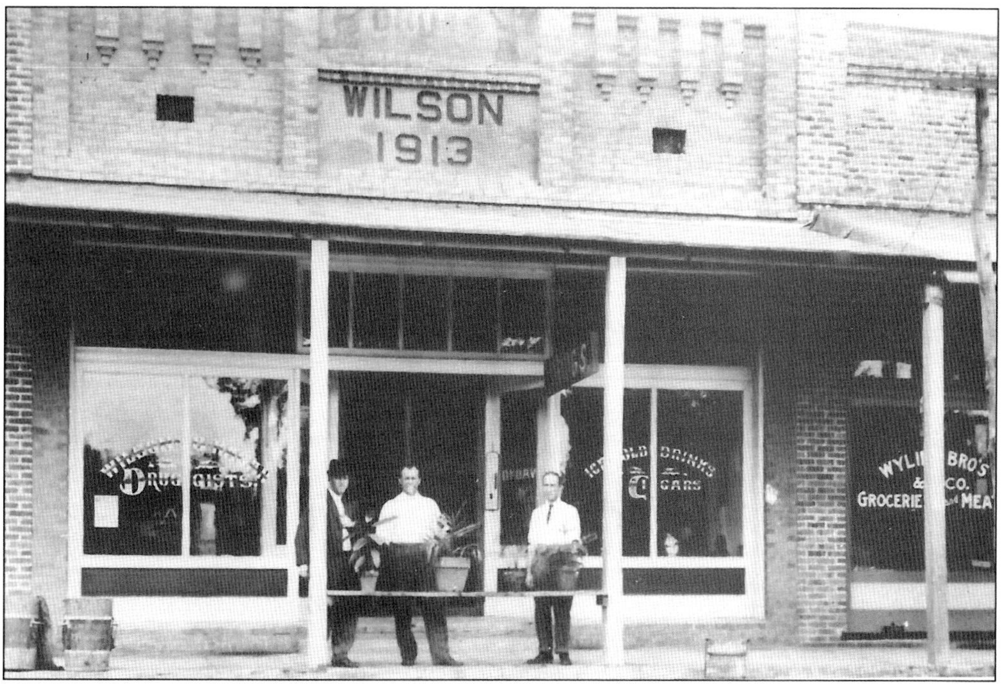

One of the early store buildings constructed on North First Street was a structure known as the Wilson Building. Built in 1913, the brick structure housed an important city business, Wilson and Hagan Drug Store. The building and store occupied the site of the current city courts structure.

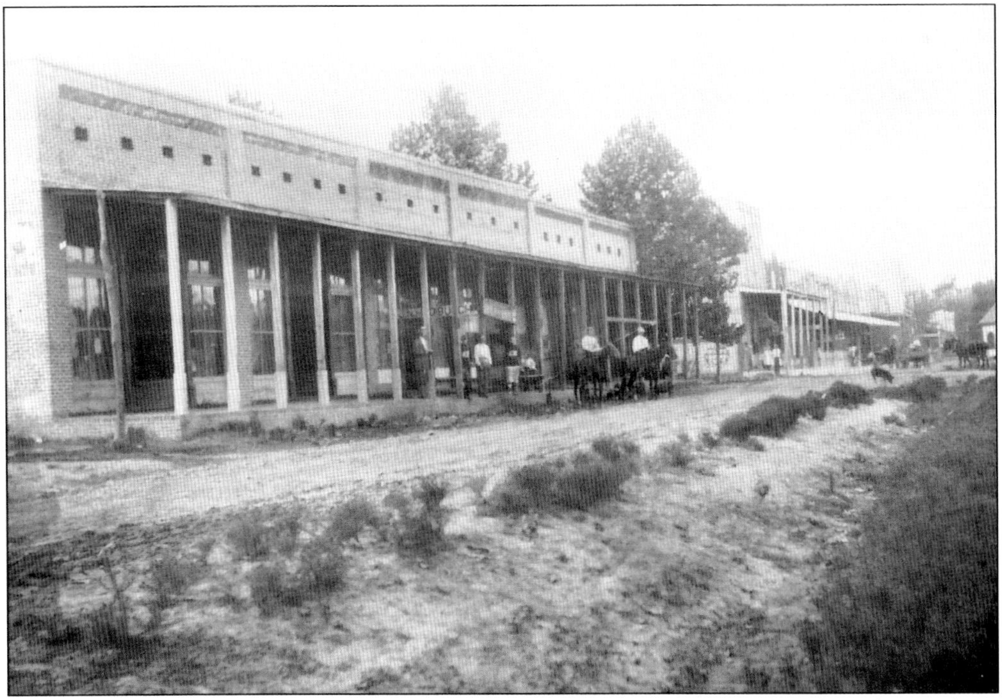

By the early 1900s, the downtown business district alongside the railroad tracks, with its many brick buildings, was a major part of the growing community. All of these buildings were eventually demolished.

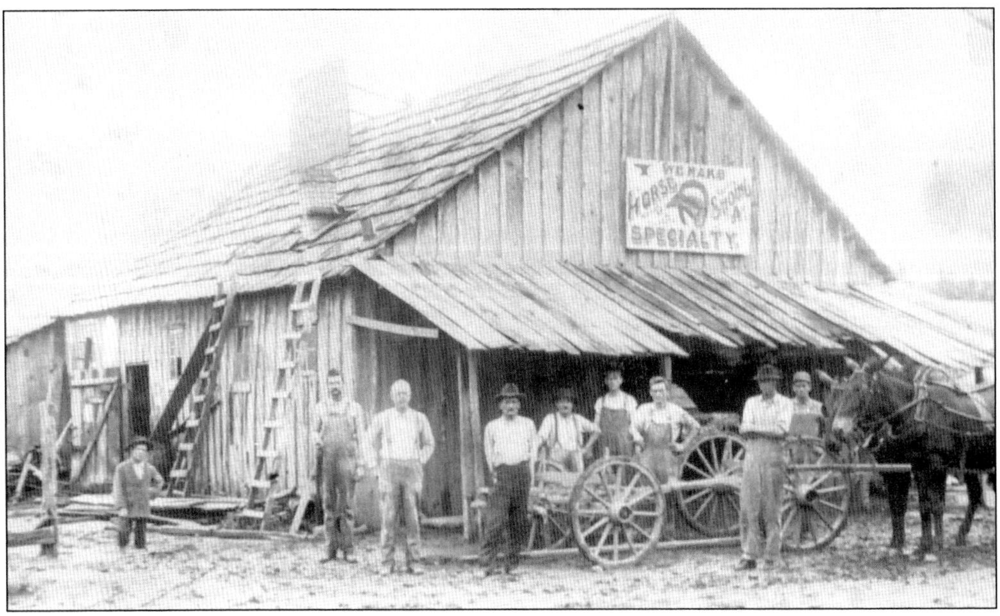

During the 19th century and much of the early 20th century, a blacksmith and wagon repair shop was essential to a growing farm community. The horse and wagon were major components for both trade and transportation. One such shop, the Fox Edwards Wagon Yard, was located in the downtown business district where Wood's Feed Store now operates.

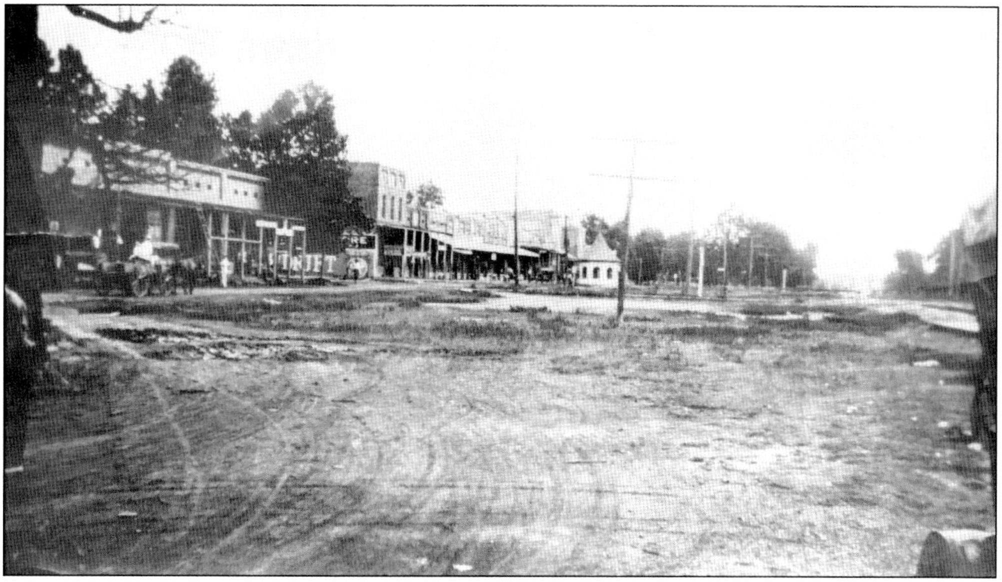

Problems with flooding in the low-lying areas of downtown can be seen in this early image. A large pool of water surrounds much of the gazebo covering the town cistern. Just behind this structure is where present-day Highway 89 crosses the railroad tracks.

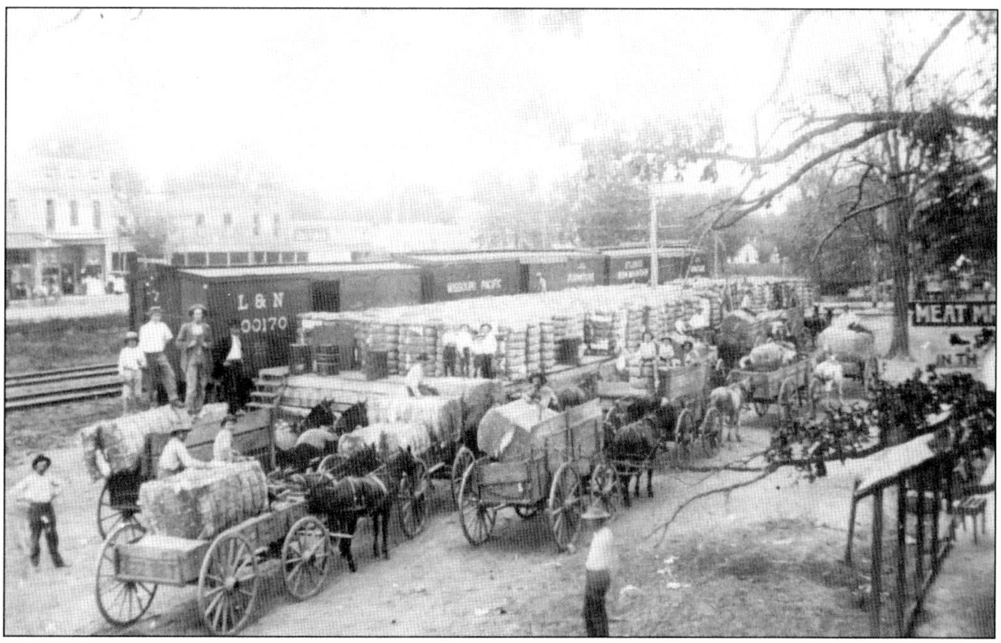

In its early days, Cabot was a bustling farming community with the railroad serving as the means of shipping crops. Cotton, which is rarely grown in the area today, was a major cash crop before the Great Depression. Here, the railroad tracks are lined with wagons loaded with hundreds of bales of local cotton awaiting shipment by rail to markets throughout the United States.

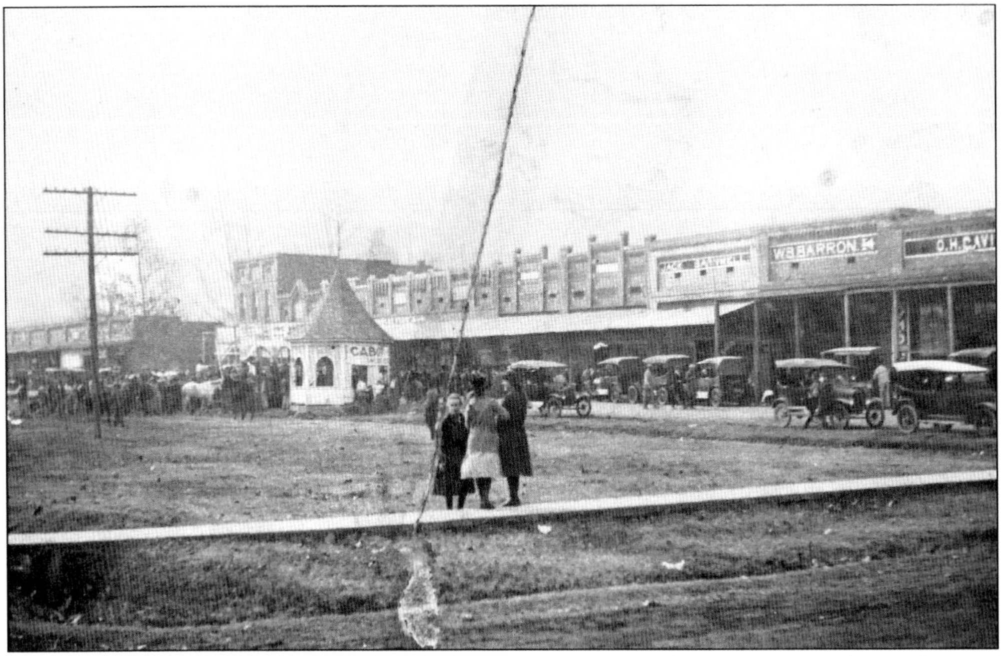

Long before a city water system was installed, water was obtained by city residents from individual wells. In downtown Cabot, water for public use came from a city cistern located on First Street near the main businesses. The Cabot cistern is shown here, covered with a decorative gazebo, in the early 20th century.

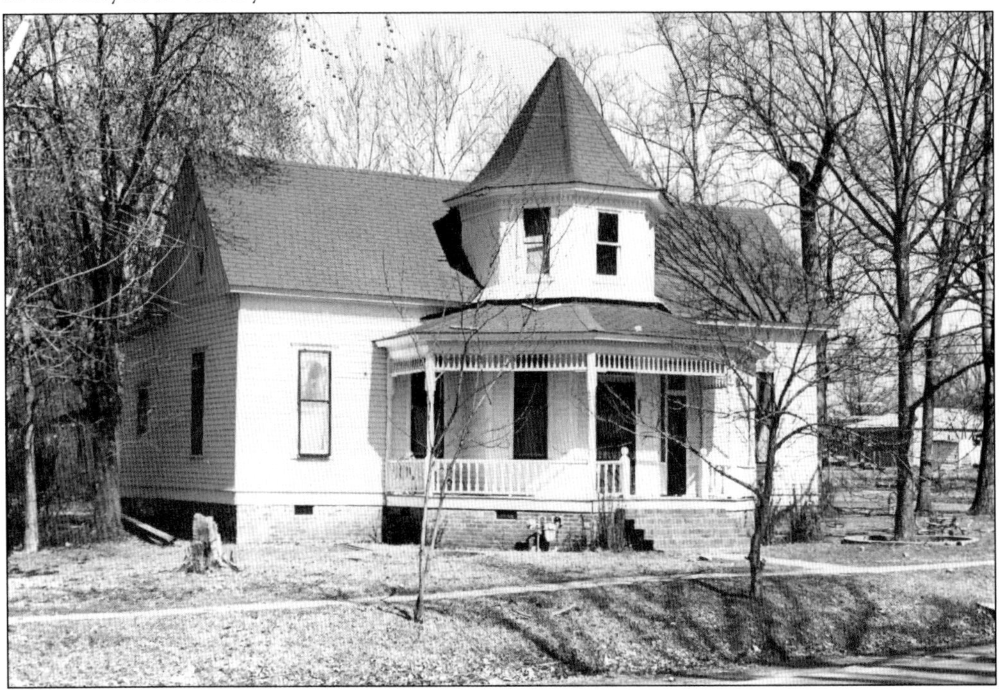

The Ray House, located on Main Street, was one of the few Victorian houses remaining by the late 20th century. Constructed by the early 1900s, it once served as a Baptist parsonage and later may have been a funeral home. The house was destroyed by fire.

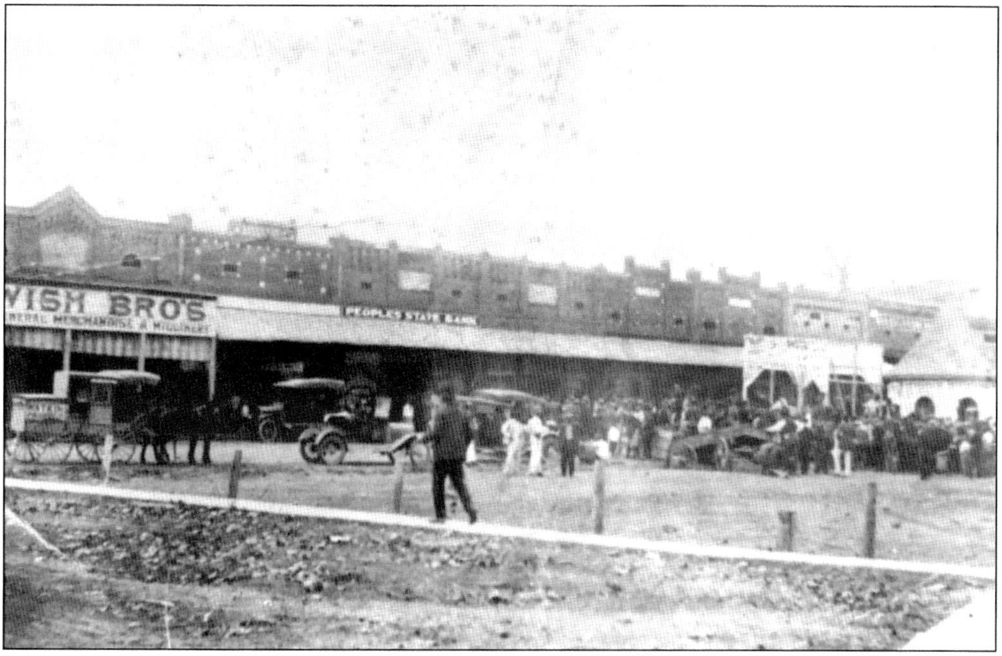

A large crowd gathers near the downtown gazebo-covered town cistern, not far from some of the town's first cars parked along First Street. Located in the center is the Peoples Bank, founded in 1916; the financial institution merged with the Bank of Cabot in 1926.

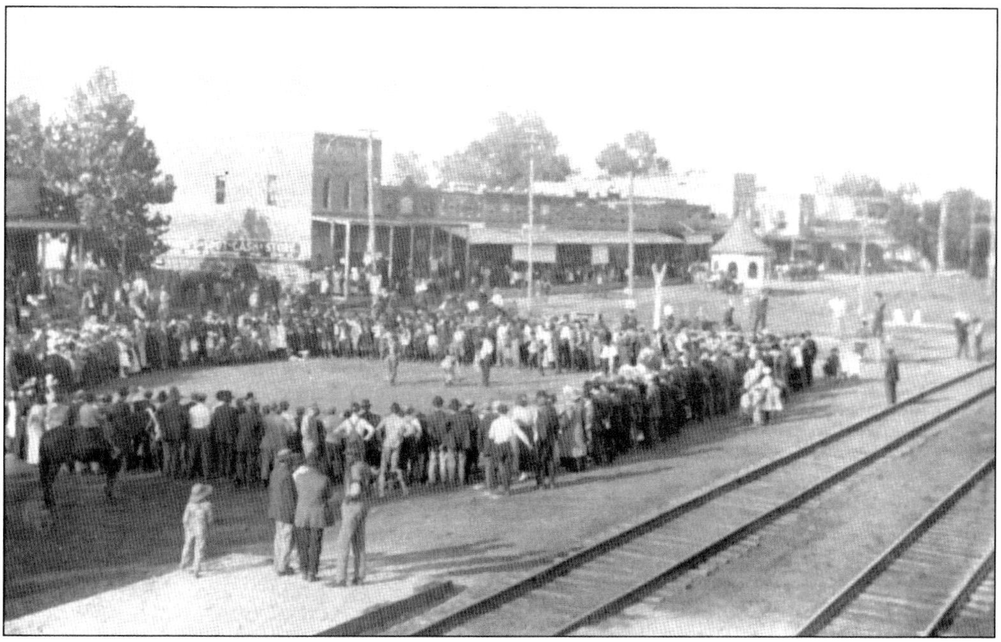

These citizens are apparently engaged in a competitive game of croquet. The game, which was introduced into the United States during the early 19th century, experienced a decline by the end of the century but saw a reemergence about the time this photograph was taken in the early 1900s.

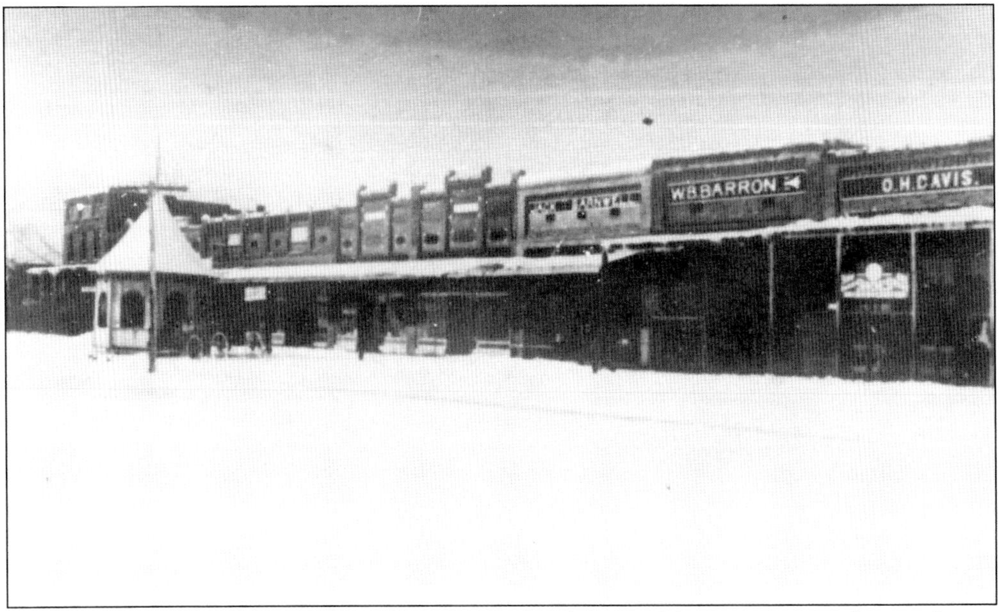

During the winter of 1917–1918, Arkansas experienced some of the worst accumulation of snow in the state's history. Some areas received more than 60 inches during the season. It is believed that this photograph documents downtown during that terrible winter season.

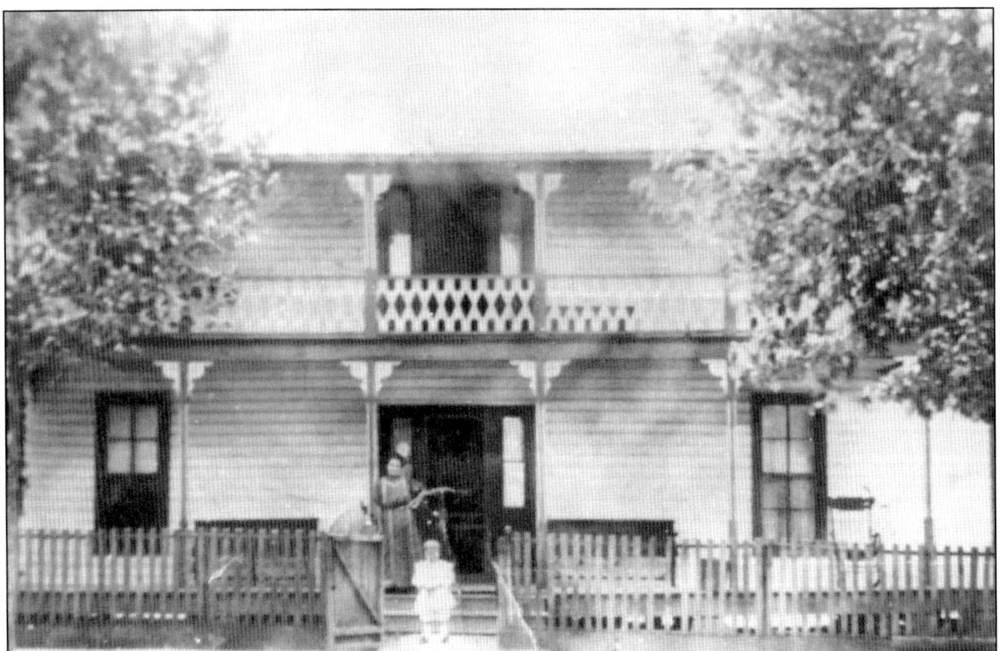

Long before chain motels became commonplace, visitors to Cabot stayed at boardinghouses, such as the Traveling Man's Hotel, located on Main Street. Jennie Howell and Reymon Glover are standing at the doorway. The building was destroyed by fire in 1968.

Two

1920s, 1930s, and 1940s

As the United States and Arkansas emerged from World War I, Cabot, now supporting a population of almost 450 residents, experienced steady growth. Within the next few years, electricity came to the city in the form of a generator that operated approximately four hours a day. Soon, a telephone system and city water were also installed. Its status as a railroad shipping station was secured with the increase in area farm production, but just as the rest of the nation, the community was hit hard by the Great Depression before recovery came in the 1940s. Many local men served in the armed forces during World War II, and the area economy slowly recovered, due partly to jobs at the nearby Arkansas Ordnance Plant. The city prospered, and by 1950, the population had grown to almost 1,200.

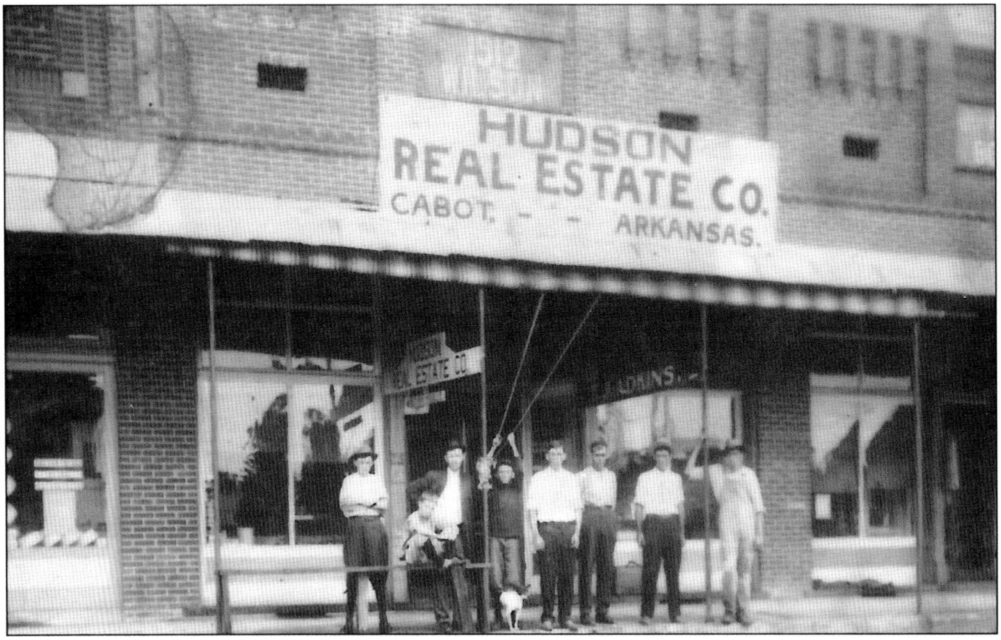

Cabot is one of the fastest growing towns in Arkansas, with real estate offices dotting the modern landscape. One of the early-20th-century real estate offices was the Hudson Real Estate Company located in downtown.

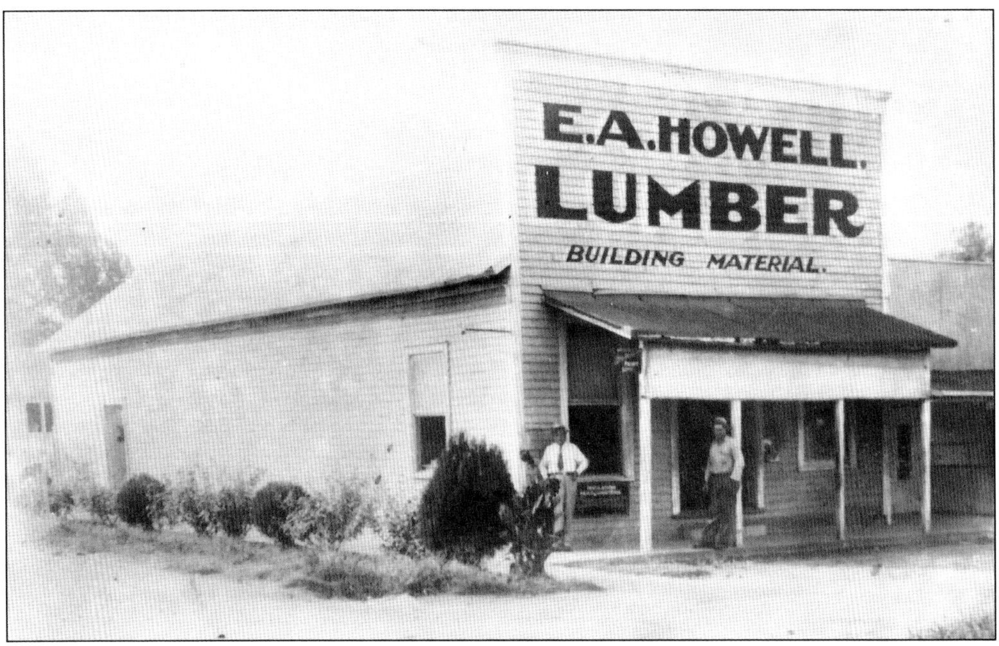

E.A. Howell provided lumber and building materials necessary for the growth of Cabot. Shown here are the Howell brothers, Emmett (left) and G.D.

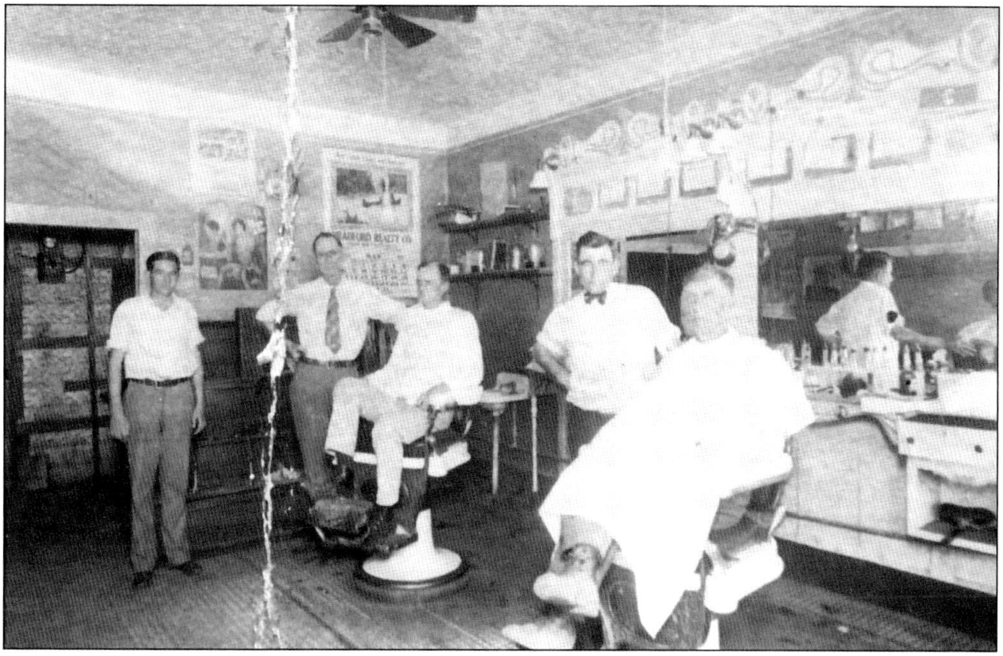

For most towns, the city barbershop remains a traditional gathering place for local males to discuss current affairs. Just behind the two men standing near the shop's second barber chair is also the typical shoeshine stand. While in most modern shops the stand has long disappeared, it was an all-important fixture when this photograph was taken in the 1920s.

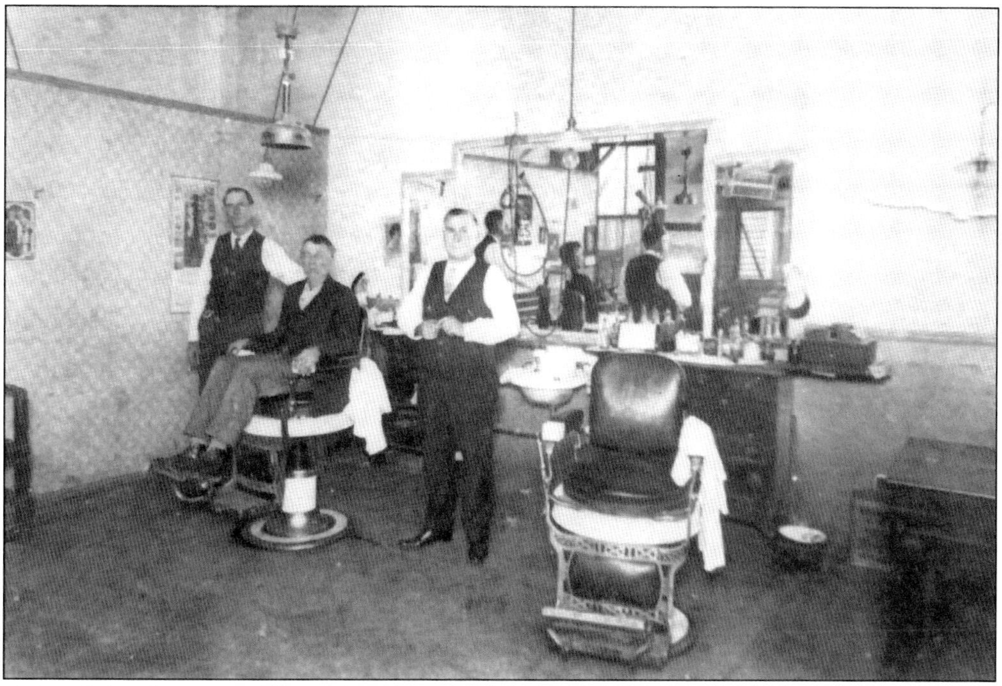

Today, Cabot has several hair salons but is still home to at least one traditional barbershop. In this photograph are, from left to right, owner William Burks, Dave Orr, and prominent local doctor F.E. Utley.

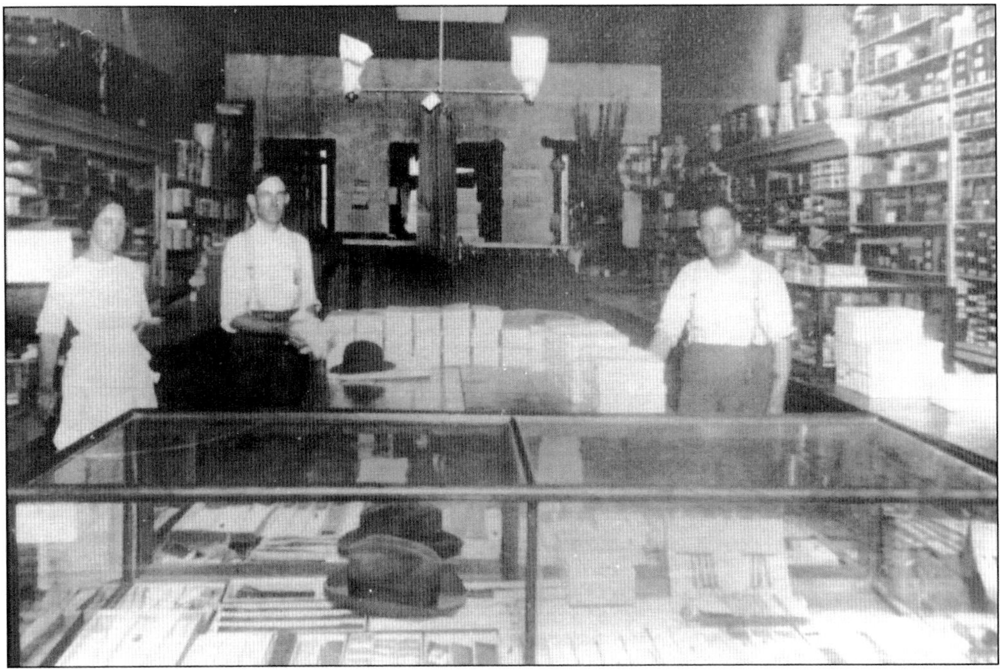

Among the several mercantile/department stores established in early Cabot, See's was perhaps the most prominent. Many items that were not produced at home could be purchased from the store's well-stocked shelves. The building housing the store was destroyed in the 1976 tornado.

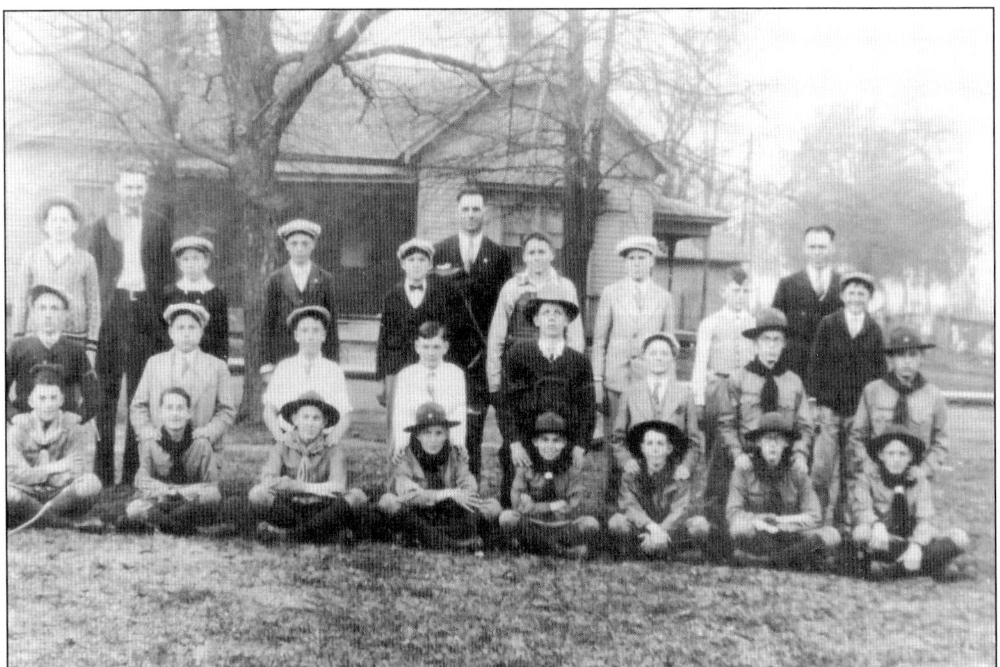

The Boy Scouts of America, which was patterned on a similar British organization, was formed in the United States in 1910. Approximately 26 years later, the first troop in Cabot, shown here, was organized. The Scouts remain an active organization in the community.

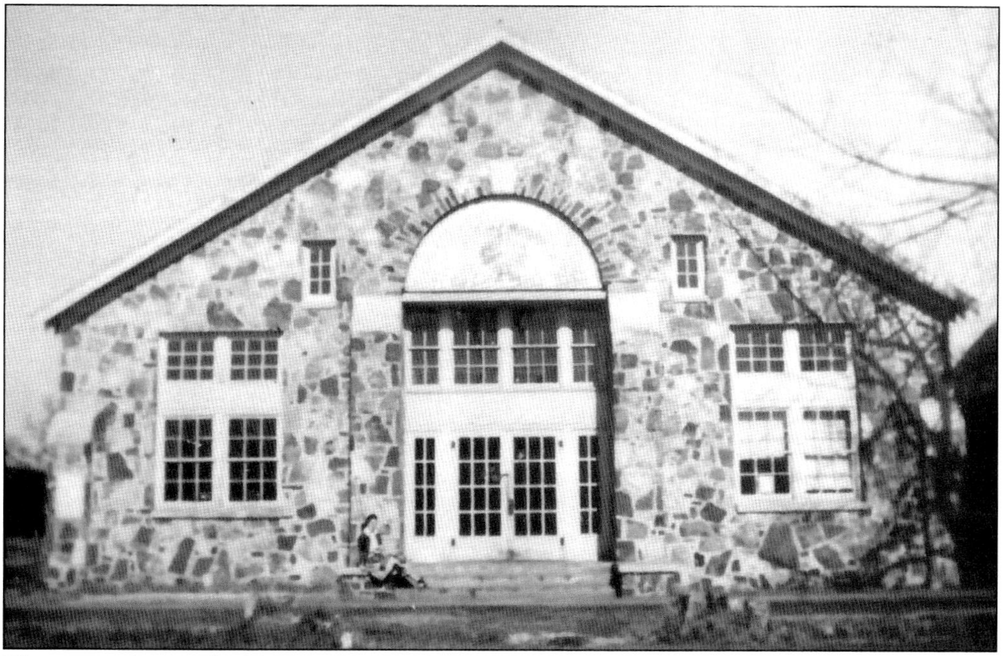

This natural stone building constructed in the 1930s under the direction of the Civil Works Administration, a New Deal program, served many purposes over the years, such as a veterans' meeting hall, gym, library, mattress factory, and a movie theater. When it was destroyed by fire in 1980, it was home to the Cabot Lumber Yard.

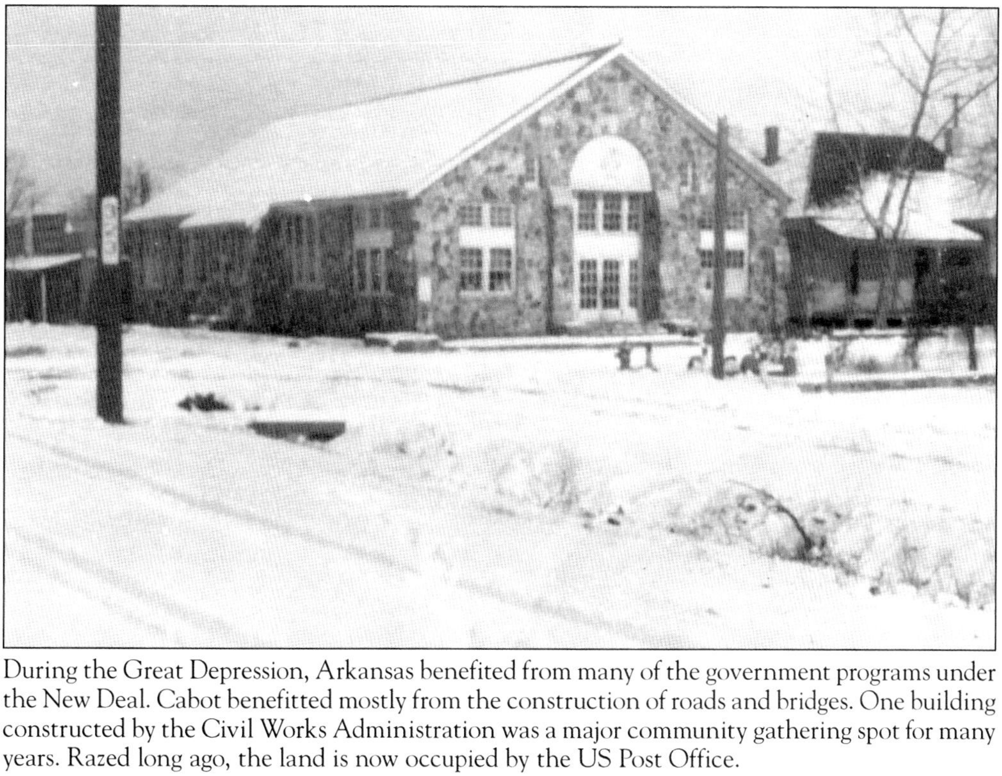

During the Great Depression, Arkansas benefited from many of the government programs under the New Deal. Cabot benefitted mostly from the construction of roads and bridges. One building constructed by the Civil Works Administration was a major community gathering spot for many years. Razed long ago, the land is now occupied by the US Post Office.

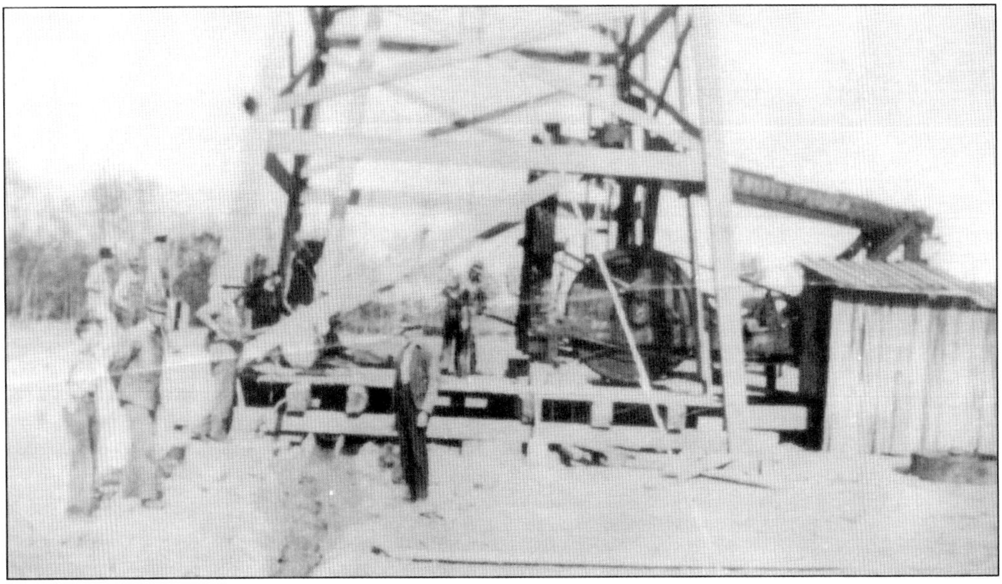

High hopes of prosperity hit the town in the midst of the Great Depression. During the drilling of a new city water well, a pool of natural gas was exposed under the city. Soon, a well, photographed here, was sunk in downtown with the expectation of a gusher. Though there was evidence of oil, unfortunately, no such wealth ever came from the ground.

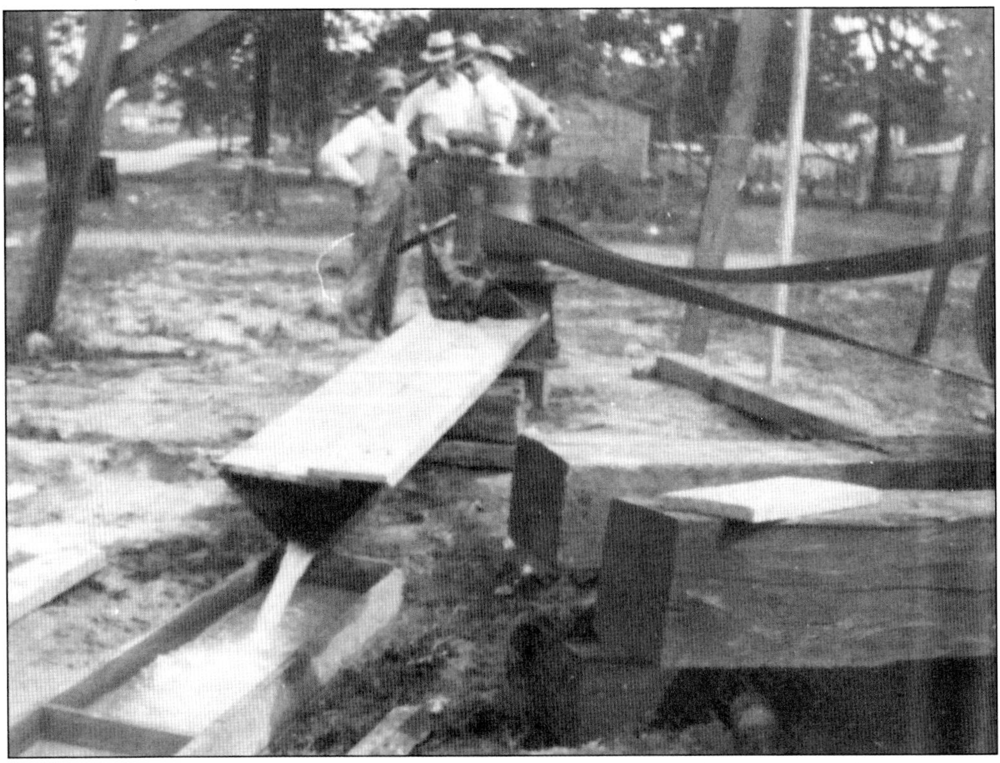

Many local citizens invested money in the Cabot Drilling Club. Though the well was sunk to over 1,400 feet, only oil-bearing sand was discovered. A small group of those investors watch in eager anticipation for the appearance of black gold.

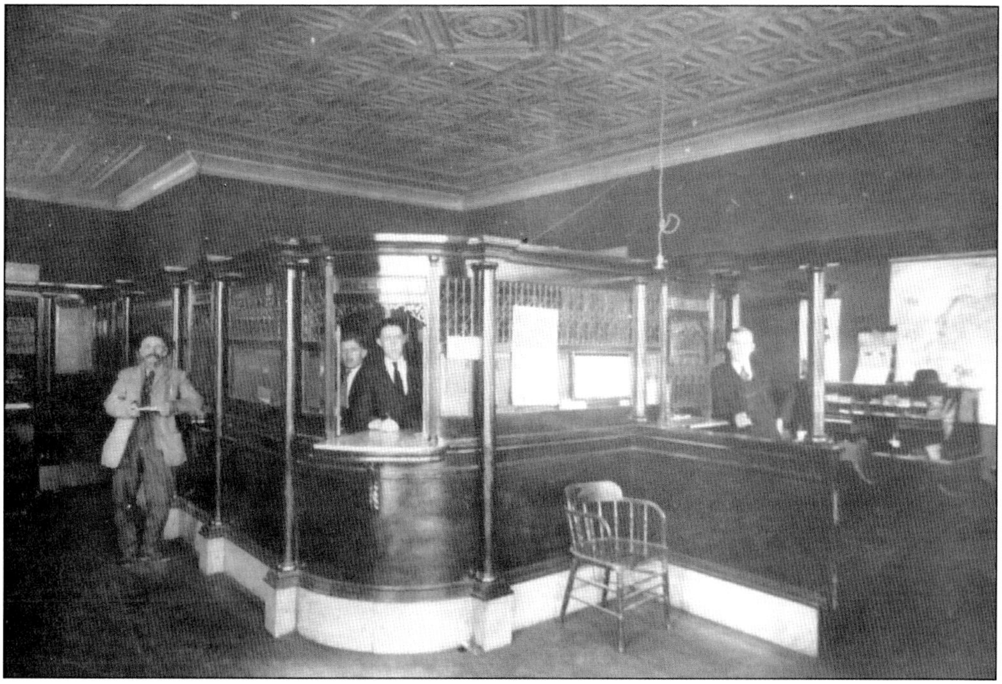

The early-20th-century ornate interior of the Bank of Cabot was typical of banks throughout the country. Employee O.H. Beasley is shown standing alone inside the teller cage at right with Hagen Shives and Fred Garlington in the center. Dandy Smith poses outside ready to conduct business.

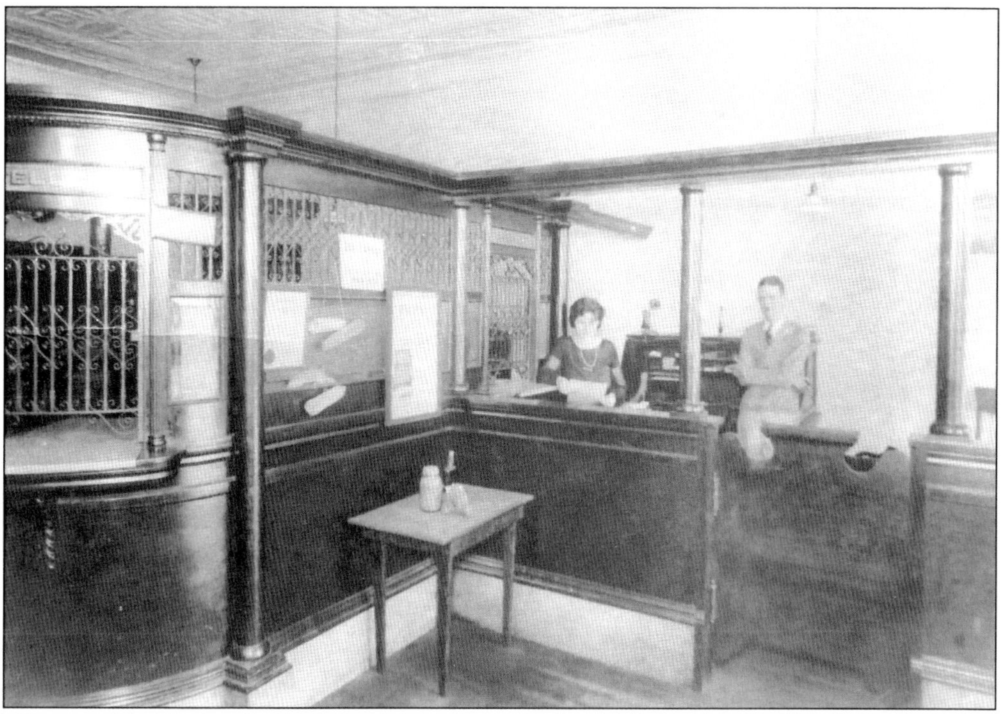

The interior of the Bank of Cabot in the 1930s, with its caged tellers, was typical of banks across the United States. Standing behind the wall is Jewell Leggett and bank president Marvin Park.

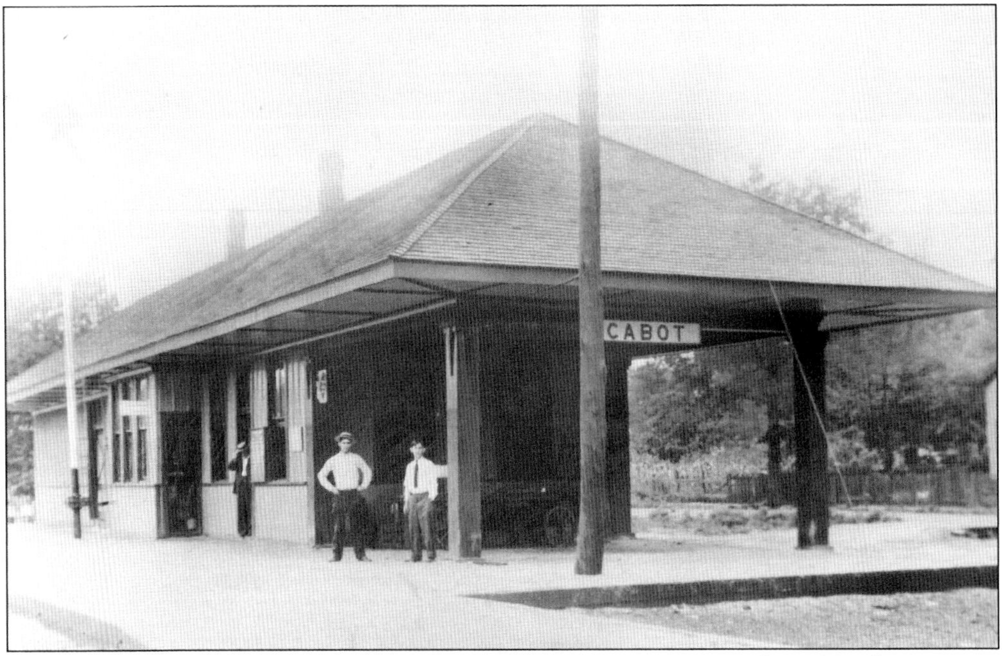

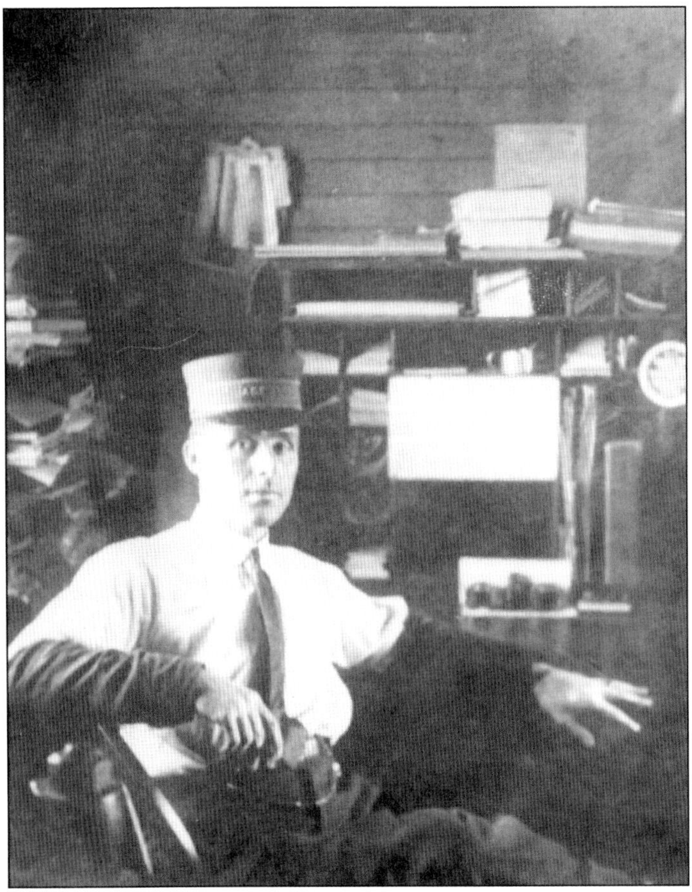

By the 1930s, the city population was approaching 700. The city's founding on the railroad was a major attraction to many people and businesses. This factor made the local train depot an important location. Each day large amounts of goods were delivered to and shipped out of the depot. Until the 1960s, many passengers also passed through the facility.

The town's existence is due to the construction of the railroad in the 1870s. Agents who conducted railroad business at the local depot were vital to the success of the company. One such unidentified Cabot agent is shown here in this early photograph.

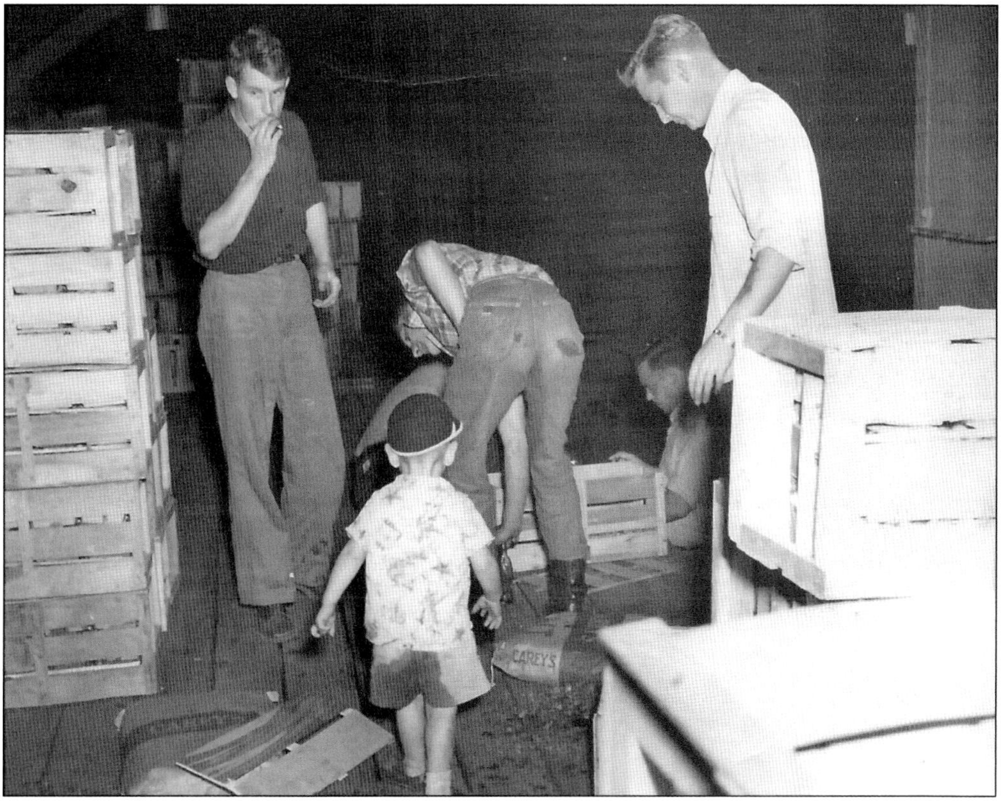

Strawberries have been commercially cultivated in Arkansas since the late 19th century and today are a multimillion-dollar crop. The fruit has been an important crop in Cabot since at least the mid-1900s. While, today, crates of the fruit are shipped by truck, as shown here in the 1940s, they were delivered to the downtown train depot and shipped by train all over the United States. (Courtesy Museum of American History.)

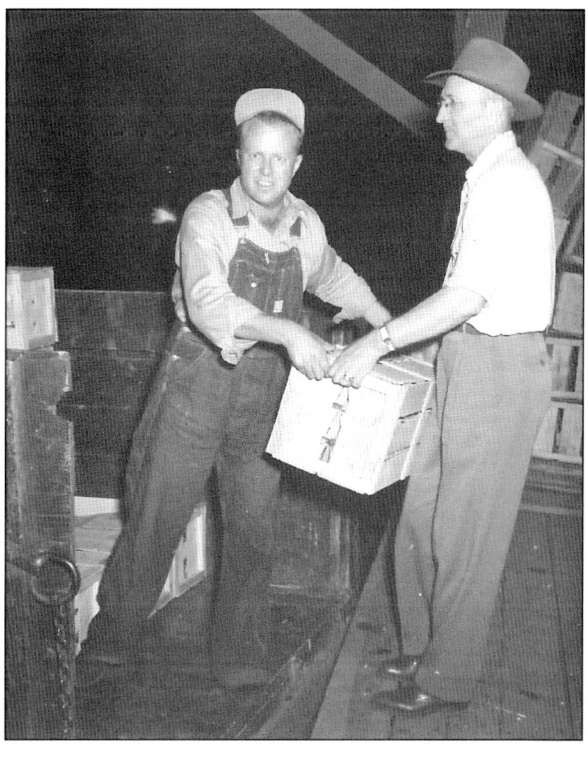

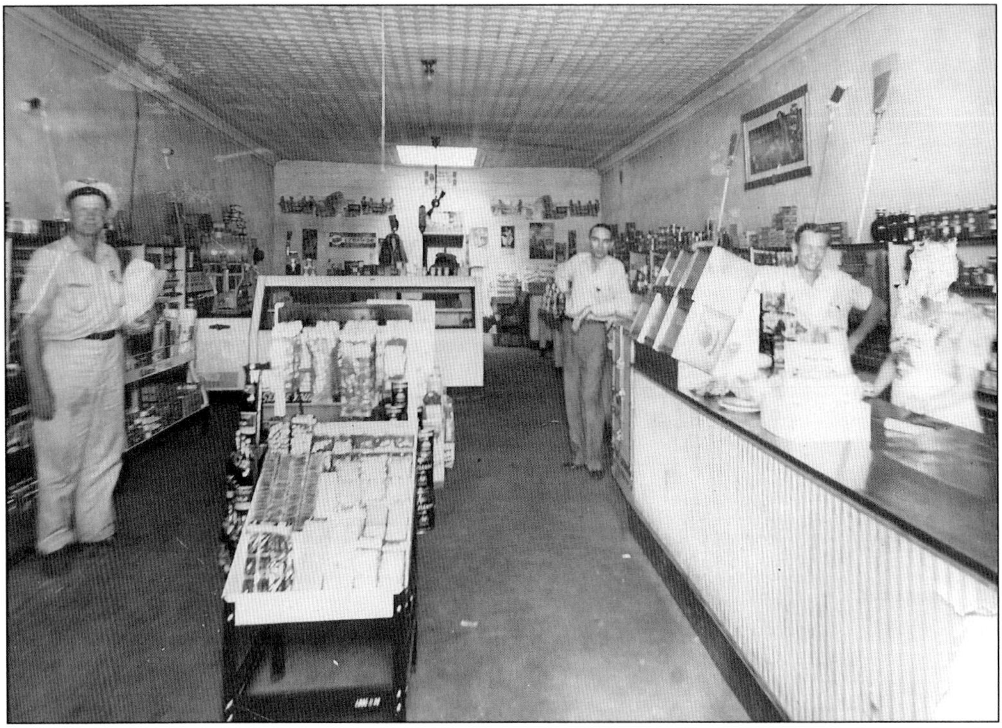

Among the many stores in the 1940s was Murphy's Grocery, operated by John Murphy. Murphy is shown leaning against the counter to the back. (Courtesy Jack and Betty Carrington.)

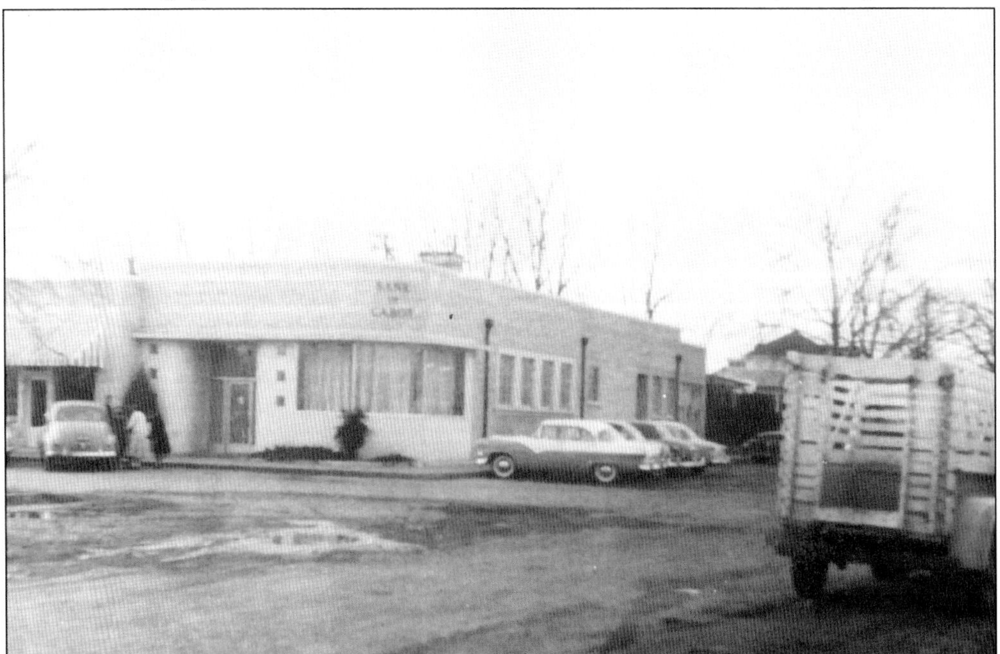

In the late 1940s, the Bank of Cabot moved into a new modern building located on Main Street. The bank has since moved to another location with the building now housing the offices of the City Water Department.

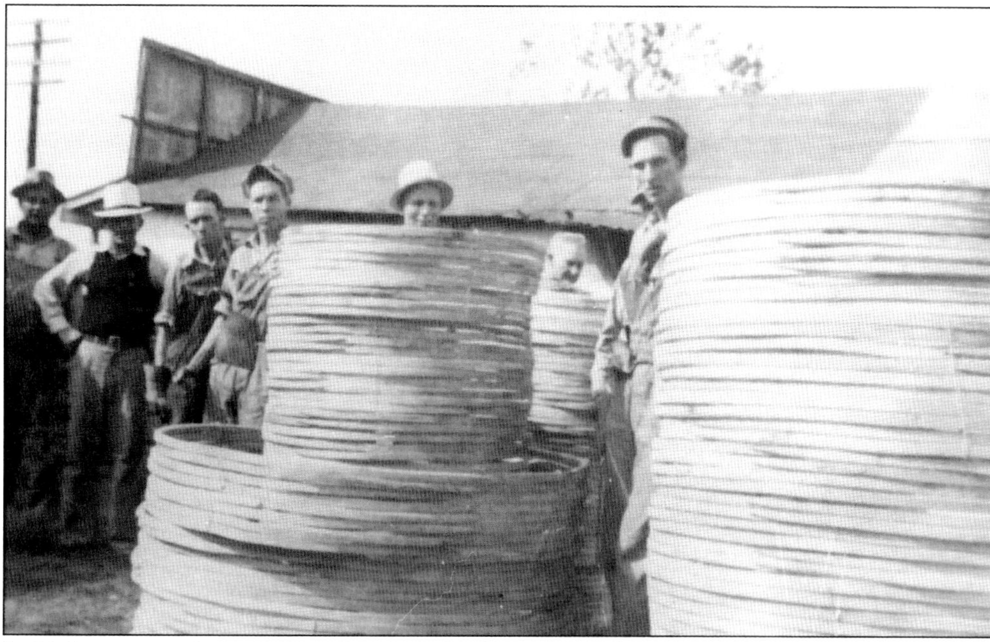

In 1948, a unique factory was in operation in downtown. The O.E. Collins Net Hoop Company occupied three buildings and employed about eight workers. The hoop fishing nets were shipped to consumers all over the United States. The company remained in operation for several years.

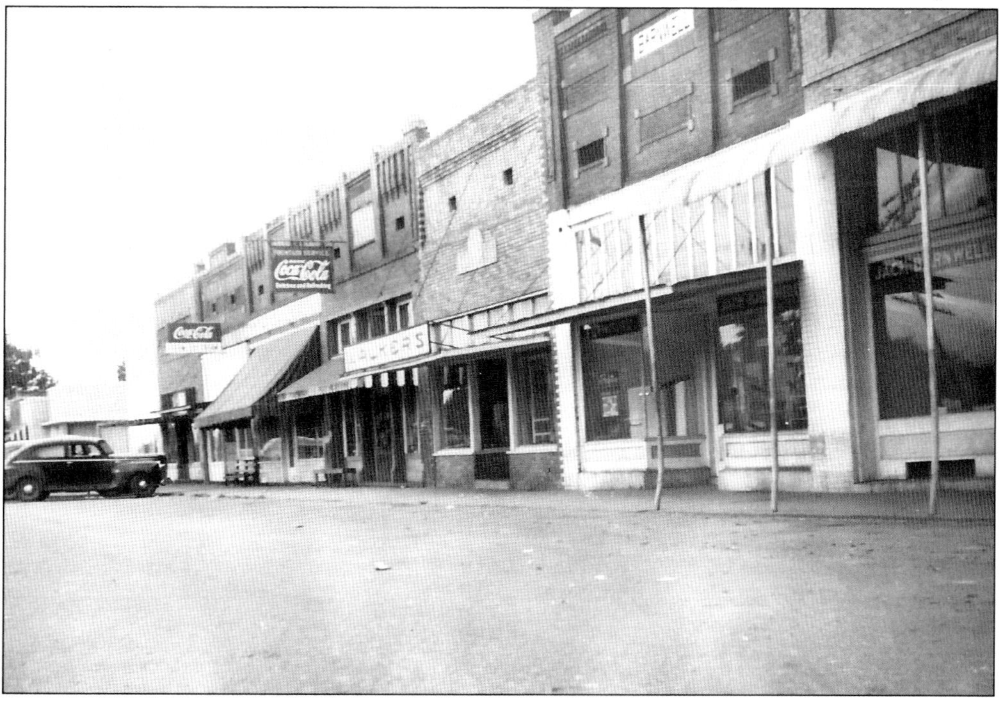

During the 1940s, downtown Cabot was home to a number of popular businesses that provided a variety of products to local customers. In those simpler days, people more often bought from local stores than traveling out of town. One such popular product bought by the locals, as seen by the signs, was the number one soft drink of the day, Coca-Cola.

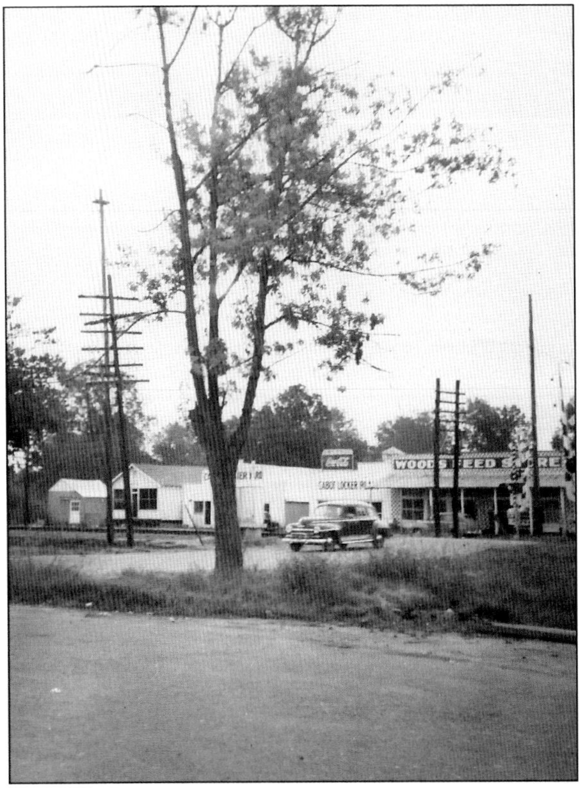

Highway 89, shown in this 1940s view, remains one of the busiest highways passing through Cabot. Today, a newer Wood's Feed Store still occupies the corner lot. The adjacent lumberyard is long gone, and the Locker Plant has moved to the other side of the highway.

US Highway 67, one of America's oldest, was a major thoroughfare from St. Louis, Missouri, through Arkansas by the early 1920s. Construction through Cabot led to growth. The road, which today is designated as Highway 367, is shown here in the 1940s or 1950s.

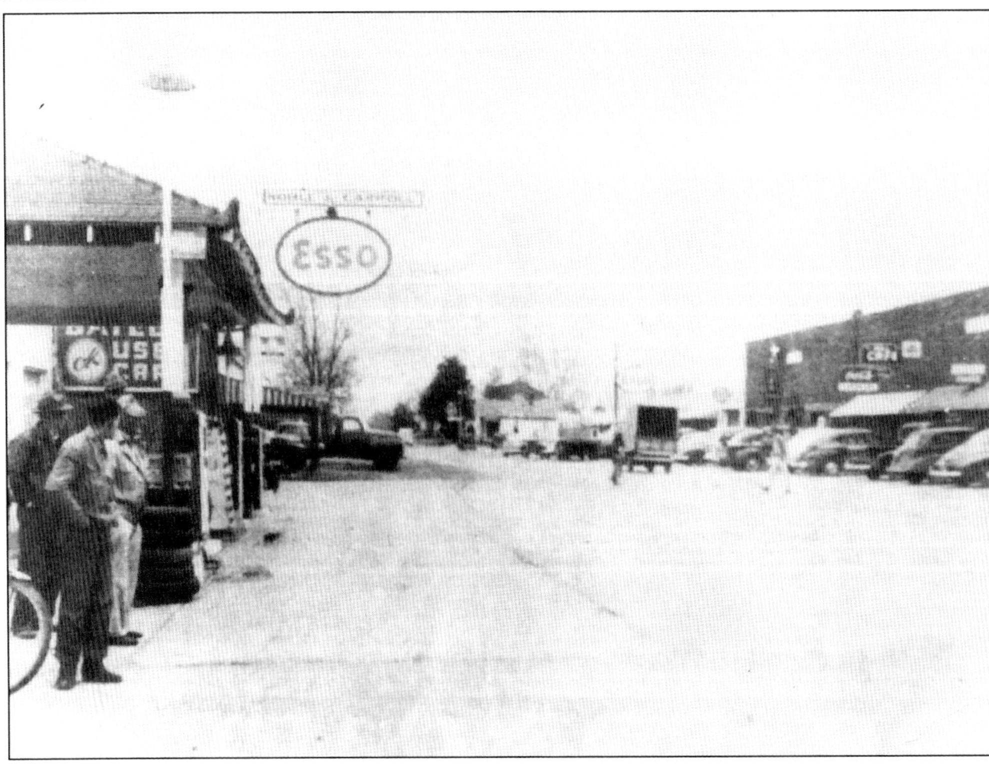

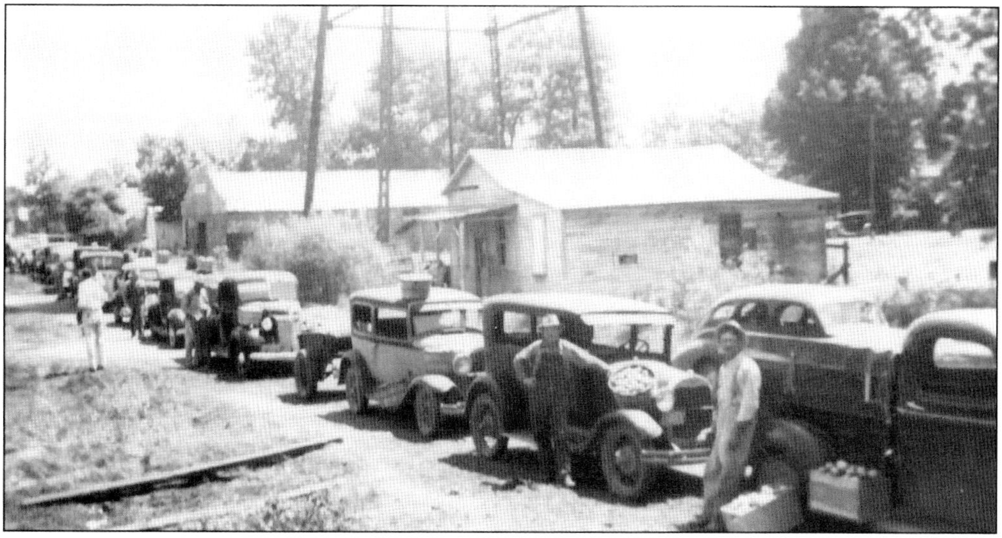

While Cabot is considered to be a modern bedroom community where residents commute to jobs in other places, it once was a thriving farm community that produced a variety of crops, including cotton and produce. Another of those crops was tomatoes. In this photograph, many of the local producers have lined up vehicles loaded with their harvest waiting for the daily train to take the tomatoes to markets elsewhere. Tomato cultivation was such an important crop during the first half of the 20th century that a group of farmers, under the sponsorship of the Young Man's Business Club, organized a marketing group called the Tomato Growers Association. Tomatoes are still grown by local farmers, though nowhere near the scale of some 70 years ago.

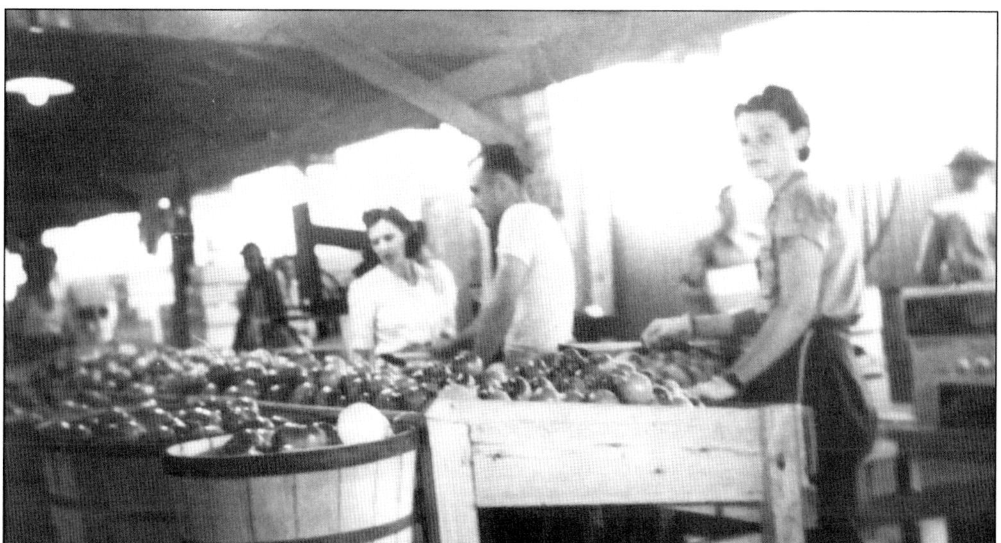

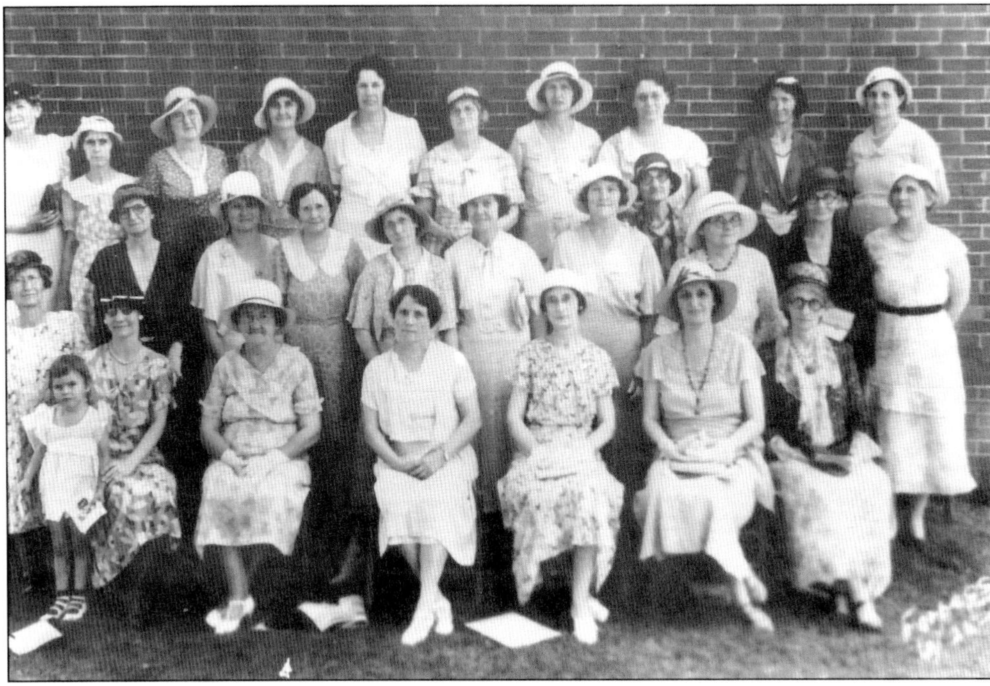

Most churches could not operate without the able assistance of their many women members. Numerous charitable activities and church services are carried out by women groups, just like the 1933 Woman's Bible Class at the local Methodist Church.

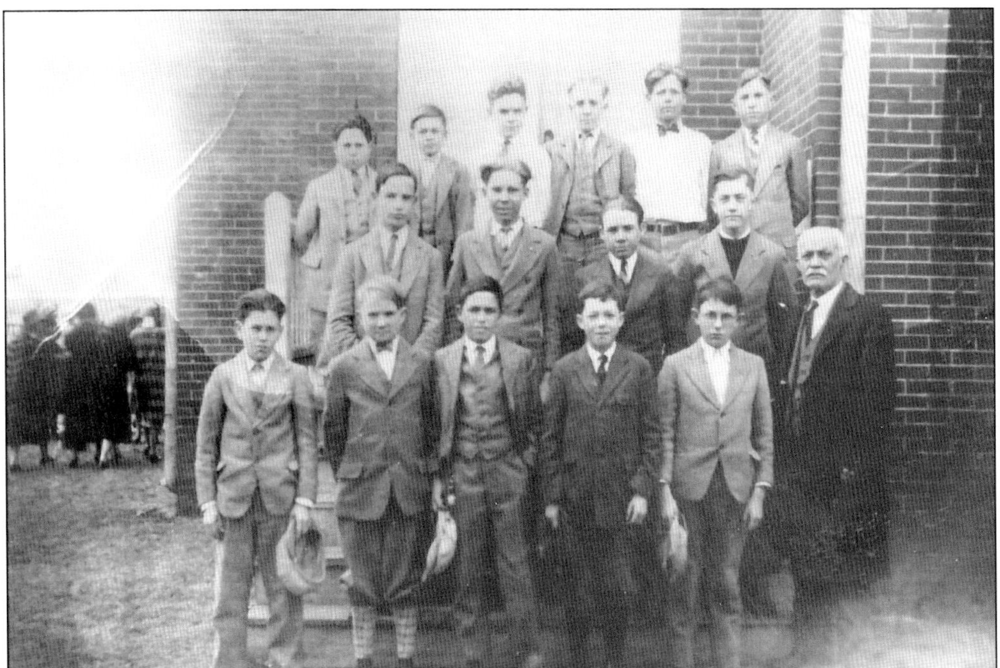

A vital part of the growth of local churches is through its youth. The churches provide a number of activities for younger members to contribute to the church and community. One such group in the 1930s was this boys Methodist Sunday school class.

Three

1950s, 1960s, and 1970s

During the next three decades, Cabot would experience the beginnings of a growth that, by the early 21st century, would make it one of the fastest growing cities in Arkansas. Much of the growth was stimulated by the construction of the four-lane Highway 167, connecting the city to Little Rock. An additional factor was the 1955 opening of the Little Rock Air Base, less than 10 miles away. The small community seemed to be on the verge of significant growth. But just as everything seemed to be moving in the right direction tragedy hit the city. On the afternoon of March 29, 1976, as the nation celebrated its bicentennial of independence, a tornado ripped through the city, resulting in millions of dollars of damage and the death of five people. The recovery from that tragedy would define the community and set it on the path to record growth by the start of the 21st century.

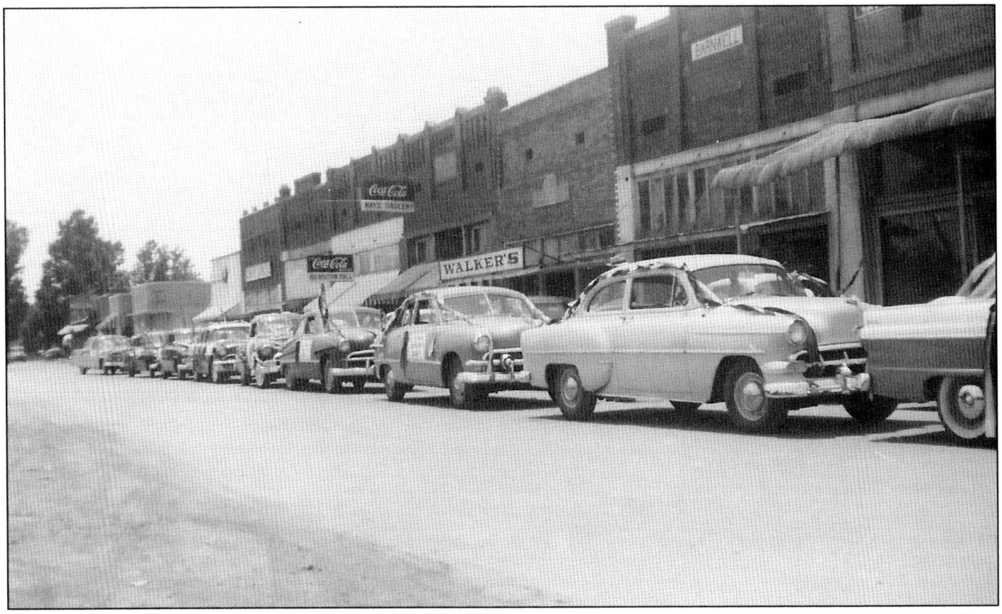

Parades in downtown have always been popular events, drawing large numbers of spectators. One such procession is shown here on First Street about 1955.

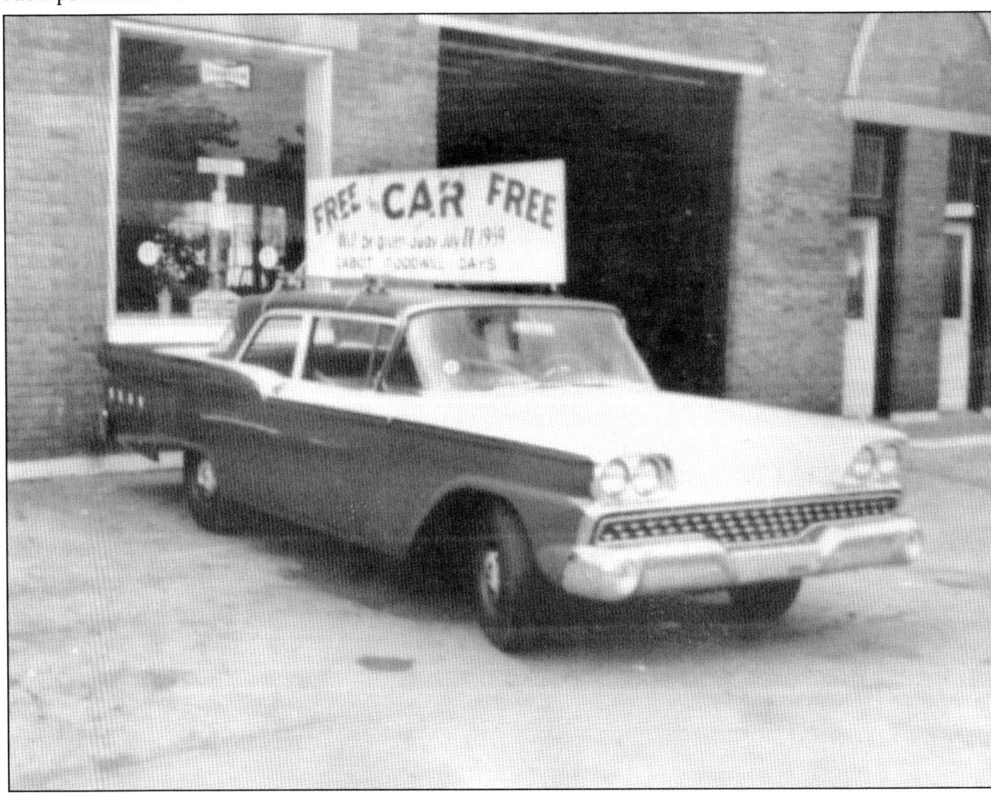

Several different programs have been used by local businessmen to attract customers. By the 1950s, Cabot Goodwill Days was initiated as such a program. On this occasion, the local Ford dealership went full force by offering this new car as a prize to one lucky customer.

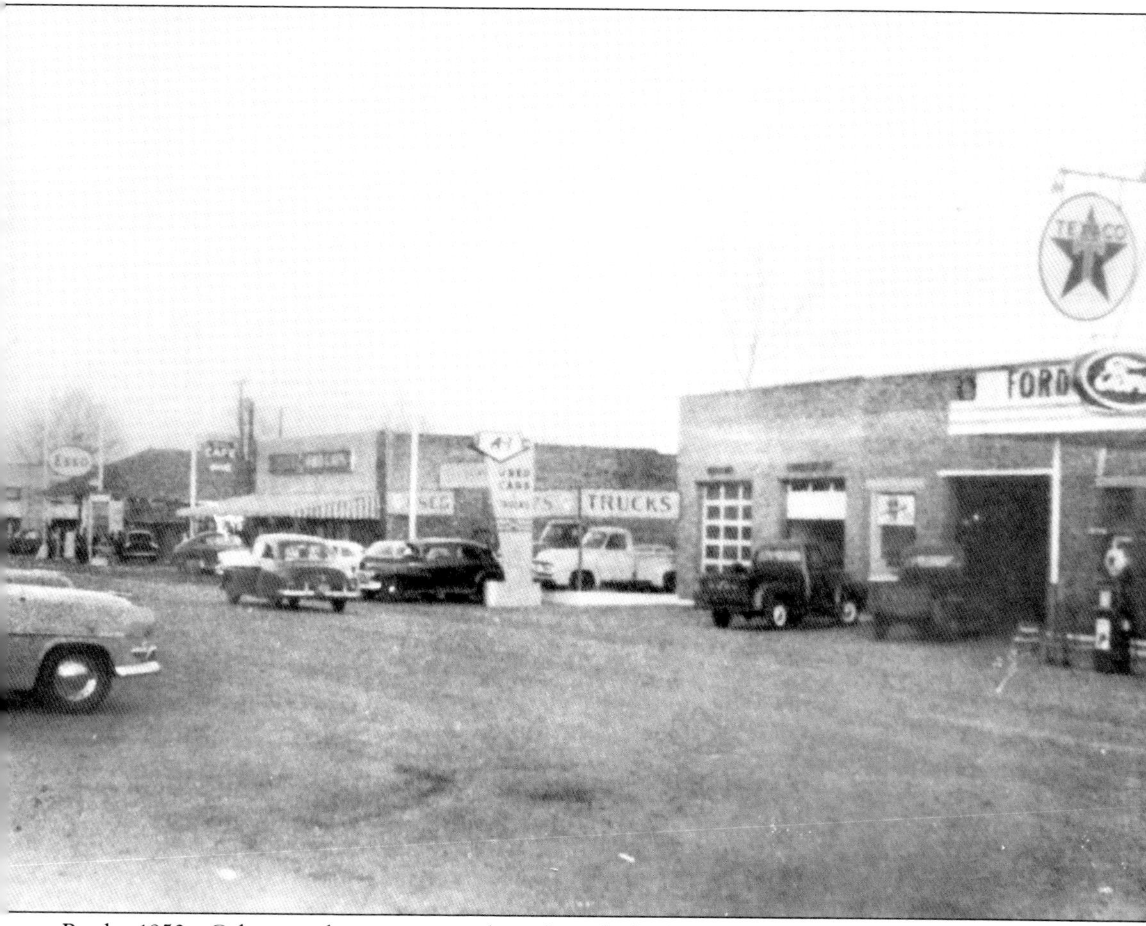

By the 1950s, Cabot was home to a number of car dealerships, such as the one located here on Second Street. It is interesting to note that some of these dealerships, along with offering the newest fad on four wheels, also doubled up as a gas station.

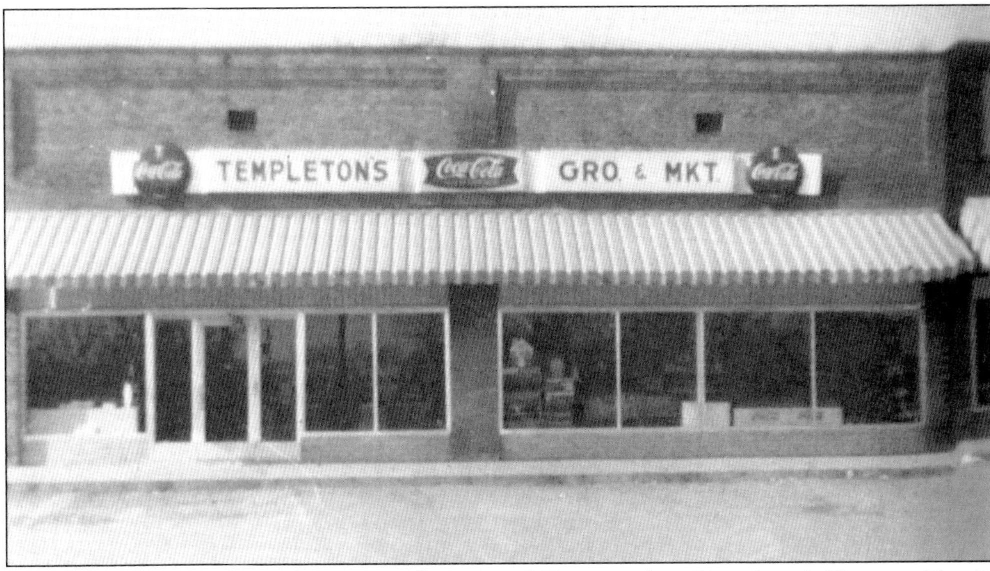

Anyone who has lived in Cabot since at least the 1960s remembers Templeton's Grocery. Charlie Templeton was one of the most highly respected businessmen in the city. A loyal supporter of the city and the school, Templeton was owner of the main grocery store in downtown. Templeton's was a typical grocery store of the times, supplying a wide variety of products to the many customers who patronized the store. Templeton's Grocery was one of the first businesses to locate south of town on Highway 89. The expanded location is today occupied by another grocery store, Knight's. (Above, courtesy Museum of American History.)

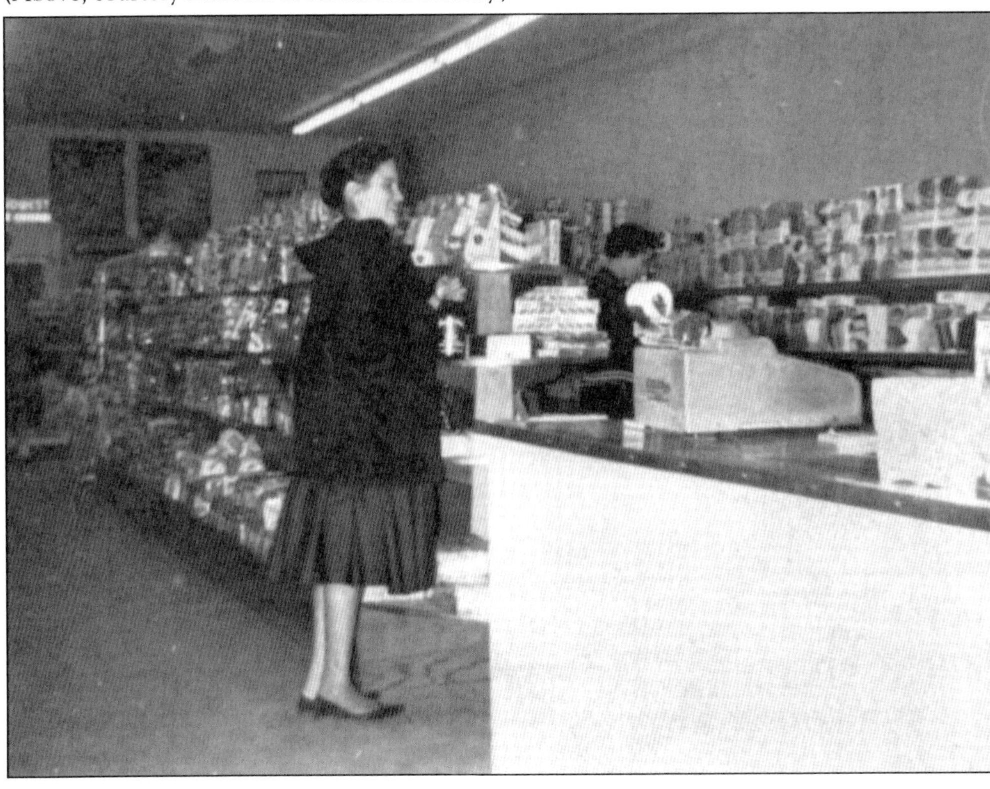

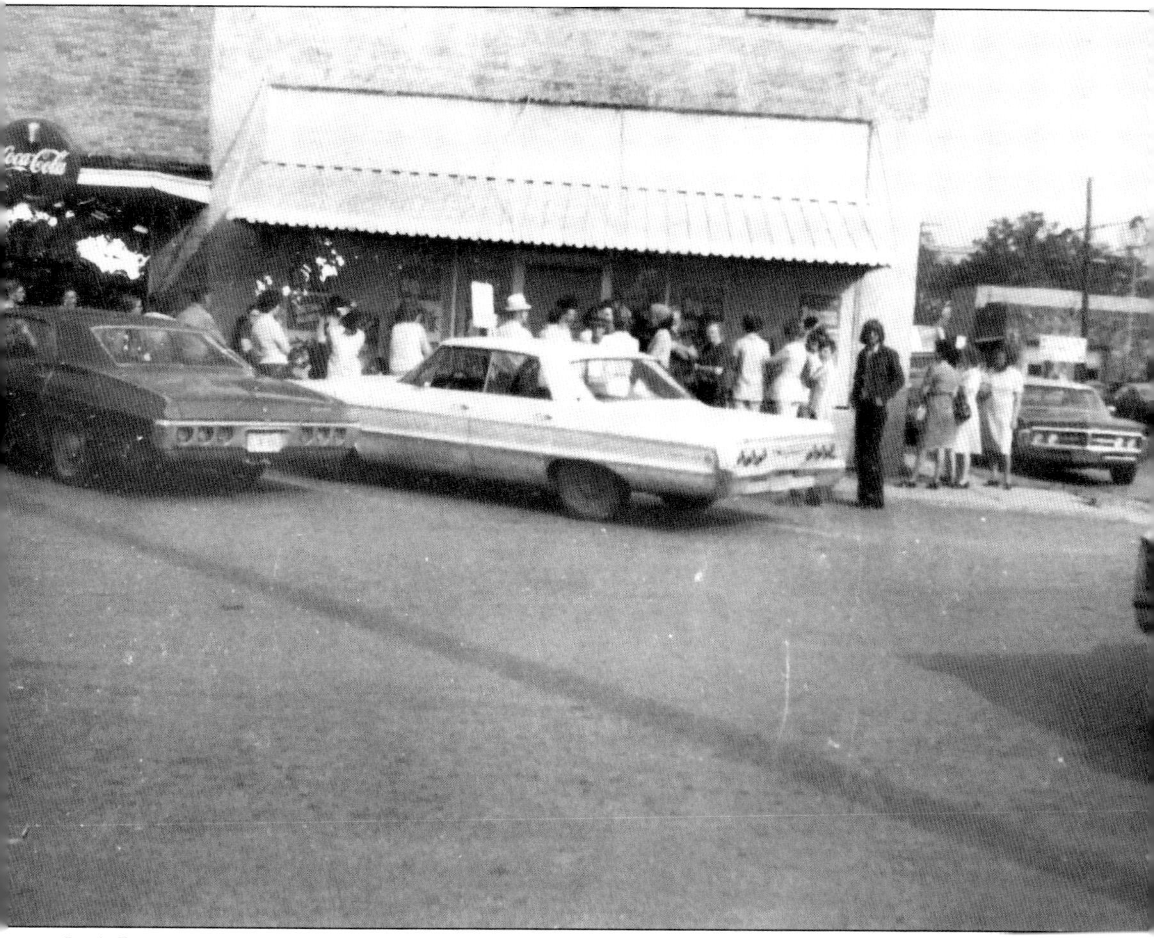

See's Department Store, which was established around 1900, is shown here sometime prior to its destruction by the 1976 tornado. The rock building, seen to the right behind the RC sign, is the office of longtime city doctor Jack Barnwell.

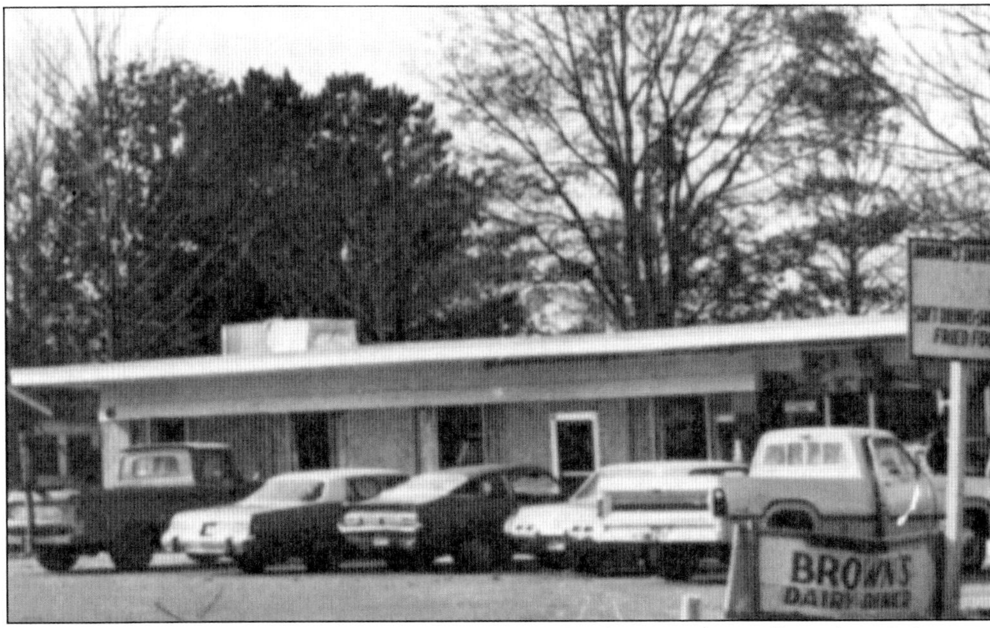

Long before the familiar fast food chains came to town, families visited a small number of what were then called "dairy bars" to obtain a quick meal. One of those early Cabot eating establishments was Brown's Dairy Bar, located on the edge of town on present-day Highway 367.

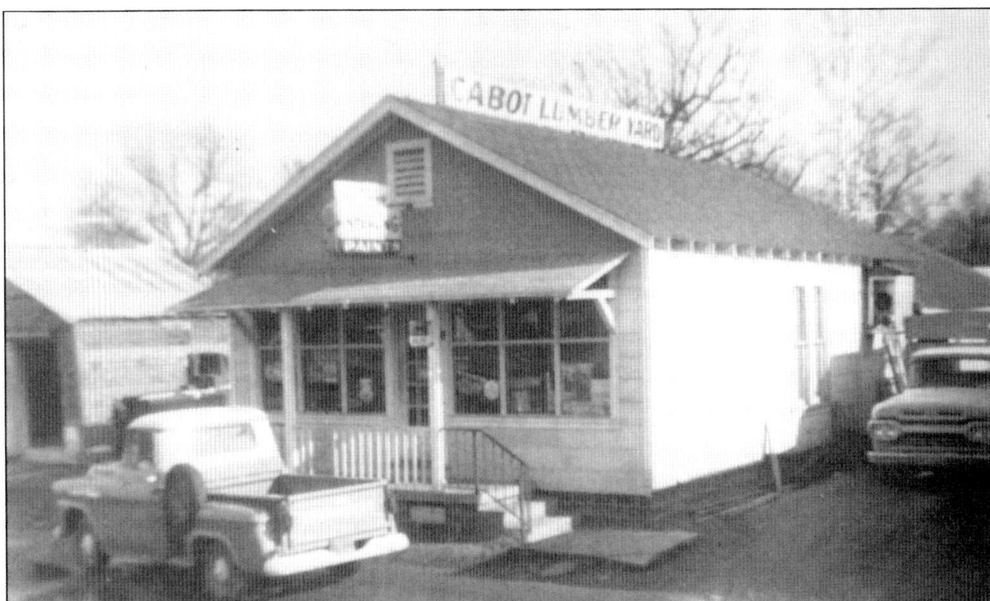

In the 1950s and 1960s, Cabot Lumber Yard contributed to the development of modern Cabot by providing building materials for local contractors. The business closed many years ago, unable to compete with the larger lumber suppliers that moved into the area by the late 20th century.

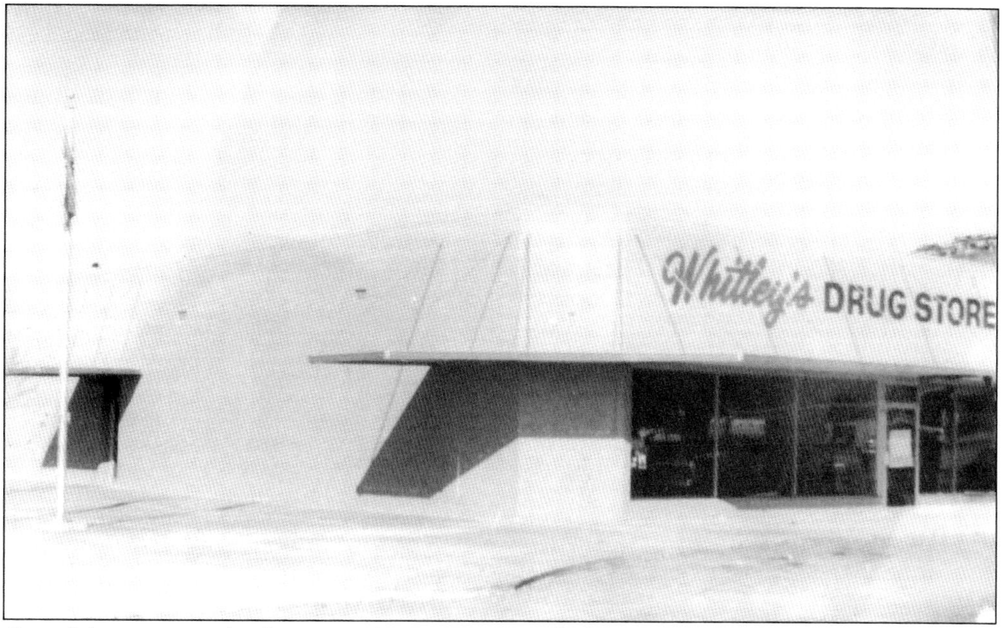

One of the most popular downtown businesses was Whitley's Drug Store. Patrons could purchase a number of items along with their medications or enjoy an ice cream soda from the store's ornate soda fountain. Today, the building is the home of a Laundromat. (Courtesy Museum of American History.)

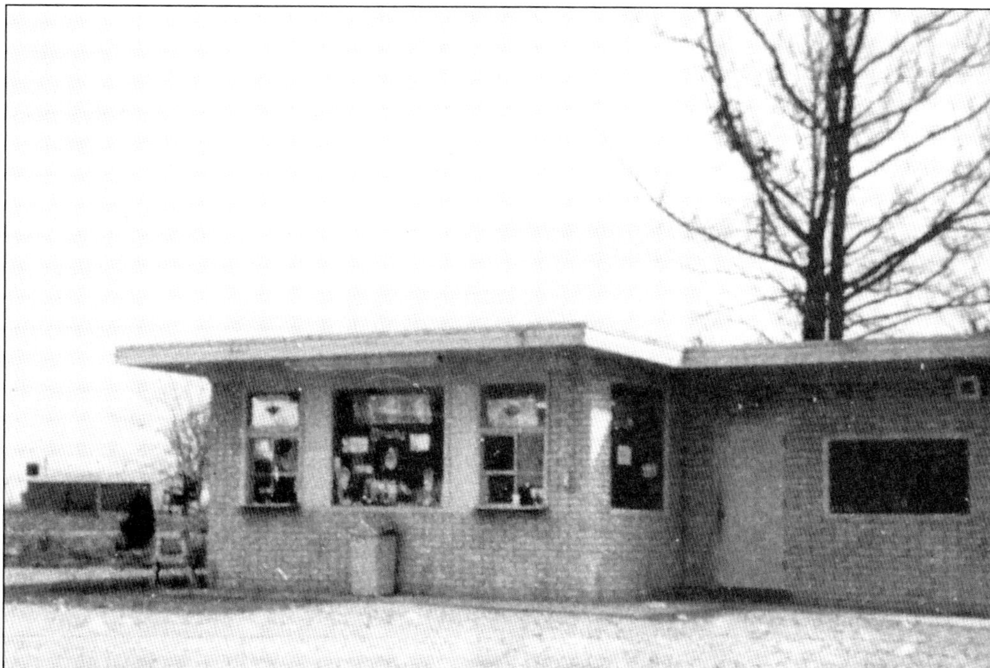

One of the early hangouts for Cabot youth in the 1960s was the Freezo Dairy Bar, located on the main drag south of town. Kids would gather to visit and enjoy one of the many frozen treats offered by the store. The building is the office of a used car dealership. (Courtesy Museum of American History.)

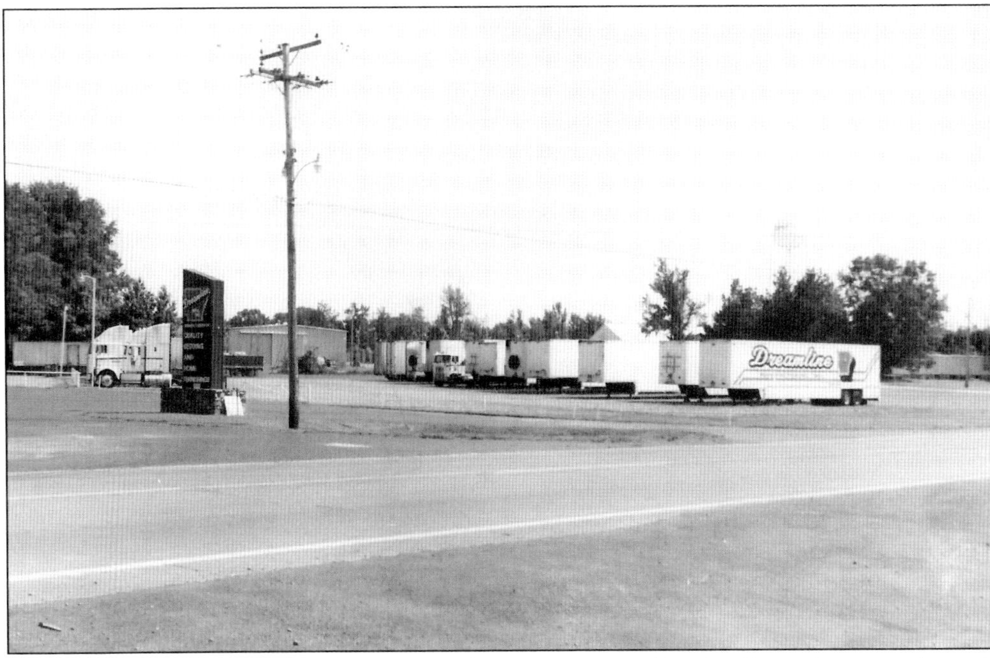

Probably the longest continuously operating factory was started by the Tipton family in the early 1960s. Founded as the Tipton Mattress Company in 1963, it has become a major producer of bedding products. Today, it operates at the same location as Dreamline Manufacturing.

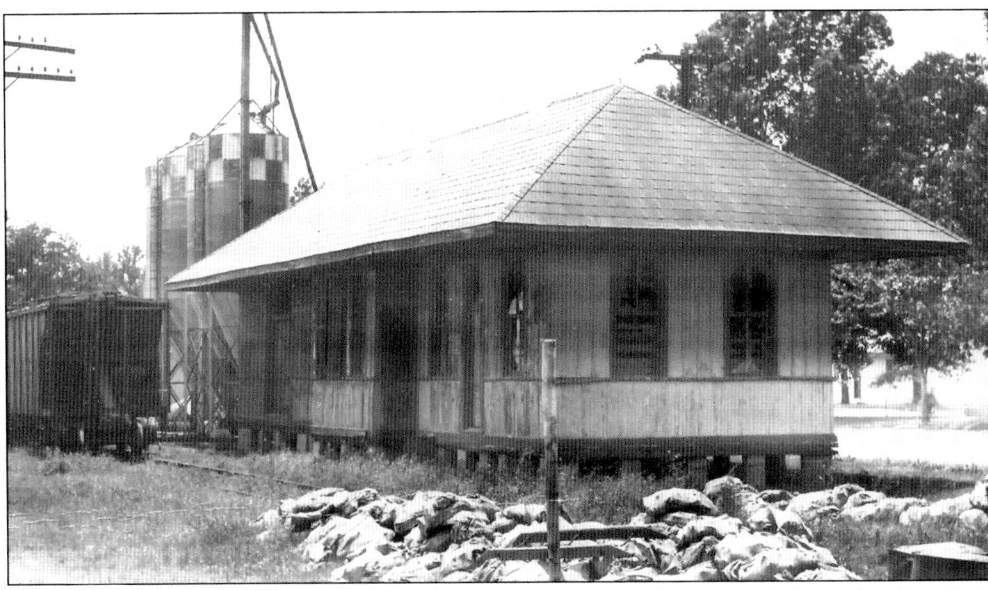

By the time this photograph was taken of the Missouri Pacific Depot in 1967, the heyday of the railroad had long passed. Long gone were the days when daily trains stopped at the depot to pick up passengers, deliver the mail, off load freight, or to pick up freight to be shipped across the United States. The once busy depot was by now just an interesting focus of conversation that would soon be moved from its location along the tracks. (Courtesy Museum of American History.)

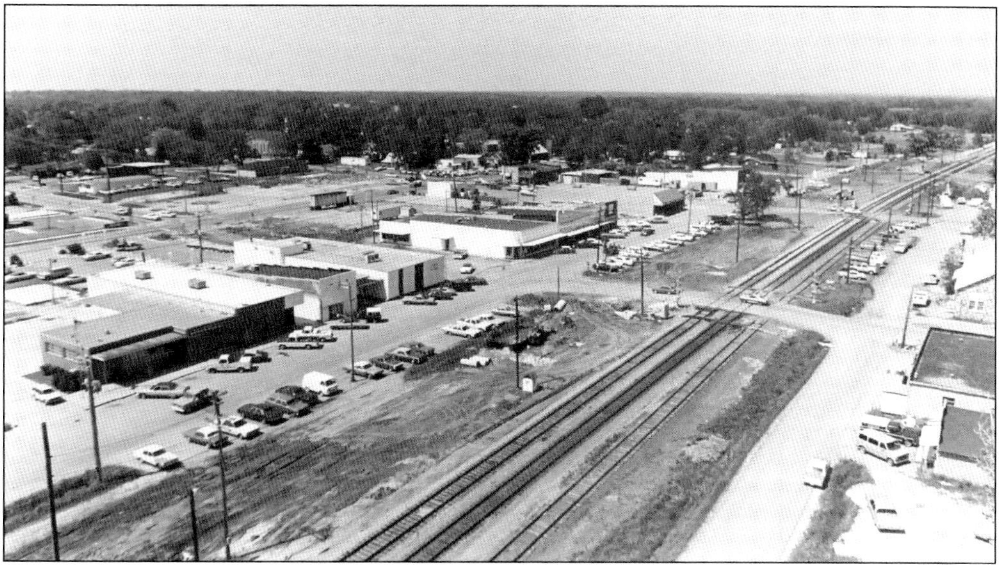

This aerial view of downtown was made approximately one year after the 1976 tornado. While the debris has all been cleared, vacant lots where buildings once stood can be clearly seen. Many new businesses have opened in this area over the years. However, much of the business growth in recent years has developed outside the former downtown business district.

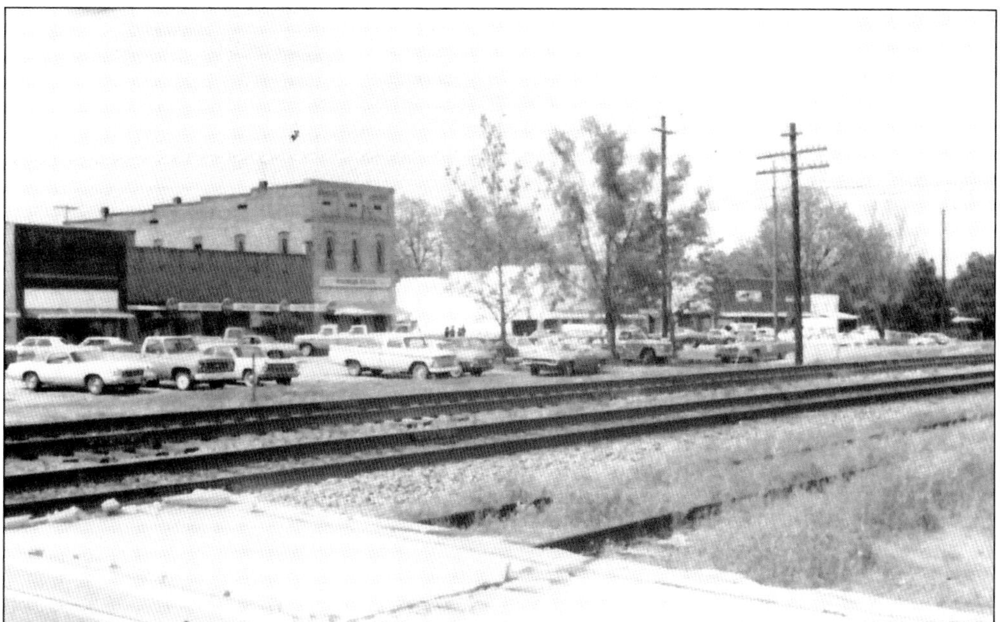

This photograph of a busy First Street was made in the early 1970s before the deadly tornado. The tall brick building near the center is See's Department Store and just to the left is Lowman's Hardware. It was in the See's where several of those seeking shelter from the tornado were killed.

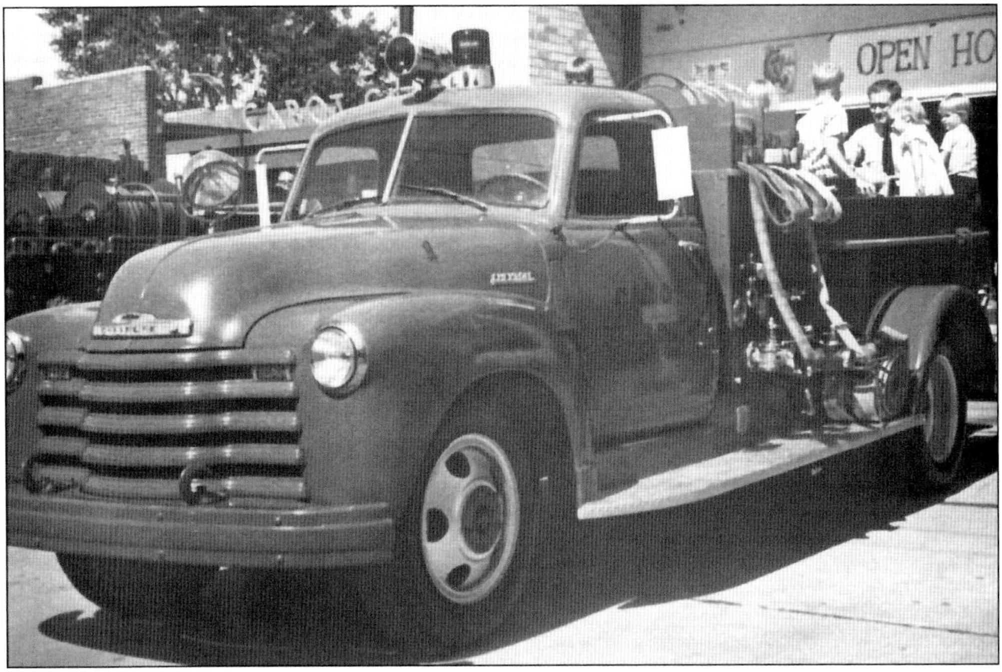

Today, the city is serviced by a number of fire stations situated throughout the city. At the time of this open house at the downtown fire station in the early 1970s, the fire department consisted of just two trucks. The old city hall can be seen to the left of the truck.

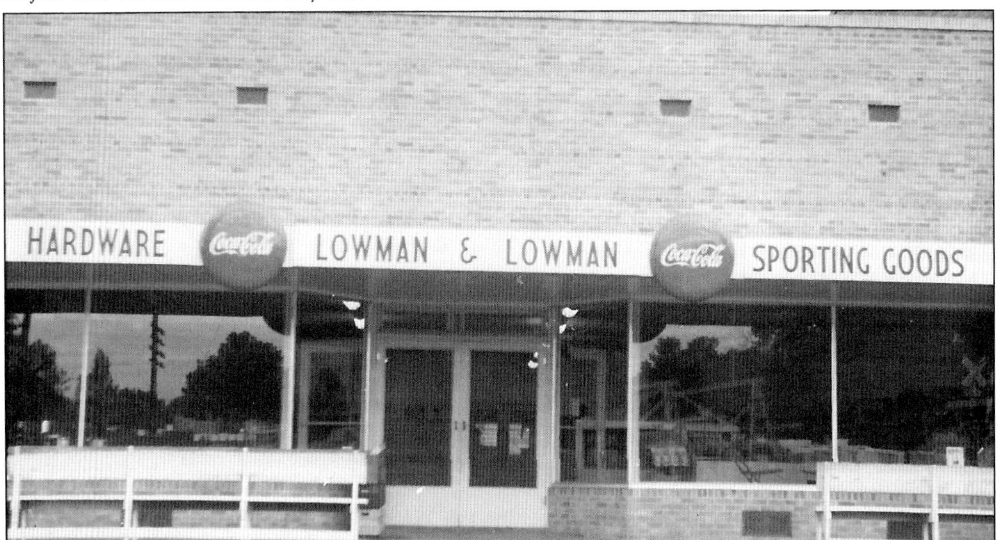

Lowmans is one of Cabot's earliest businesses. James Lowman opened the first family store in the late 1800s and operated it until its closing in 1910. In 1920, he opened a new store on First Street with son Jake in charge. By 1973, the business, then known as Lowman and Lowman, was taken over by the elder Lowman's grandsons, Jake and Jack. The business, which was sold in the early 21st century, was located in downtown until it was briefly moved to a building at Olive and Fifth Streets after the tornado.

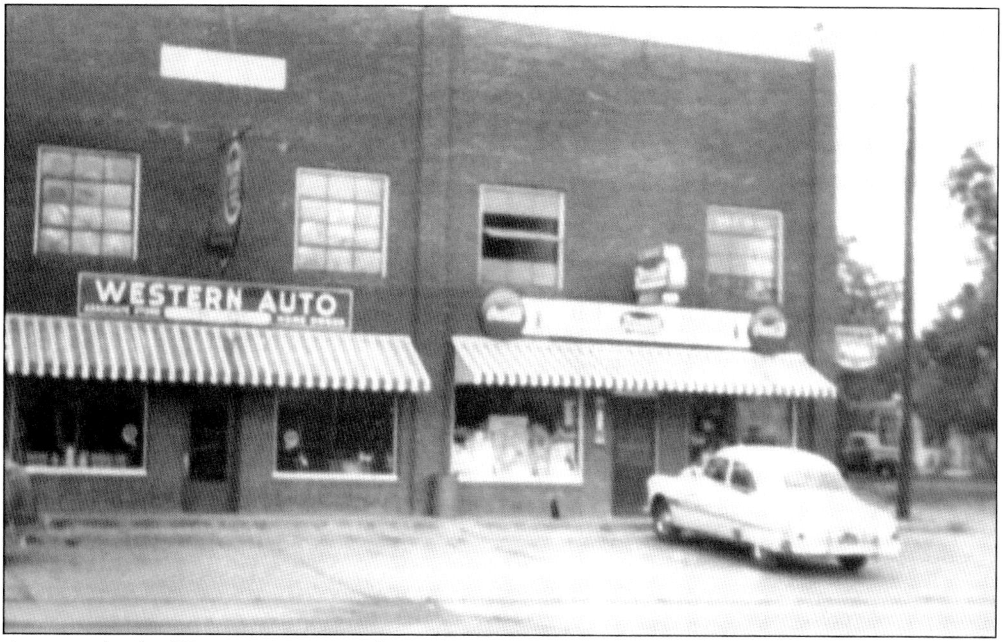

At its peak, the Western Auto Supply Company, a series of chain stores that supplied auto parts and a variety of other items, operated almost 600 stores nationwide. One of those was located on Second Street in downtown Cabot. The store, shown here in the 1950s, was destroyed by the 1976 tornado. The current Western Auto is located on Highway 89.

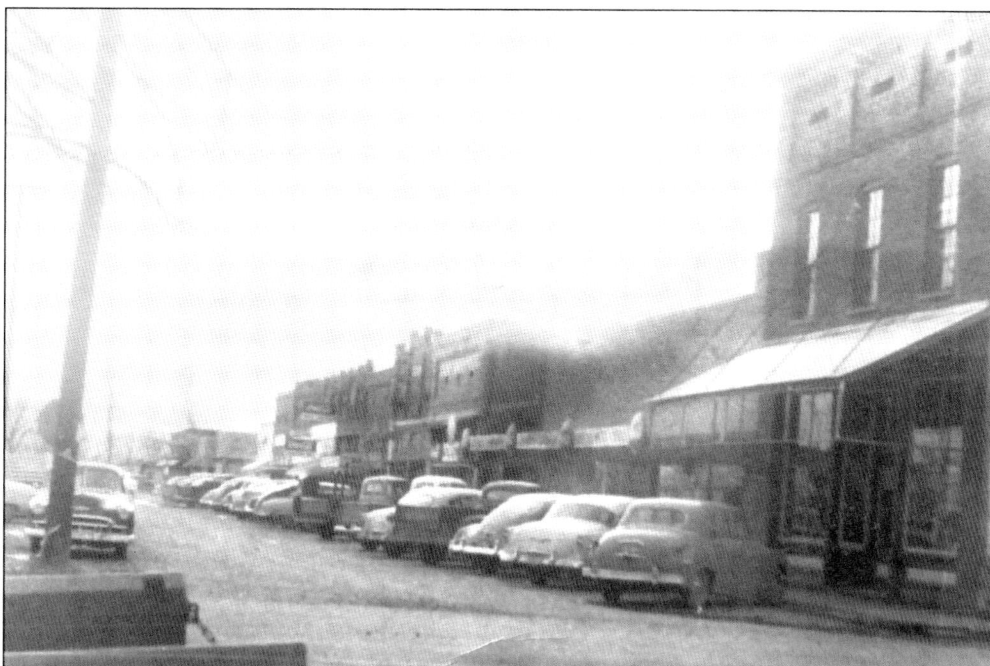

A profitable day for businesses on First Street is apparent by the many parked cars shown here sometime in the 1950s.

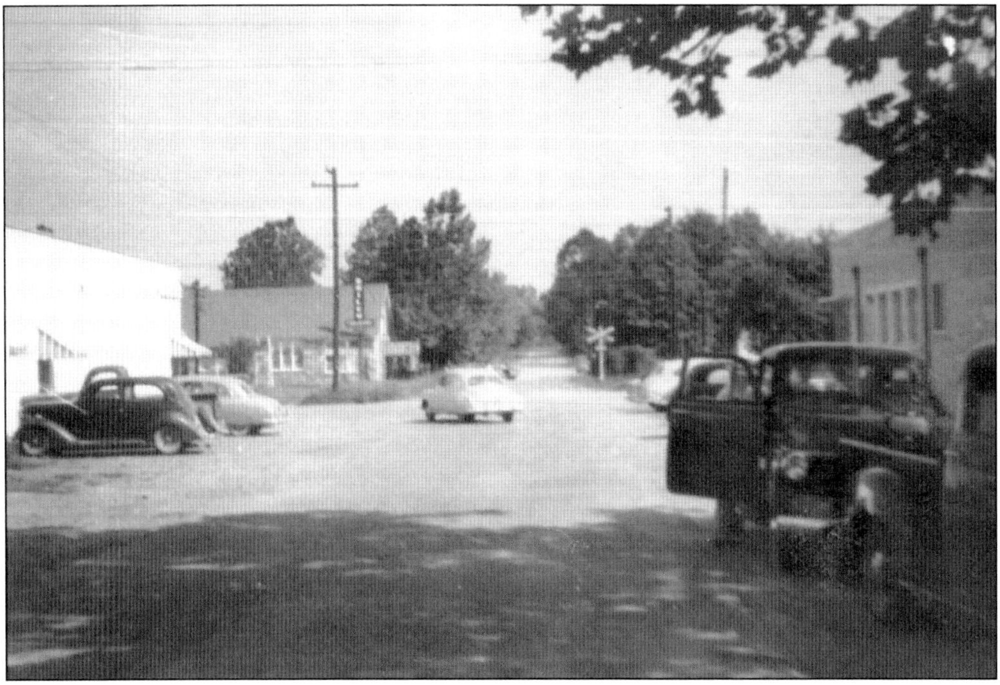

A person with this view today would be standing in the mall area behind the Willie Ray Center. To the left is Whitley's Drug Store, and to the right is the Bank of Cabot. Just across the train tracks on the left is the Legion Hut, which at the time was home to the popular Bailey's Theater.

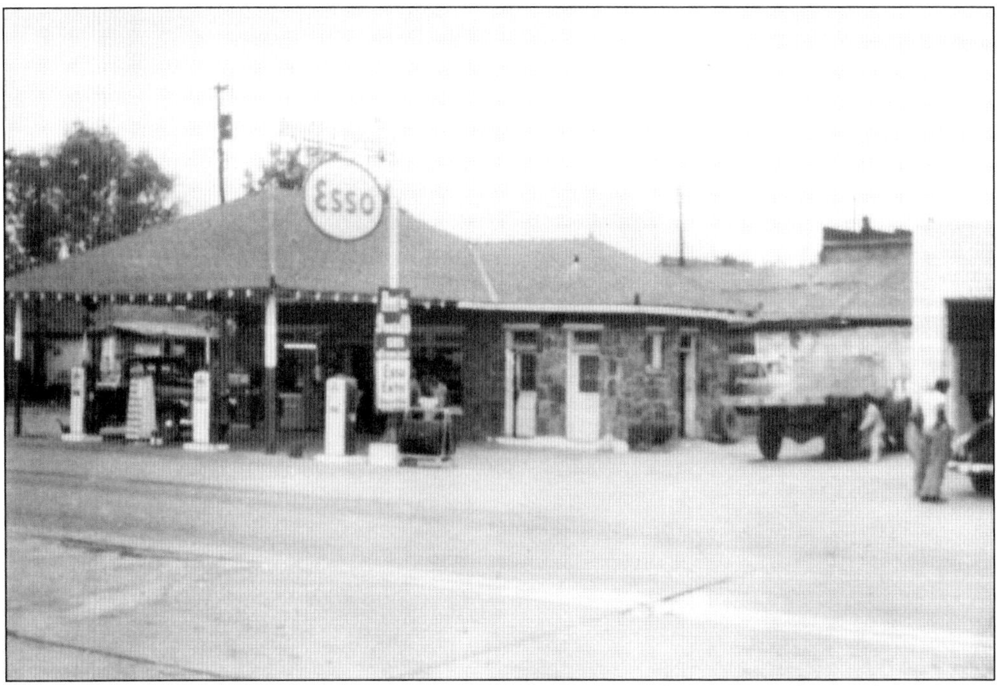

In the mid-20th century, ESSO gas stations, like the one located on present-day Highway 367 in the 1950s, dotted the American countryside. The pronunciation of the name of the popular gas station was derived from the letters S and O from Standard Oil.

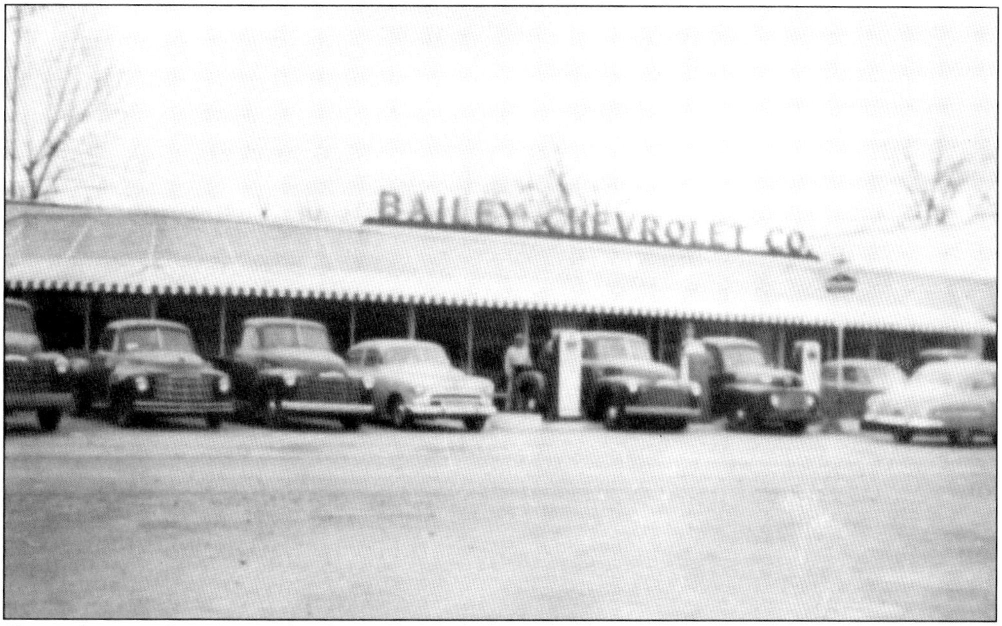

Shown here in the 1950s is the downtown Chevrolet dealership operated by the prominent Bailey family. The building was one of several that did not survive the 1976 tornado.

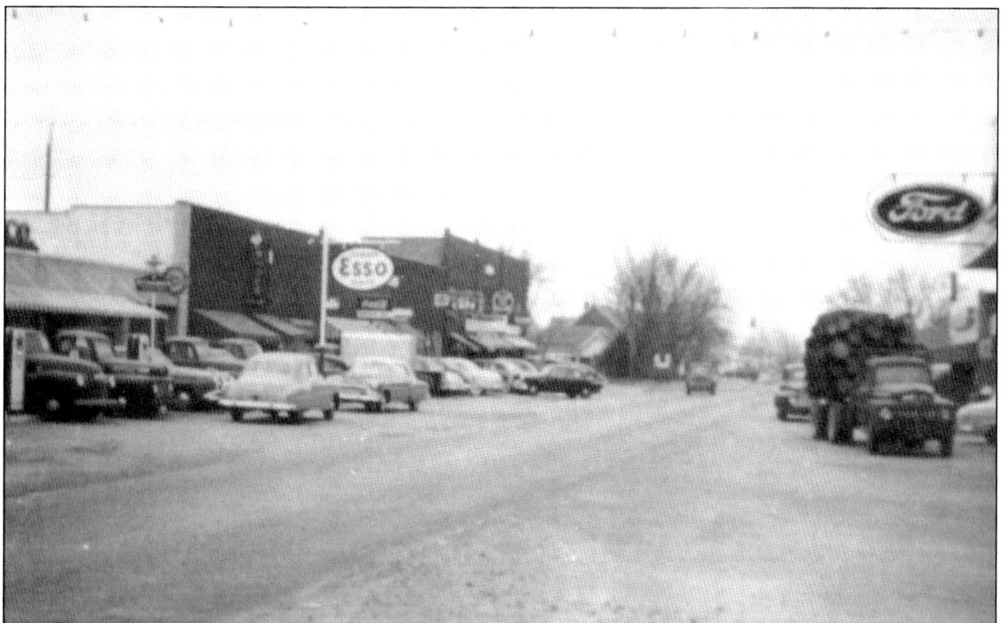

During the 1950s, present-day Highway 367 was a bustling thoroughfare. None of these buildings remain standing, with much of the present-day block occupied by First Security Bank.

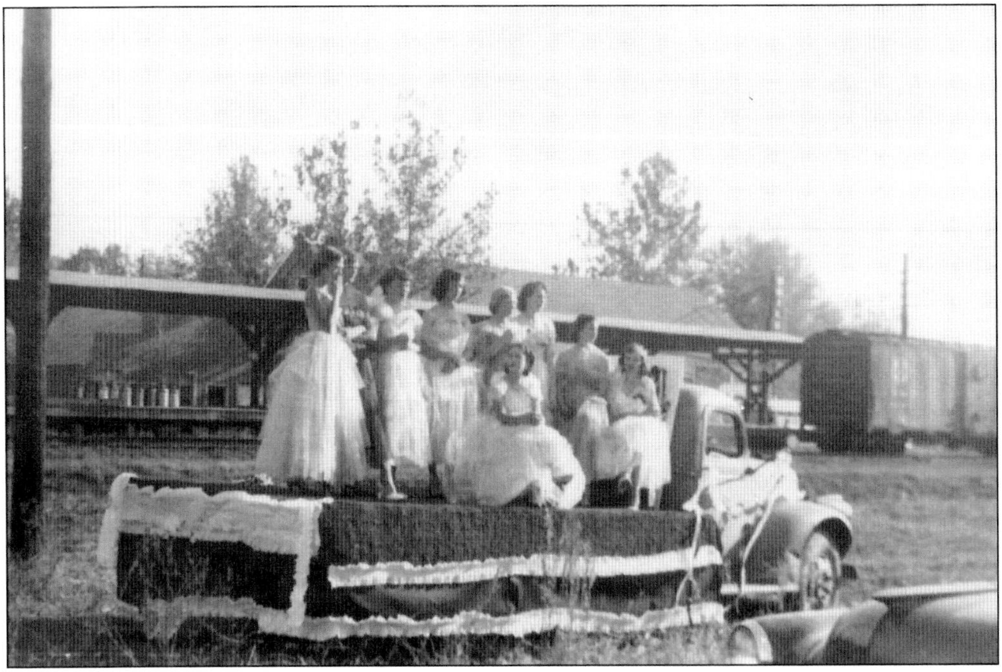

Behind the float carrying these 1950s beauty queens is the railroad loading dock used for the shipment of locally produced goods by rail. Among those goods was locally produced milk shipped in metal cans, a number of which are seen lined up on the dock.

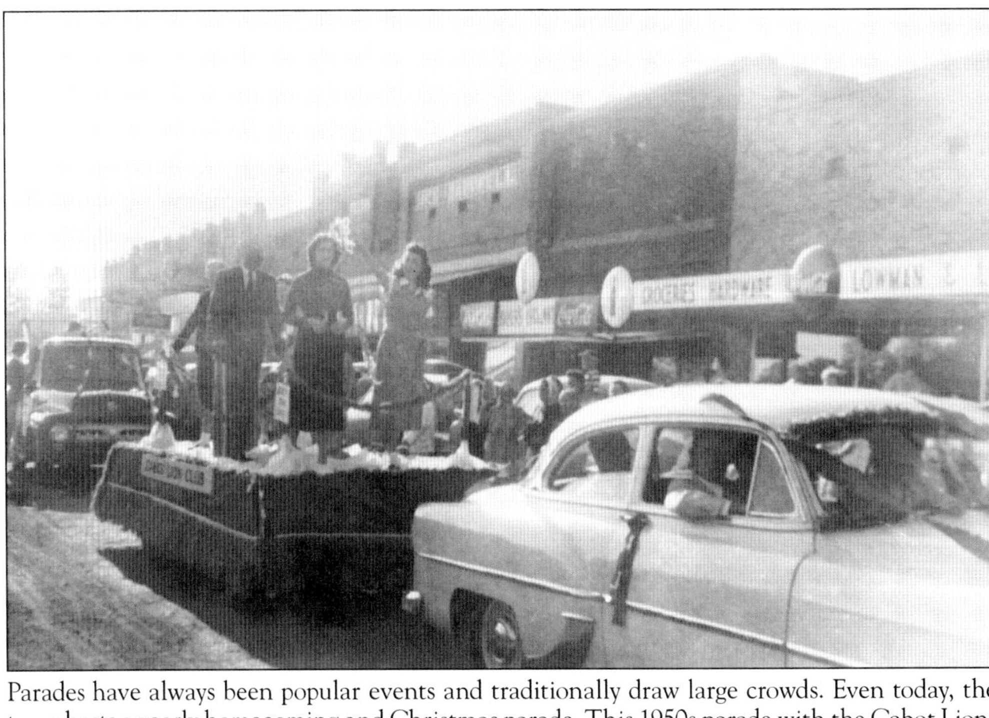

Parades have always been popular events and traditionally draw large crowds. Even today, the town hosts a yearly homecoming and Christmas parade. This 1950s parade with the Cabot Lions Club float leading the way slowly passes down the unpaved First Street.

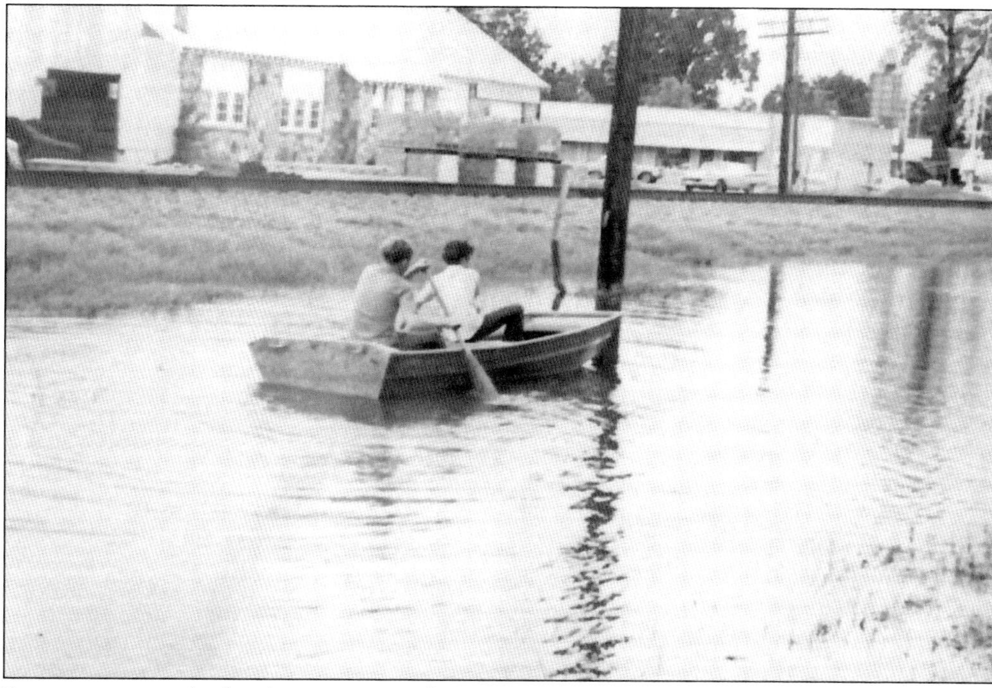

For many years, the low-lying areas in downtown were prone to flooding during heavy rain, creating problems near the railroad tracks. Many town youth, such as the Lowman boys shown here in their flat-bottom johnboat, saw the waters as more fun than trouble.

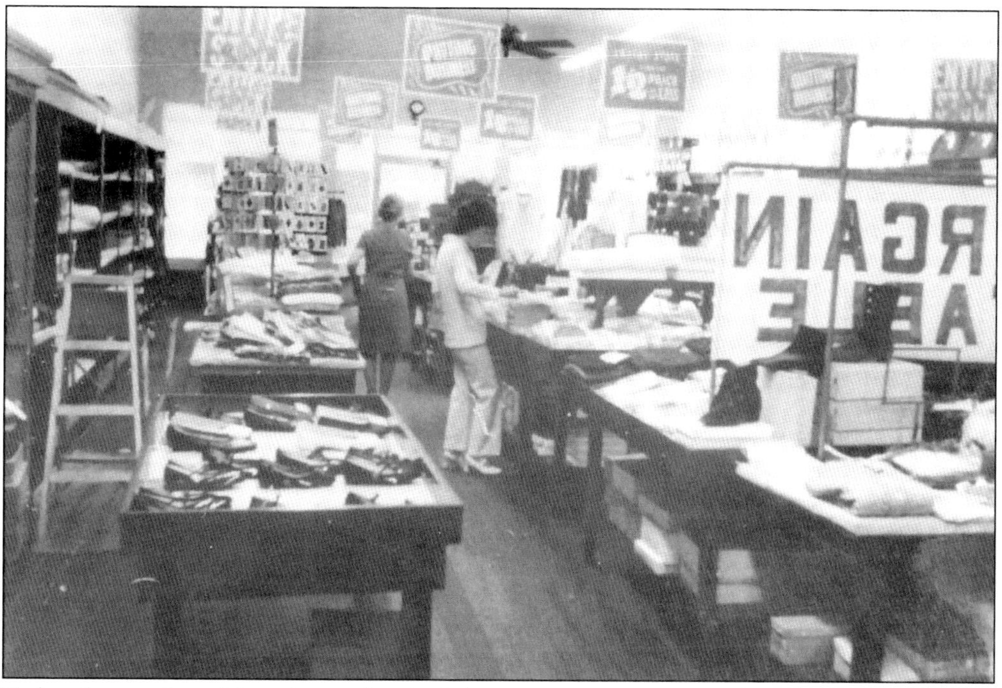

Today, the number of shopping outlets in Cabot is many times greater than they were when this photograph was taken inside See's Department Store in the 1970s. While the number may be greater, such local stores offered a wide variety of products to area customers.

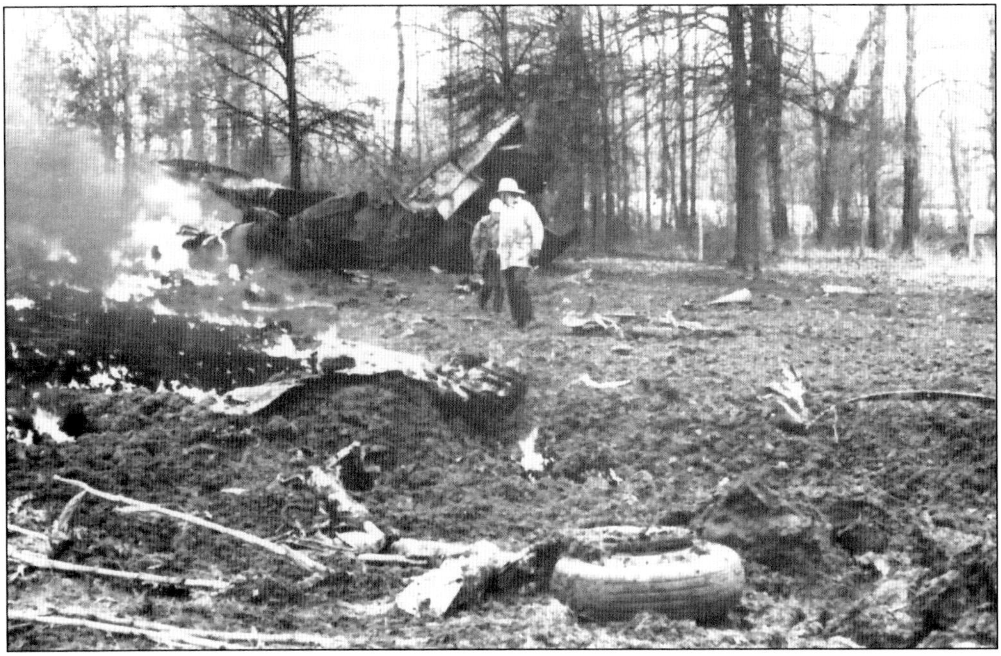

In the 1970s, the citizens of Cabot were shocked by the collision of two airplanes just south of town, off Carrington Road. Both planes were destroyed in a ball of flame, leaving a large area of destruction shown here being examined by rescue personnel. This was just one of two crashes near the town during the decade.

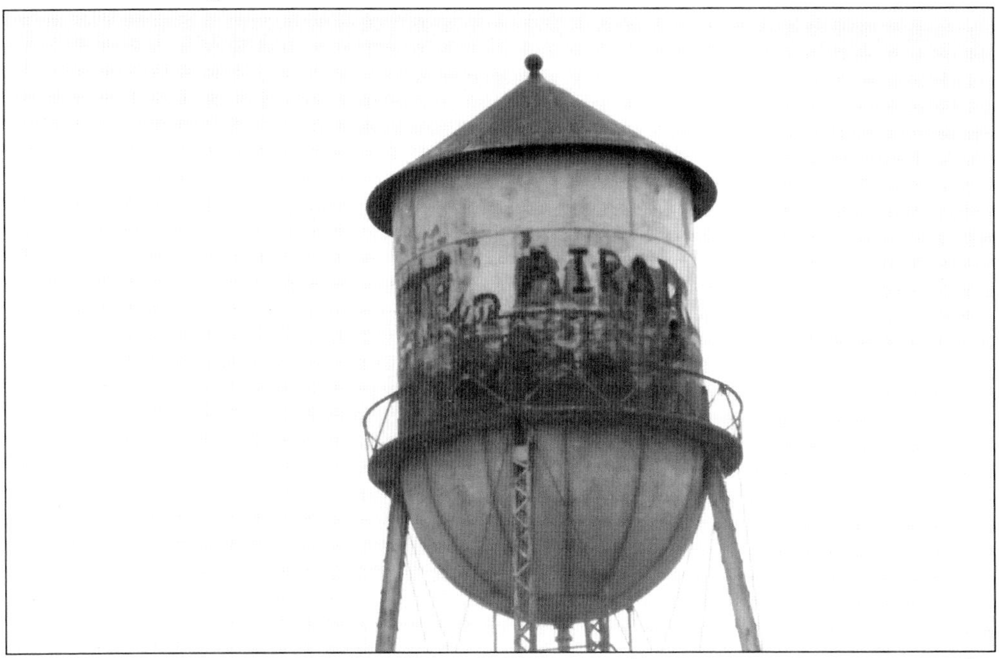

As one travels through the towns and cities of Arkansas, the water tower is a common sight. When the downtown cistern was discontinued and city water installed, Cabot began the use of a water tower to regulate water pressure. This old tower, which was located on Adams Street, was demolished in 1989. Today, the city is home to a number of much larger structures.

Four

Tornado

On March 29, 1976, the physical landscape and future of Cabot was drastically altered. On that spring day, a killer tornado tore a path of destruction through the main business section of town before lifting into the sky, narrowly missing the school. Millions of dollars in damage and five dead were left in the storm's wake. Many consider the rebuilding efforts after the storm as stimulating a rebirth of Cabot, and in 1978, the town celebrated its recovery with the slogan "We're Back" and a festival that continues today called CabotFest. Since that time, Cabot has experienced rapid growth and development, making the city one of the fastest growing and most desirable residential areas in the state.

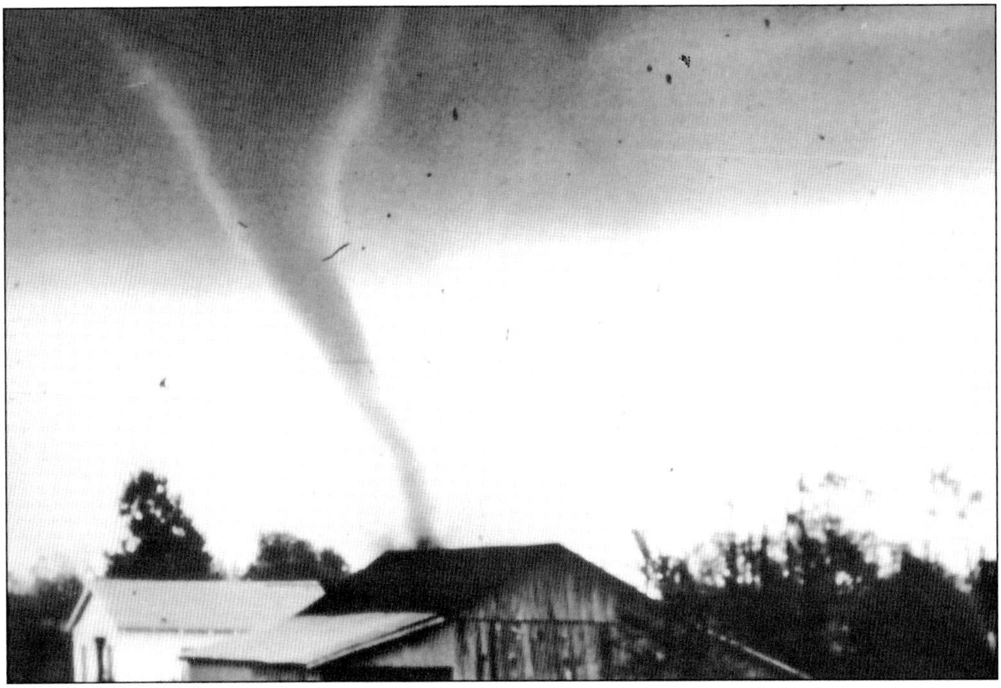

On March, 29, 1976, tragedy struck when a killer tornado ripped a path through the business section of town. Before lifting into the sky, the twister caused millions of dollars in damage and five citizens their lives. Though there is video of the funnel cloud, this is the only known still photograph to surface.

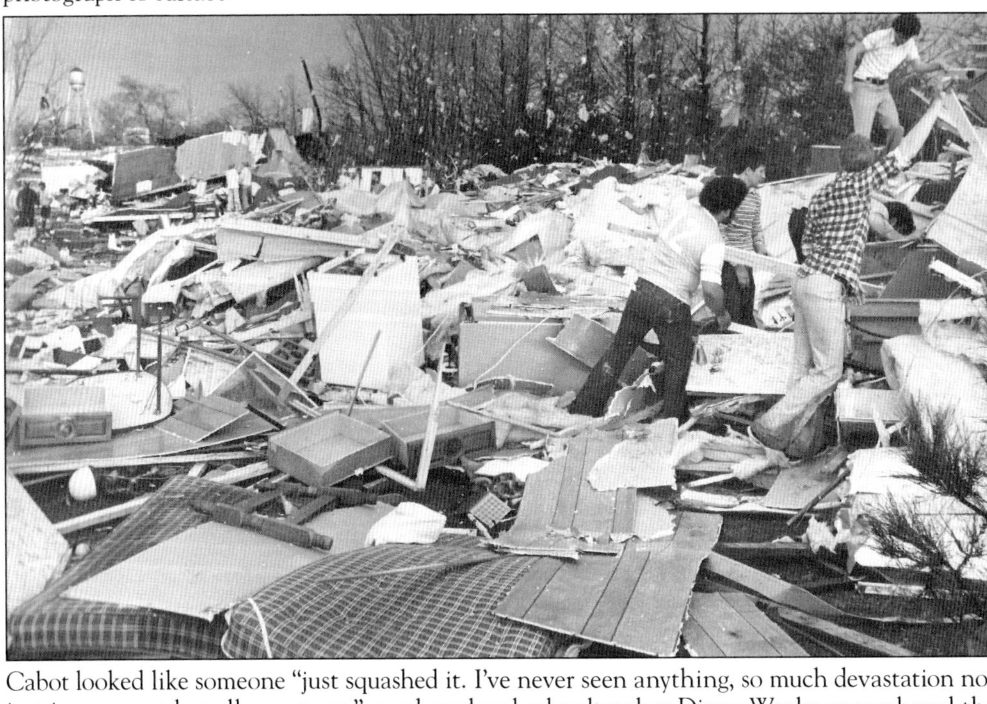

Cabot looked like someone "just squashed it. I've never seen anything, so much devastation not just in one spot but all over town" was how local schoolteacher Diane Weeks remembered the killer storm. Rescue workers are seen here among the devastation searching for survivors.

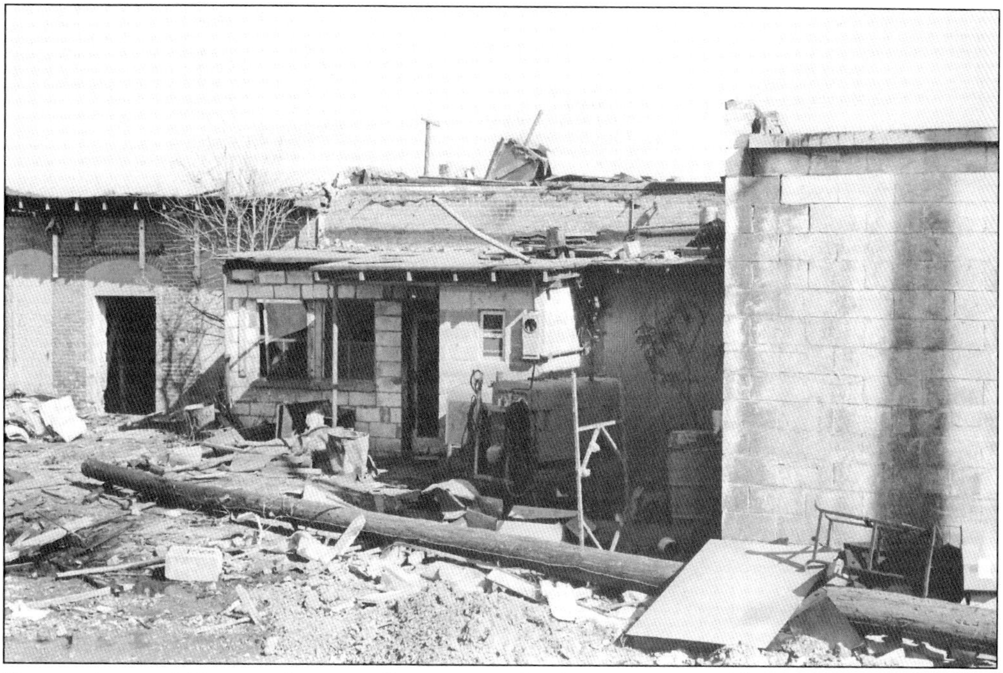

Destruction could be seen in every direction in the downtown area. Floyd Shirley said that "it didn't look like Cabot anymore. It was gone. It was destroyed."

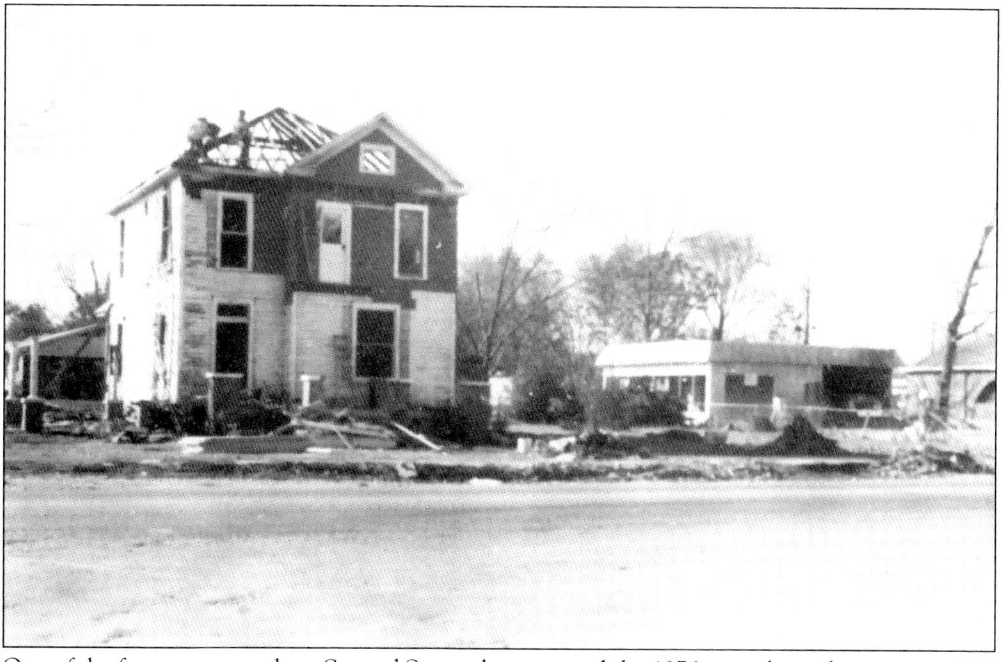

One of the few structures along Second Street that survived the 1976 tornado is what is commonly known as Mattie Anderson's house. Though the building sustained major damage, it was repaired and today serves as the offices of a title business. The car wash to the right has long since been razed, and the building farther to the right is Regions Bank.

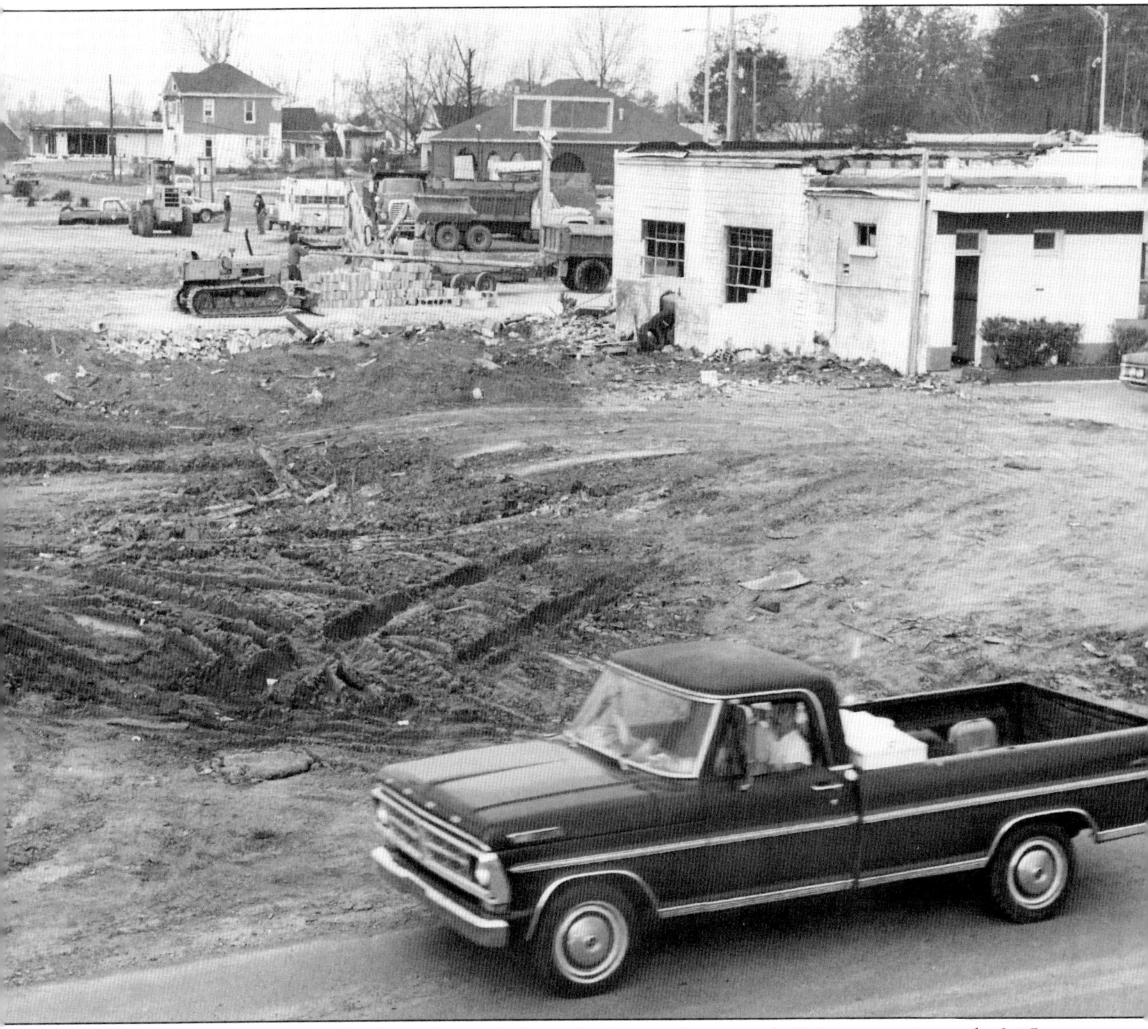

Local newspapers described it as "pure hell in the form of a tornado." At approximately 3:15 p.m. on March 29, 1976, a tornado emerged from the sky devastating much of the downtown. The destruction is clearly shown in this photograph taken near the intersection of Highway 89 and Second Street. Many of the damaged buildings still remain, including the gas station at top right and the two story house at the top.

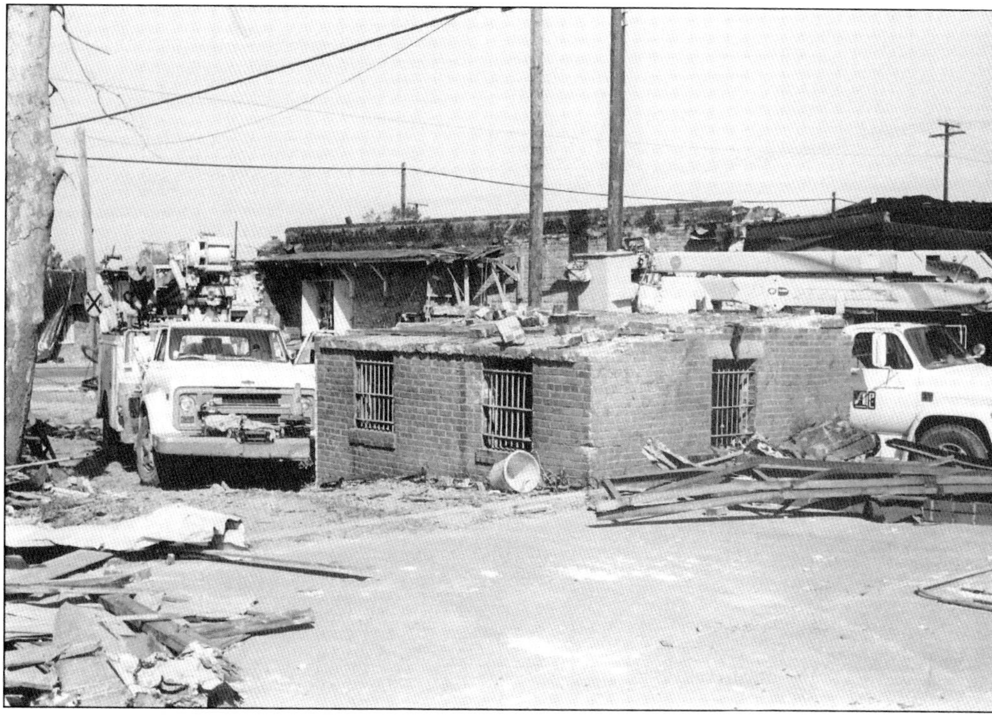

It took numerous people to clean up the area and to restore some degree of order to the city. Hundreds of local people pitched in, as did the state. The National Guard was sent in, and city was declared closed by Gov. David Pryor. Arkansas Power and Light crews are shown here working to restore a main priority to the area, electricity.

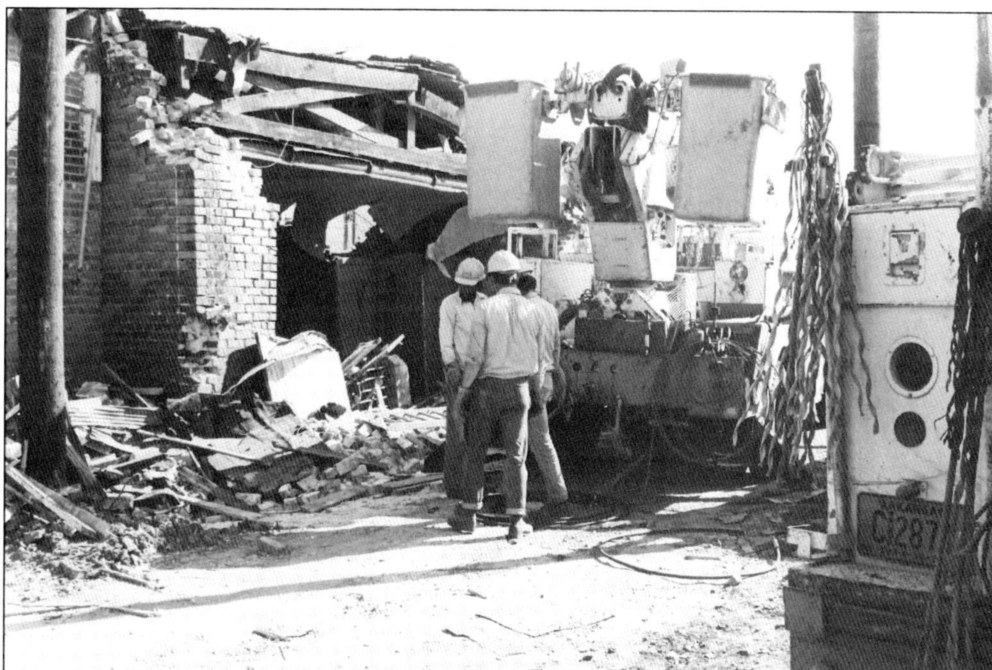

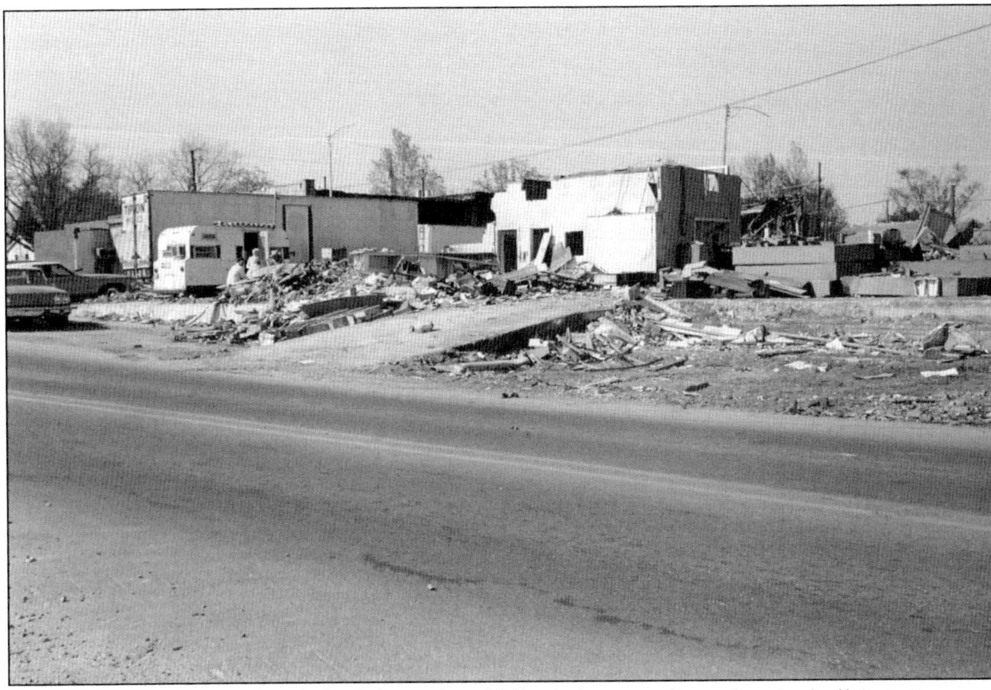

"It was just completely demolished, from the old Ford place to where the city hall is sitting now, to approximately the fire station which housed the city hall at the time," future mayor Pete Clements recalled.

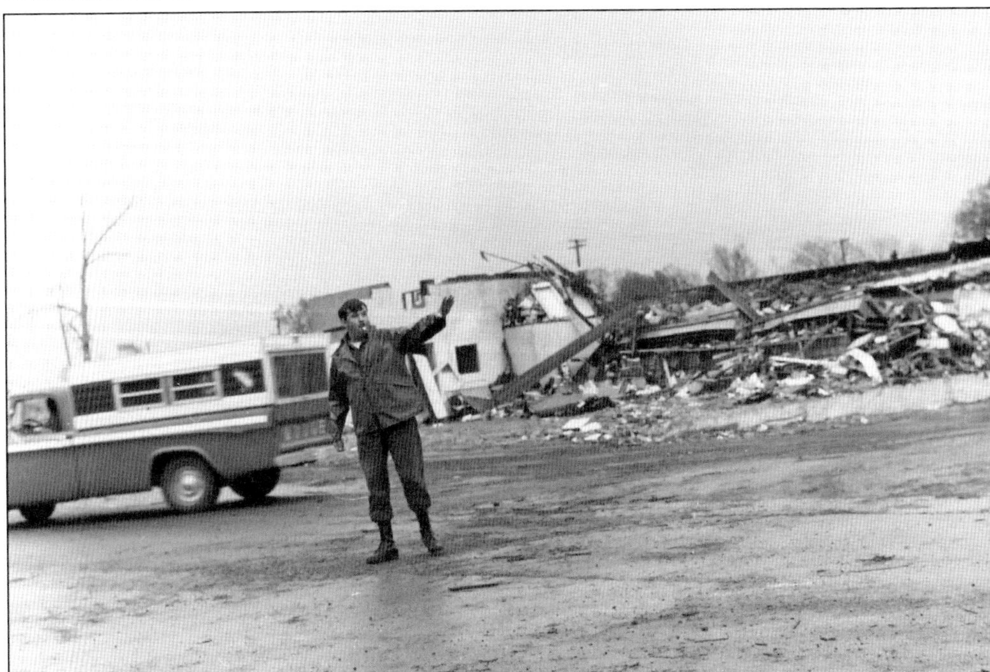

As with all major storms, necessary emergency personnel are some of the first to arrive on the scene. National Guardsmen were placed throughout the town, like the soldier shown here, to assist in the clean up and to maintain order and prevent any possible looting.

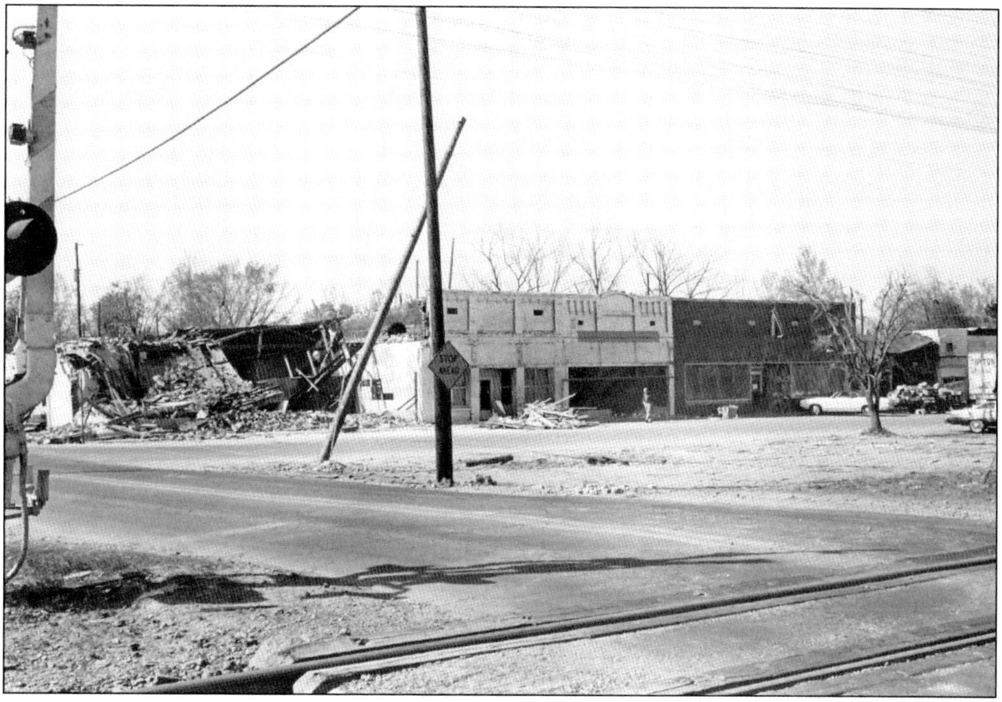

A large part of the old business and residential sections of the city were destroyed by the storm. Ray Sexton stated that it "looked like it was just a miniature town that you took your arm and knocked it all down." Many of the old buildings were damaged beyond repair and had to be removed. As a result, the storm not only destroyed lives, but also changed much of the physical landscape of the old town. While the city now appears different, many of the buildings shown in the bottom view of First Street still exist, though covered by modern facades.

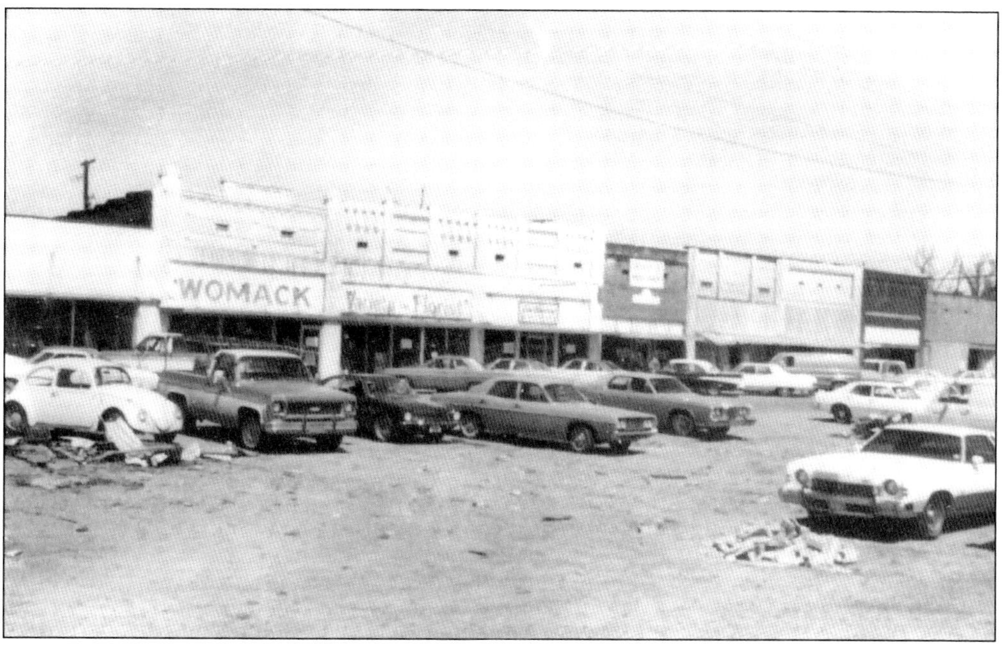

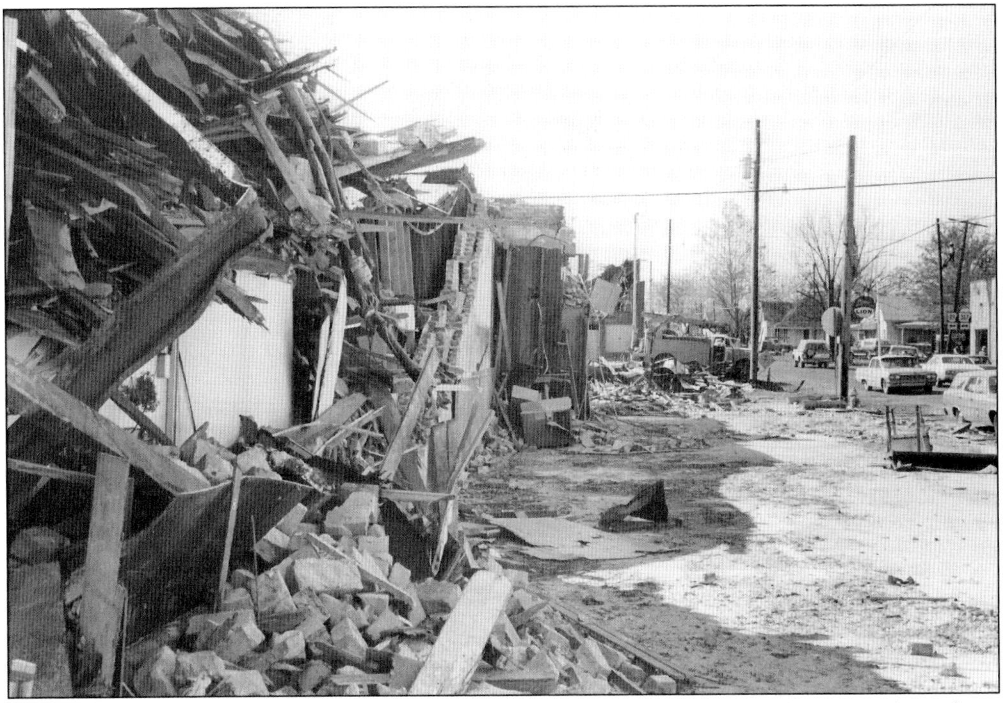

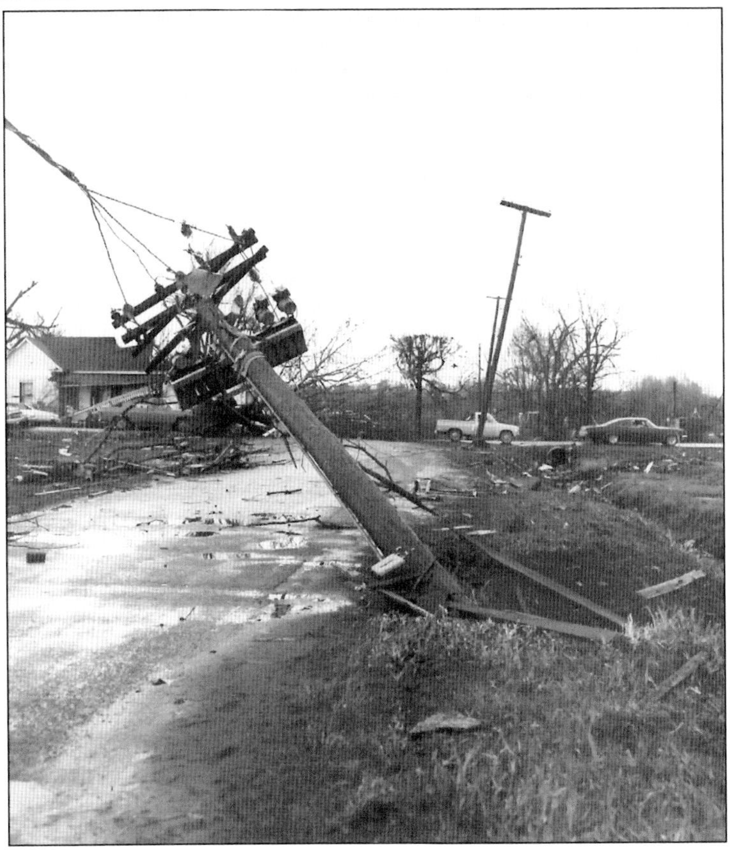

"There were lots of buildings flattened and lots of rubble, some buildings were still standing, but maybe the building next to it might be a pile of bricks. Pieces of things everywhere, stuff hanging out of trees, just debris everywhere," said Marva Verkler

Power was out all over town, with many of the power line poles snapped by the winds as if they were nothing more than twigs. Electricity was not restored to the entire town for several days, with many rescue workers and local citizens removing the rubble and looking for survivors in the dark.

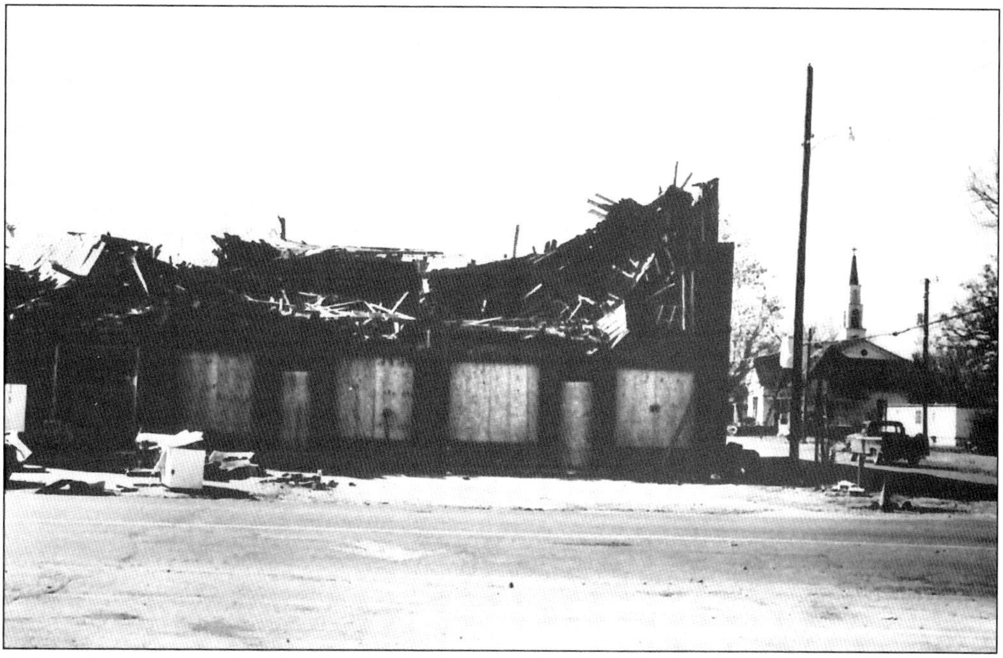

Before the storm would lift into the sky, five people were killed; at no other time has the city experienced such a loss. Many people took refuge in the downtown buildings. Many of those buildings, such as the one shown here on Second Street, were determined to be a complete loss and removed.

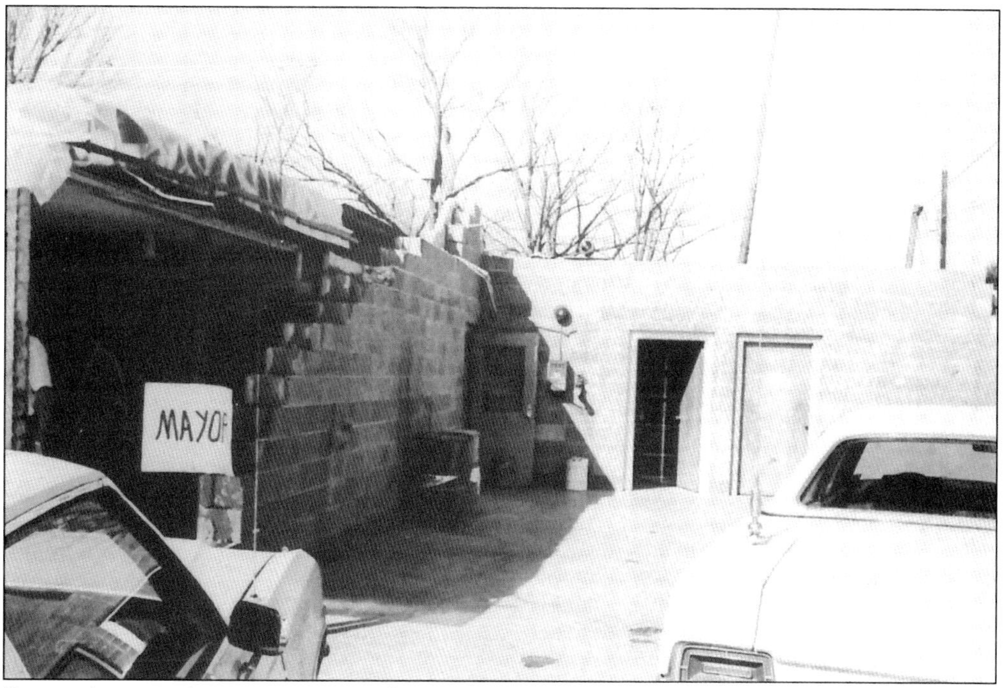

During the crisis, longtime mayor Willie Ray directed the city out of this badly damaged building simply marked with a cardboard sign. While the job seemed almost impossible at the time, Mayor Ray was a major contributor in the recovery of the city and its future growth.

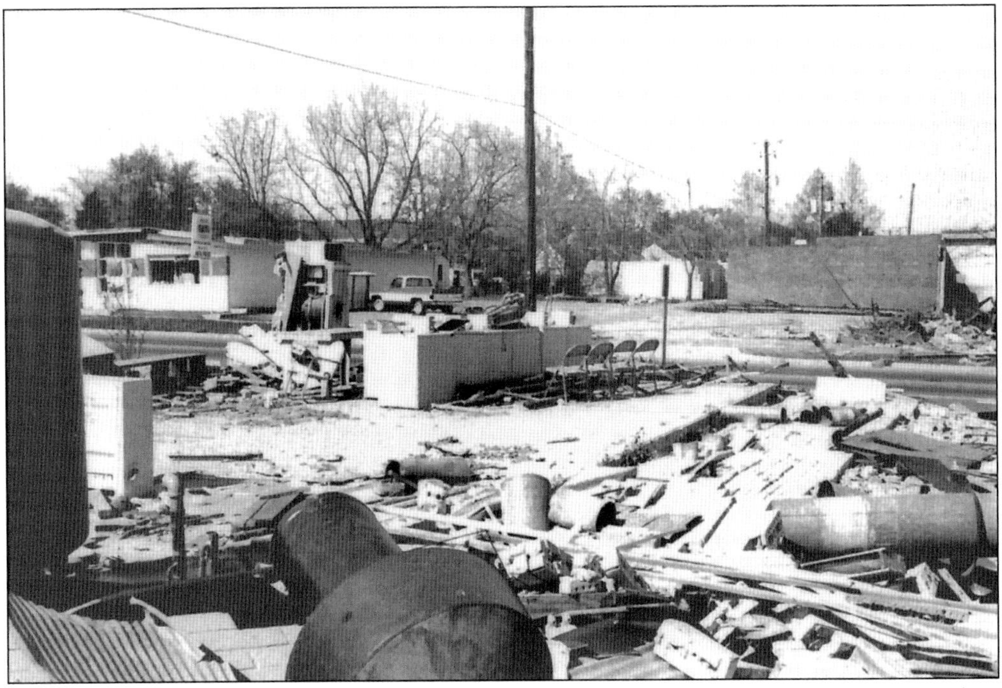

Quite often odd things are seen in the devastation of killer tornadoes. While the surrounding buildings have been flattened, four folding chairs sit in the aftermath, unmoved as if nothing has happened. One witness recalled how strange it was to see complete automobiles sitting on top of buildings.

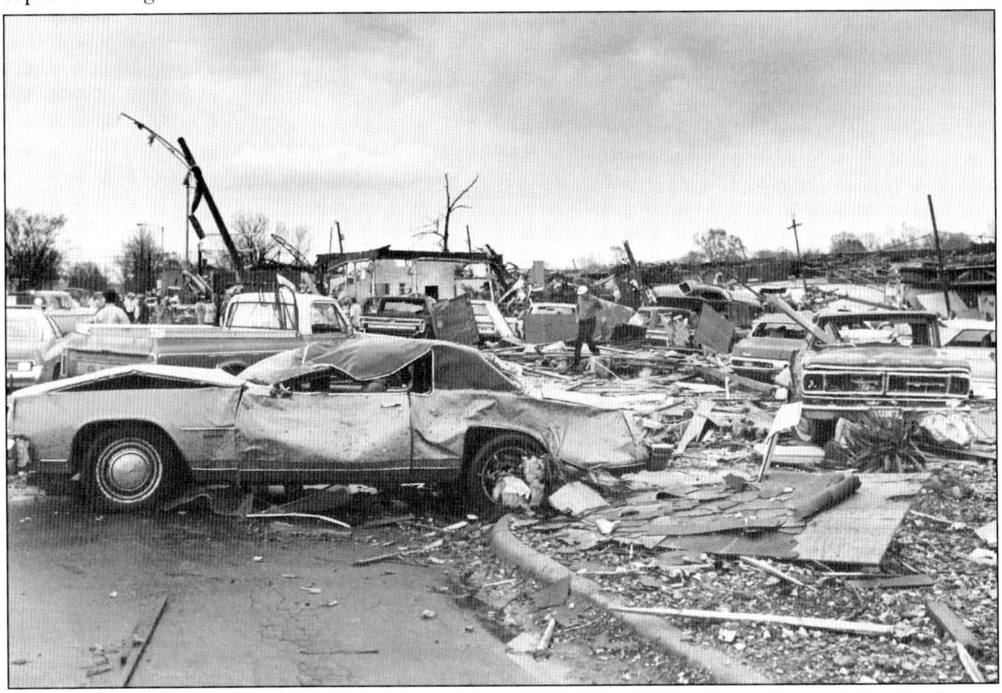

Wanda McManus said, "It really looked like a bomb had dropped right in the middle of it. It was just debris everywhere, and you couldn't get through the streets. It was just a mess."

Five

Boomtown

Behind the slogan "We're Back," city leaders began a campaign to rebuild Cabot in the late 1970s. Little promotion was required due to the city's country atmosphere and its location on a four-lane highway just miles from the state's capital city. People could enjoy slower-paced living while working in the metropolitan Little Rock area. Soon the city began to grow with the population approximately doubling every 10 years. The highly regarded public school system also grew; today, it is one of the largest and fastest growing in the state. Businesses began to move from the traditional downtown area, building on Highway 89 south and north and along newly constructed Highway 321. By 2009, the Internet publication *Businessweek* designated Cabot as an "Arkansas boomtown" and the third fastest growing city per capita in the state. Steady growth continues in the city that now numbers over 25,000 residents.

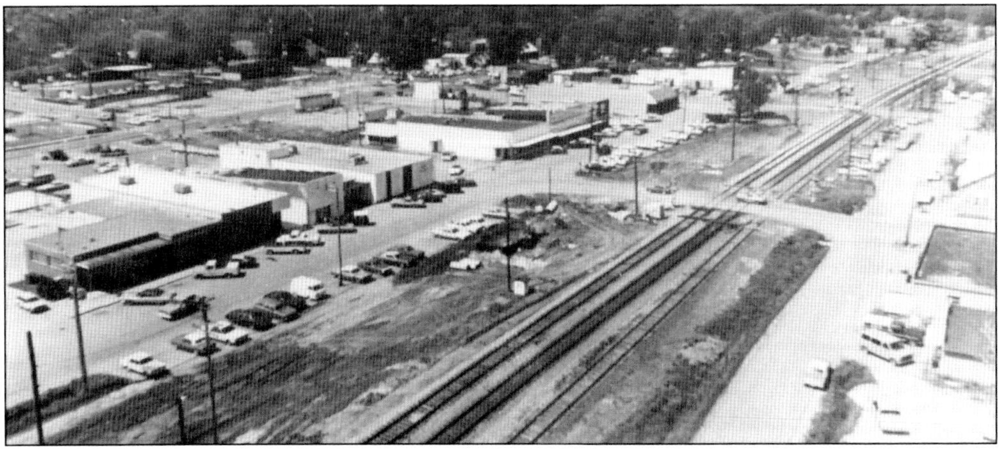

This aerial view of downtown was taken a few months after the 1976 tornado after the debris had been removed. In the top left, on Second Street, vacant lots mark the destructive path of the tornado. The center street is Main Street before it was closed by the construction of the Willie Ray Community Center.

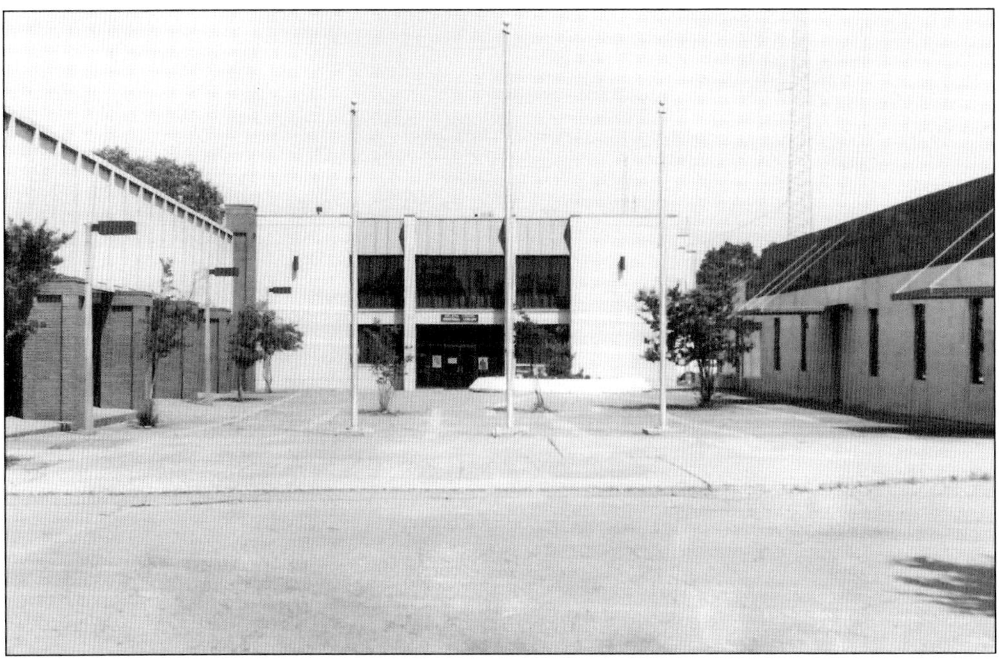

Not long after the killer tornado, a city hall/community center was constructed. Its construction required the rerouting of State Highway 89. The building, which today houses city government offices, was named in honor of Mayor Willie Ray. The back of the building is viewed here from what is commonly called the mall.

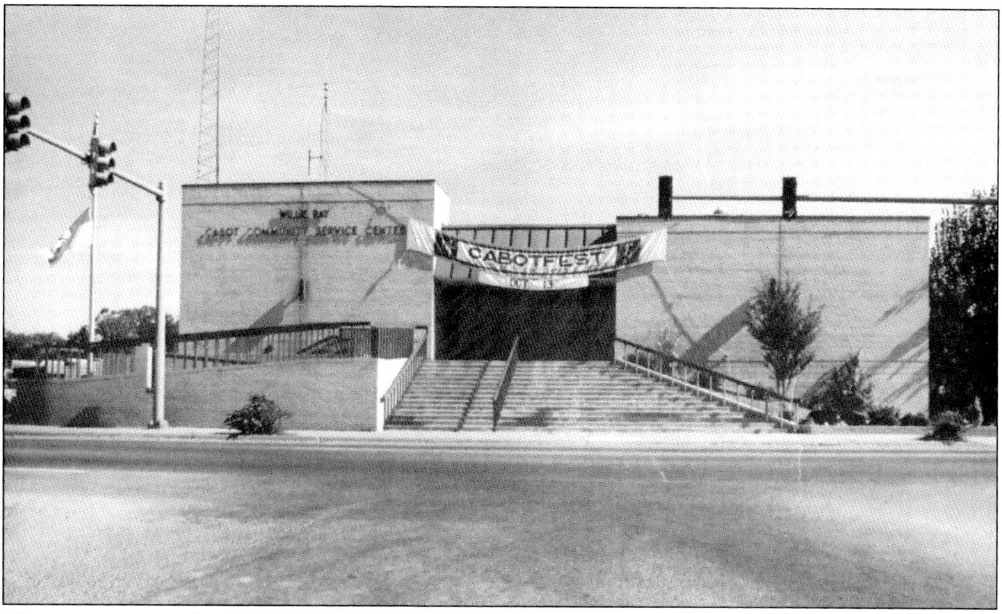

The entrance to the Willie Ray Community Service Center is shown here shortly after it was occupied, decorated with a banner advertising an early CabotFest. Some 30 years later, the building remains much the same.

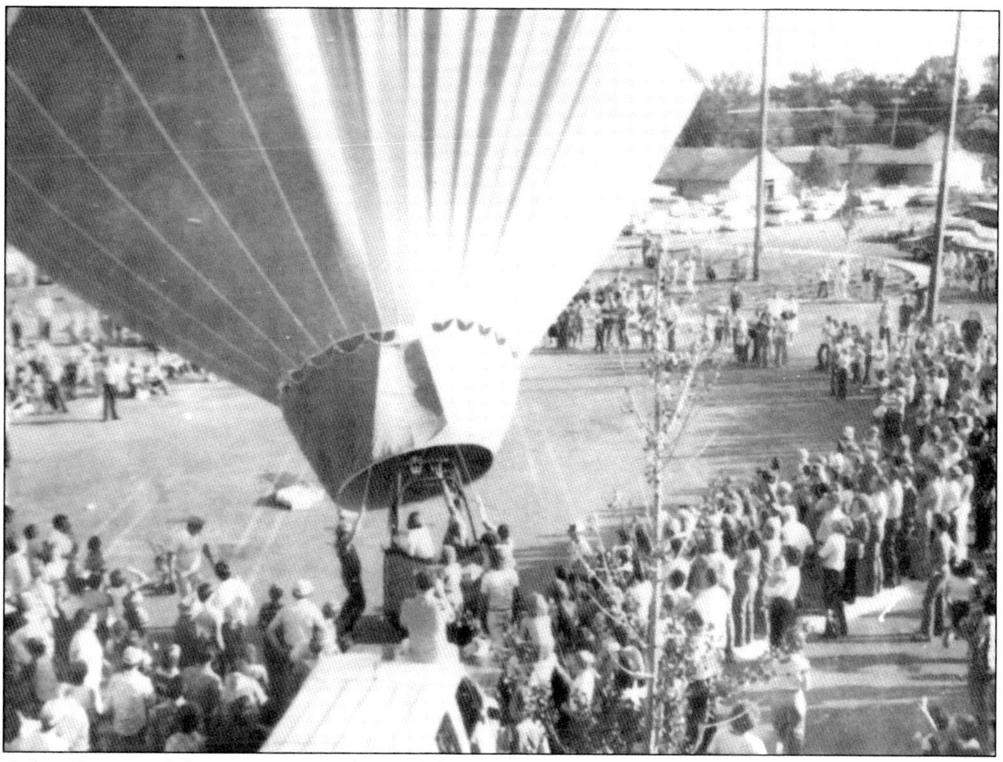

CabotFest, a celebration initiated to celebrate the city's comeback from the tornado, was first held in 1978. Many activities are enjoyed by participants in a carnival like atmosphere. Included in the festival were hot air balloon rides.

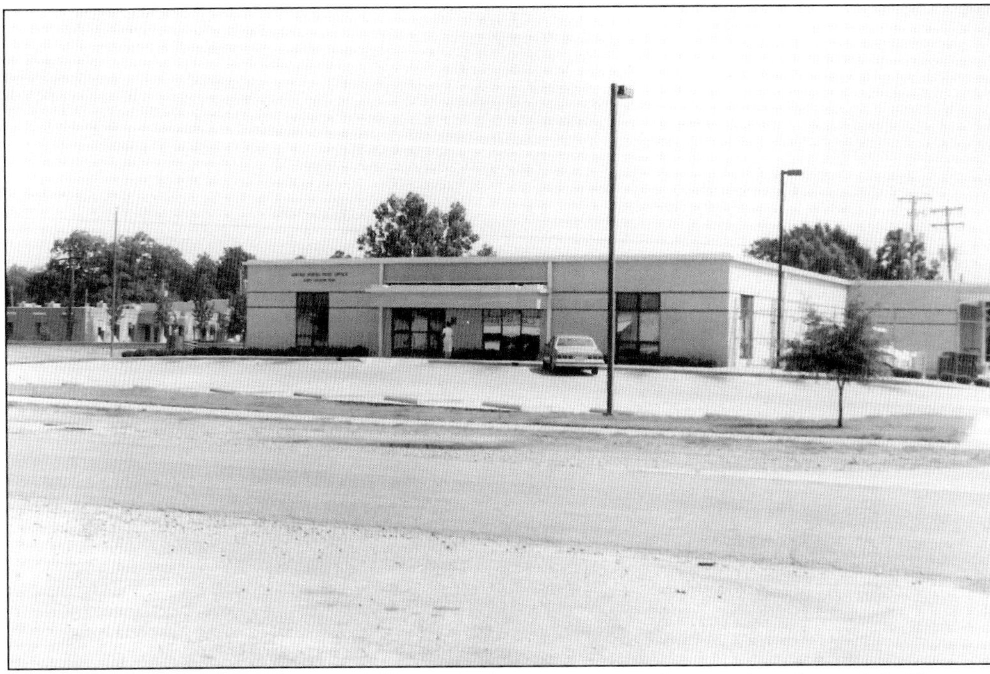

In 1986, a new, modern US Post Office, which continues as the town's only mail facility, was constructed in the downtown area.

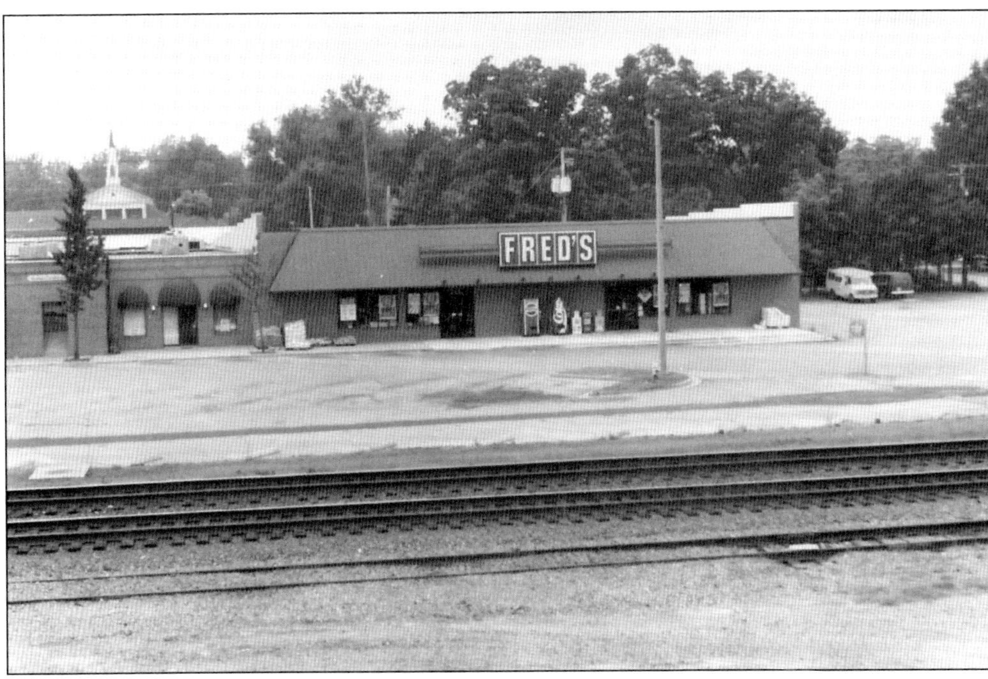

With the completion of Highway 67/167 as a four-lane highway by the 1980s, Cabot began to grow steadily. A growing population attracted new businesses. One of the few new businesses to open in downtown was Fred's. Though relocated about three blocks from this location, it is still one of the town's leading department stores. The former building is home to the local courts system.

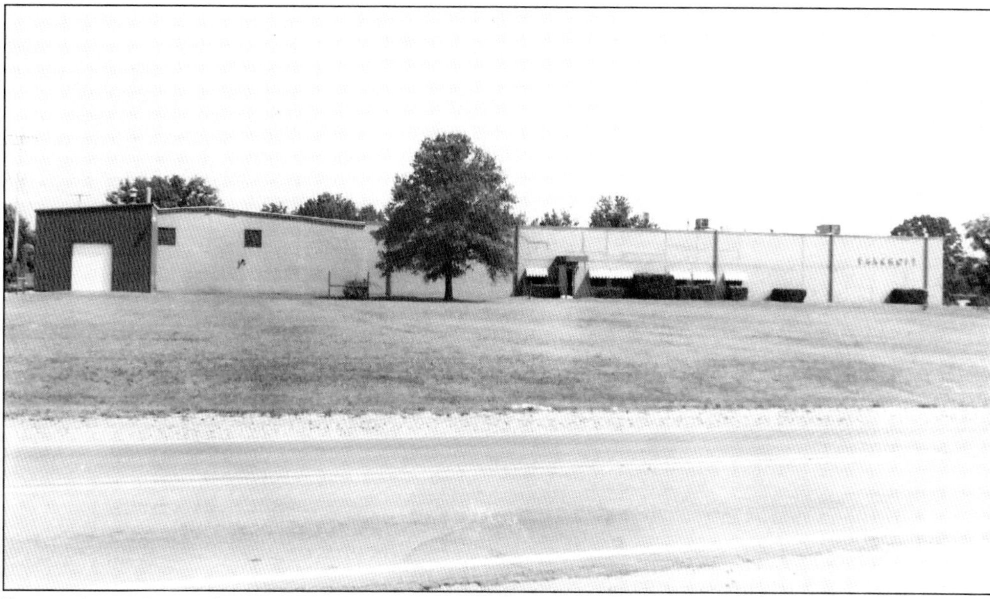

Bancroft, on Second Street, was one of the first industries to locate in Cabot in the 1970s. At one time it was a major manufacturer of military hats, supplying military forces all over the world. The company maintained a flock of sheep from which wool was collected for producing many of the hats. The factory closed in the early 21st century.

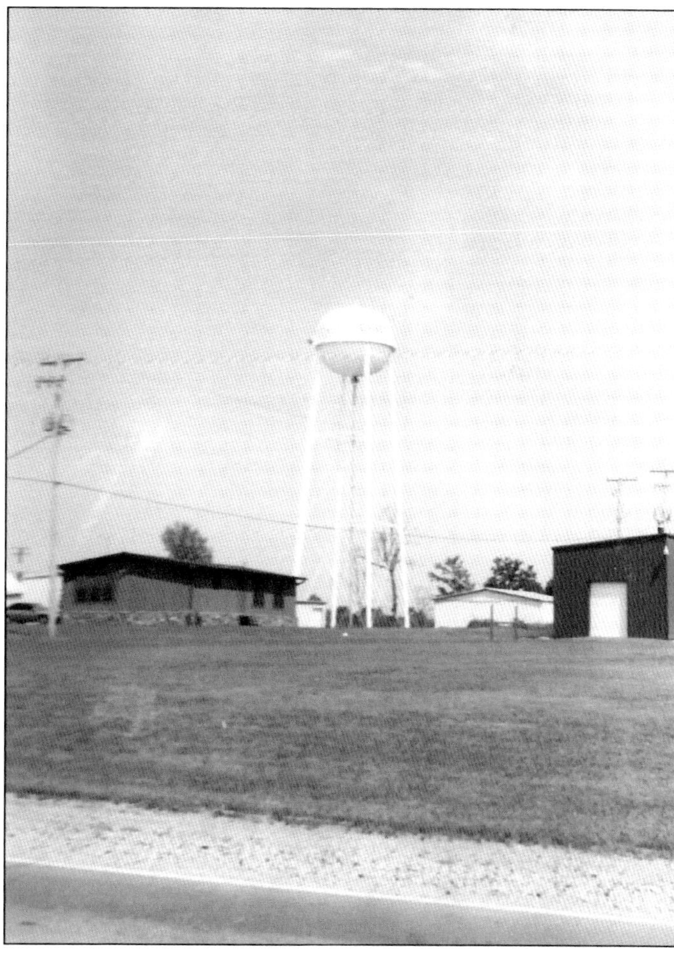

Though tall buildings have been constructed in recent years, nothing stands taller than the familiar town water tower. The town's second tower, shown here, still stands in the old industrial park area. The first tower, located in downtown, was removed many years ago.

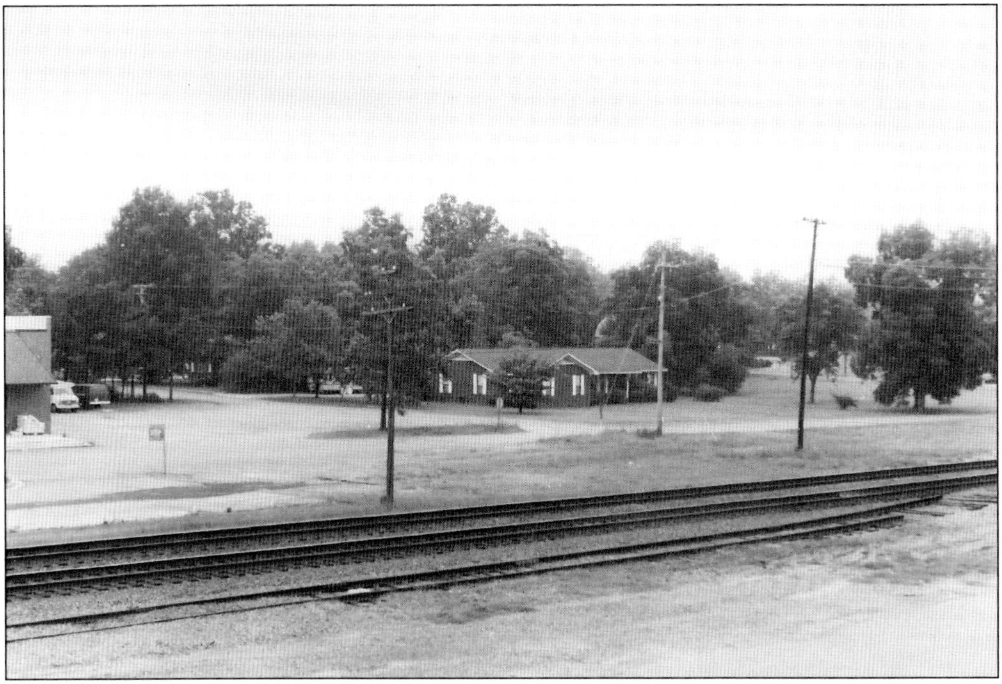

While the traffic might be more congested, the north end of First Street has changed little since this photograph was taken in the 1990s. The building to the left, Fred's at the time of this photograph, is today the city annex. The house in the center is still occupied.

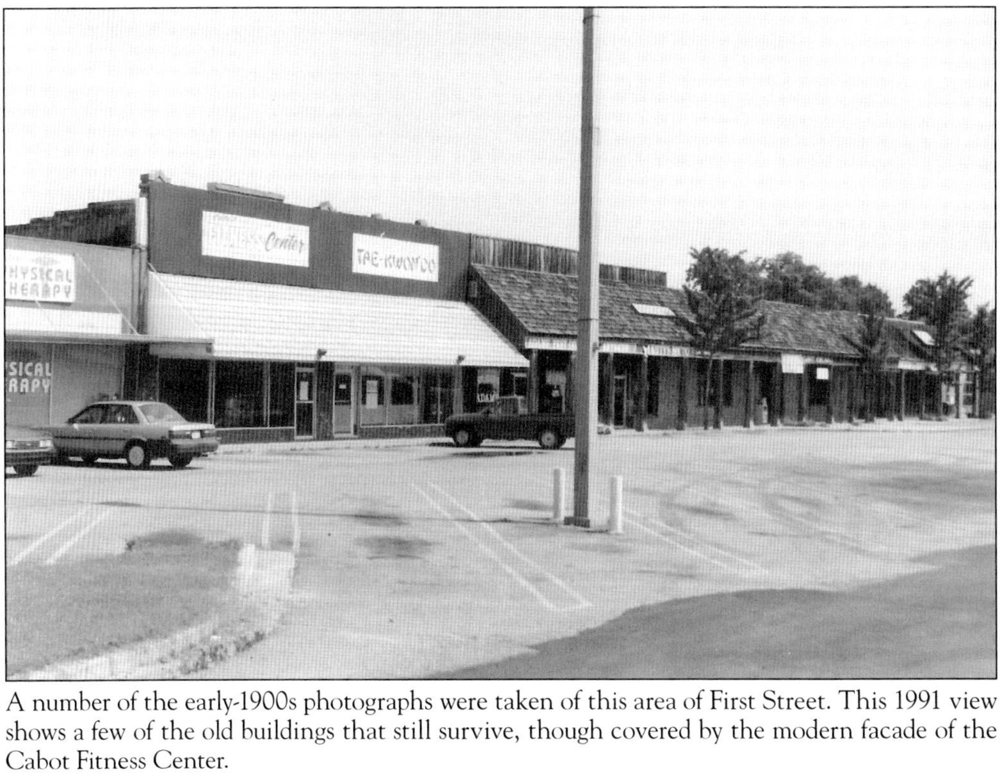

A number of the early-1900s photographs were taken of this area of First Street. This 1991 view shows a few of the old buildings that still survive, though covered by the modern facade of the Cabot Fitness Center.

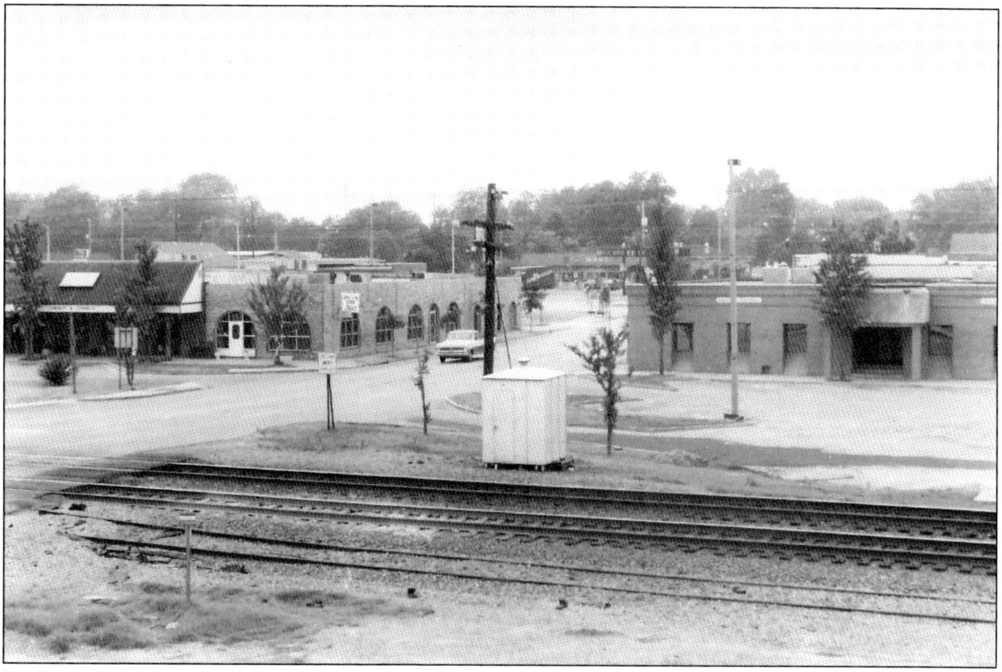

Highway 89 is one of the two main highways to pass through Cabot. Here, it is shown at the main railroad crossing. In the mid-20th century, See's Department Store occupied a building on the left corner, while the old Bank of Cabot structure was on the right corner.

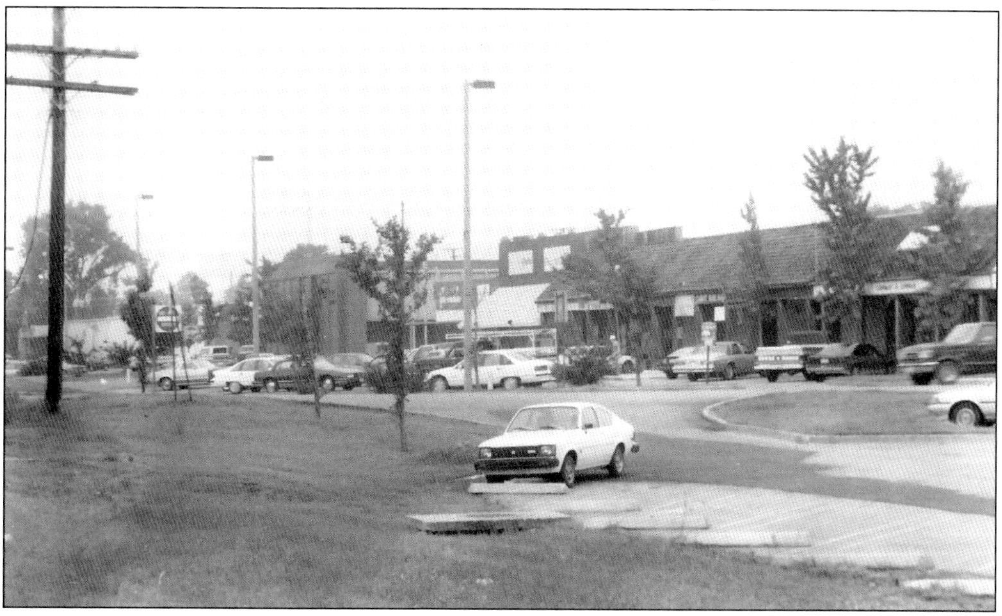

By the 1990s, much of the downtown business began to be overshadowed by new growth along Highway 89, extending to Highway 5. All of the businesses shown in this 1990s photograph have closed, though a hardware store under different ownership is still open in the old Lowman and Lowman building to the extreme right and the City Water Department occupies the old Bank of Cabot location. Unlike many Arkansas downtown business districts, most of the buildings in downtown Cabot remain occupied, though growth continues elsewhere.

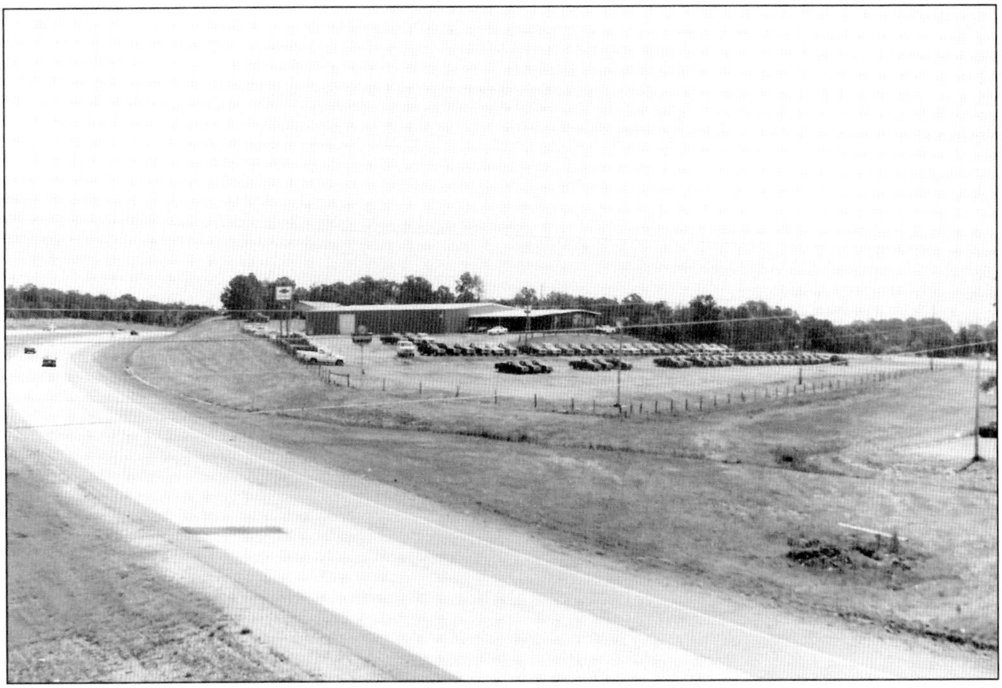

Four-lane Highway 67/167, which connects Cabot with Little Rock, has been a major factor in the rapid growth of the town. In the center is Ray Chevrolet, a longtime car dealership closed as a victim of America's economic problems in 2010.

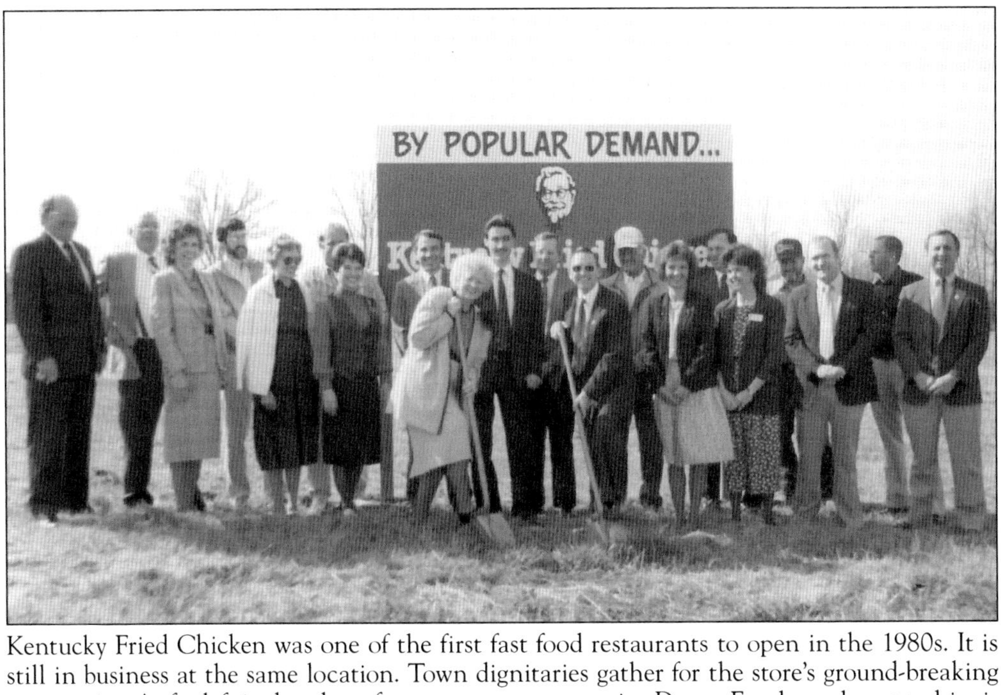

Kentucky Fried Chicken was one of the first fast food restaurants to open in the 1980s. It is still in business at the same location. Town dignitaries gather for the store's ground-breaking ceremonies. At far left is chamber of commerce representative Dewey Faught and next to him is school superintendent Don Elliot. The woman with the shovel is Gene Ray, wife of the former mayor. To the far right is local banker John C. Thompson.

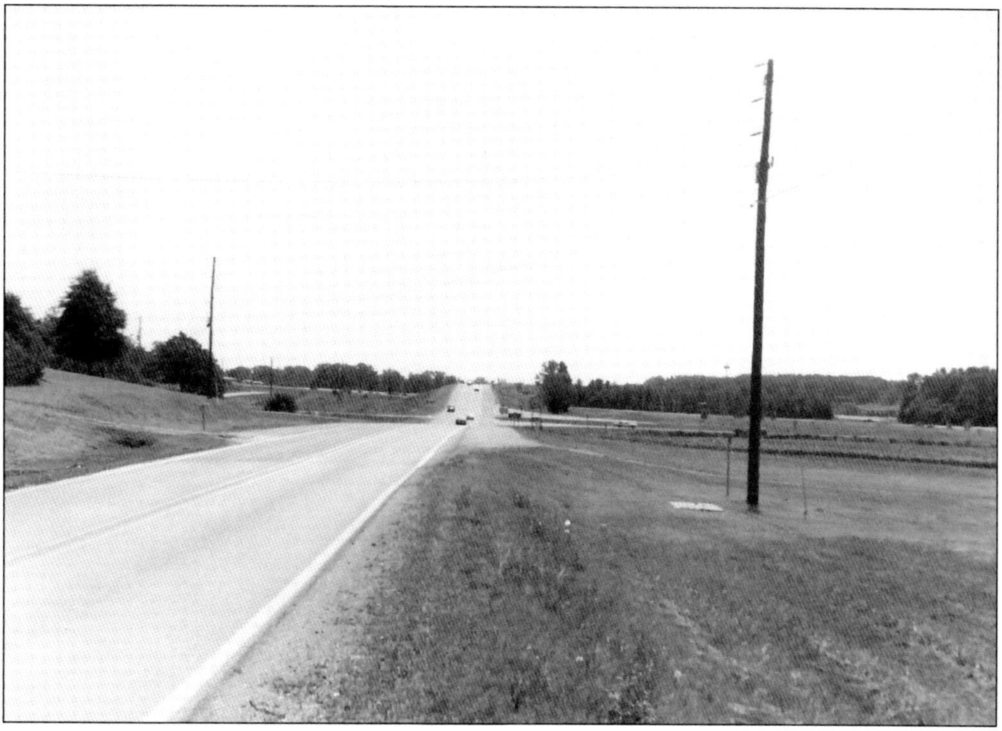

This stretch of Highway 89 is one of the busiest in present-day Cabot. A number of businesses have built along the roadway in recent years as the town's business sector continues to grow.

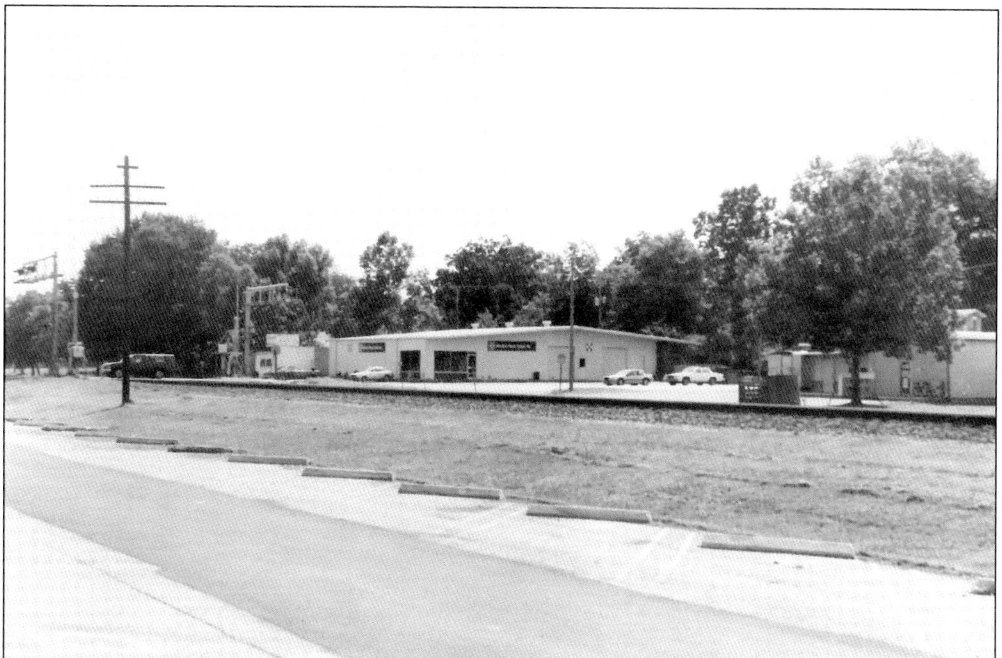

This view of Woods Feed Store in the center and the Cabot Locker Plant to the right has changed little since this photograph taken in the early 1990s. Both remain important downtown businesses.

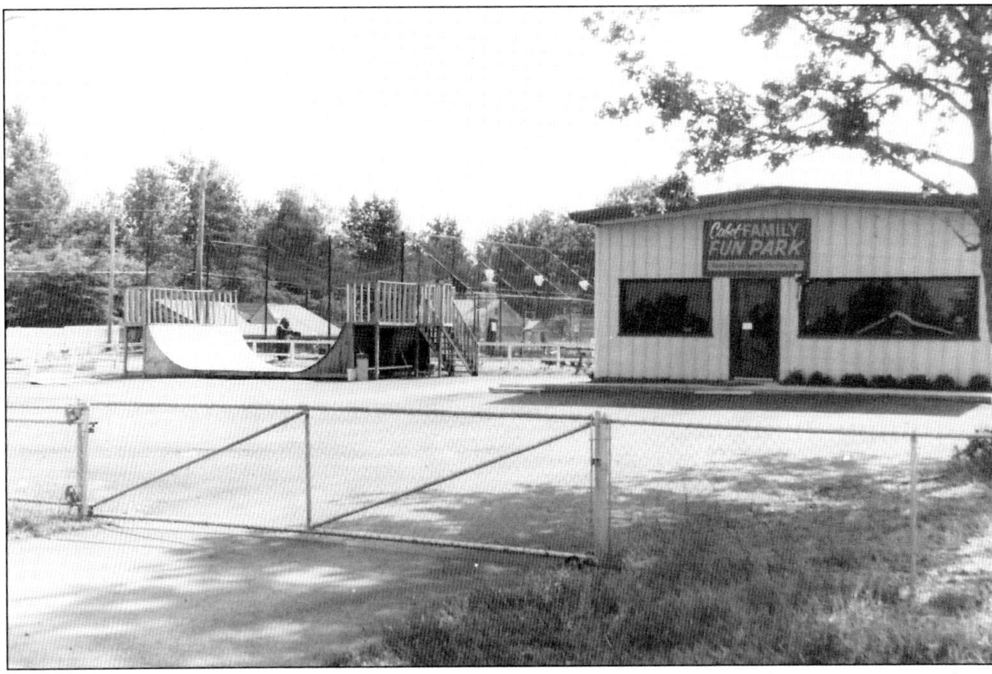

With its opening in the 1980s, Cabot Family Fun Park became a popular attraction with its miniature golf course, game room, batting cages, and, unique for the time, skate board ramp. It remained open for only a few years.

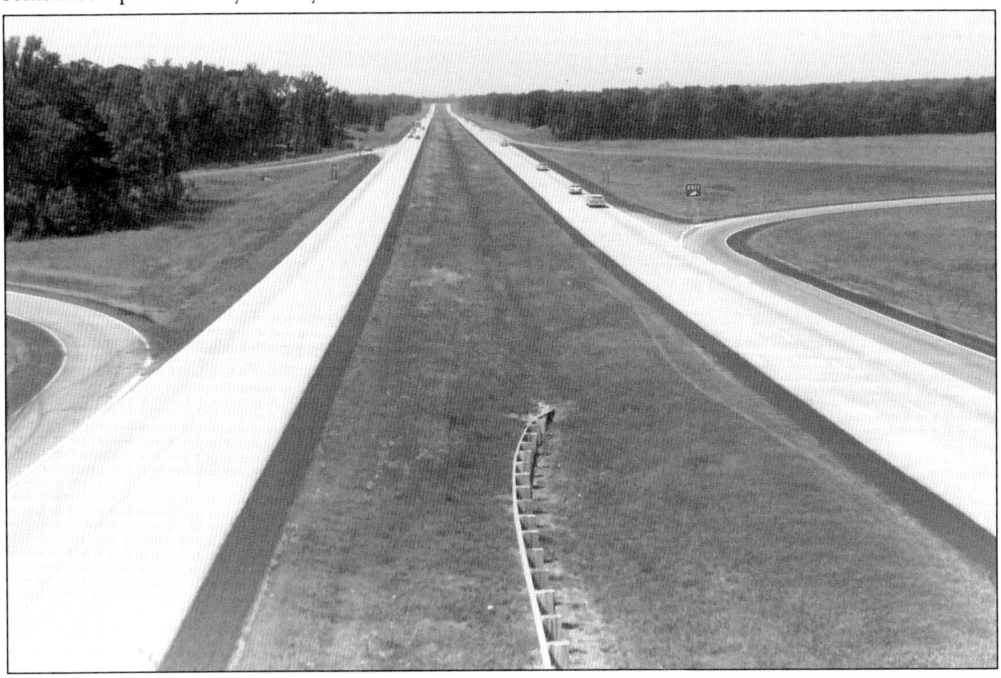

A major factor contributing to the rapid growth of Cabot was the completion of the four-lane highway designated at Highway 67/167. Connecting the city with Little Rock, it quickly became a busy artery providing people with easy access to jobs and entertainment while living in the "country." Today, it is one of the most used highways in central Arkansas.

Six

Schools

New residents of Cabot are often heard to say, "We moved here because of the quality schools." The school system, one of the state's largest and most respected, had humble beginnings in 1875 with the establishment of a school by Prof. G.W. Newton. Just as in present-day Cabot, Professor Newton's school grew rapidly, resulting in the construction of a two-story frame building in 1893 followed by a massive brick structure affectionately known as Old Main in 1912. The school continued to grow and grow, adding more buildings and campuses over the years. From those simple beginnings, the highly regarded district has grown to a system that includes a charter school, nine elementary schools, two middle schools, two junior high schools, and one high school, all of which provide a quality educational opportunity for almost 10,000 young people.

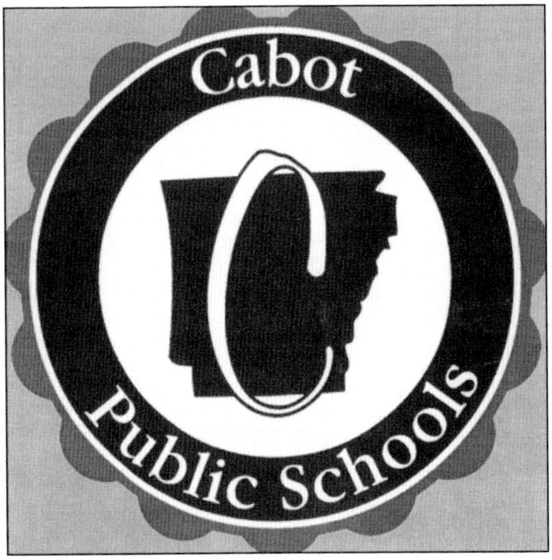

Long gone are the days when students at Cabot Public Schools were educated on a central campus. Today, the school consists of one high school, two junior high schools, two middle schools, a charter school, and nine elementary schools. Shown here is the current official school seal. (Courtesy Museum of American History.)

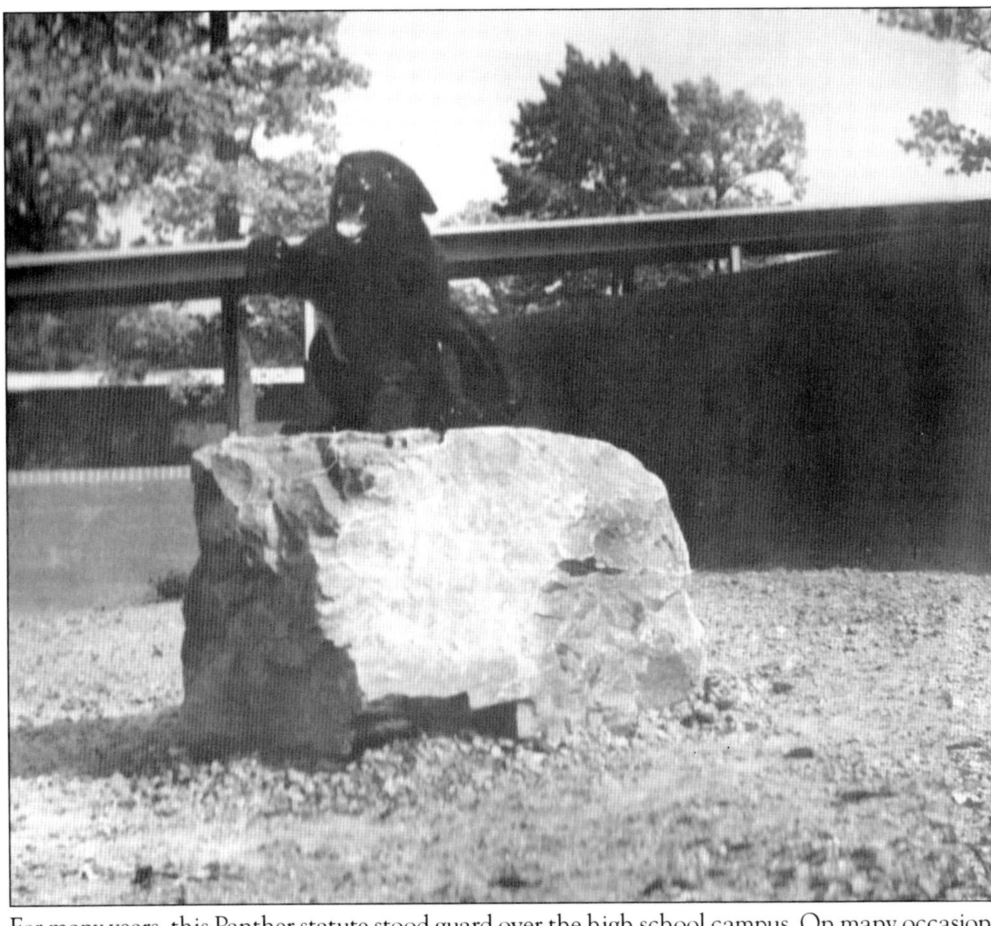

For many years, this Panther statute stood guard over the high school campus. On many occasions students from rival schools would sneak onto the campus and paint the mascot with their school colors. At one time, it was moved in the front of the gym and today rests on a platform in the entrance hall of the main high school building. (Courtesy Museum of American History.)

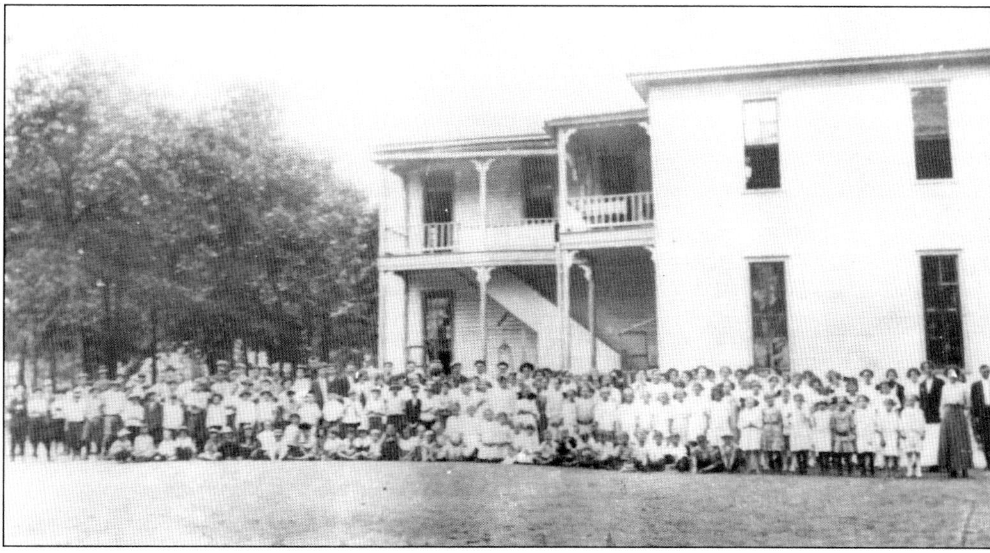

Cabot is well known for its schools, with the first school being founded by Prof. G.W. Newton in 1875. Approximately 18 years later in 1893, this two-story frame building located on Jackson Street housed the public school. While, today, several hundred teachers are employed by the district, there were only five at the beginning of the 20th century.

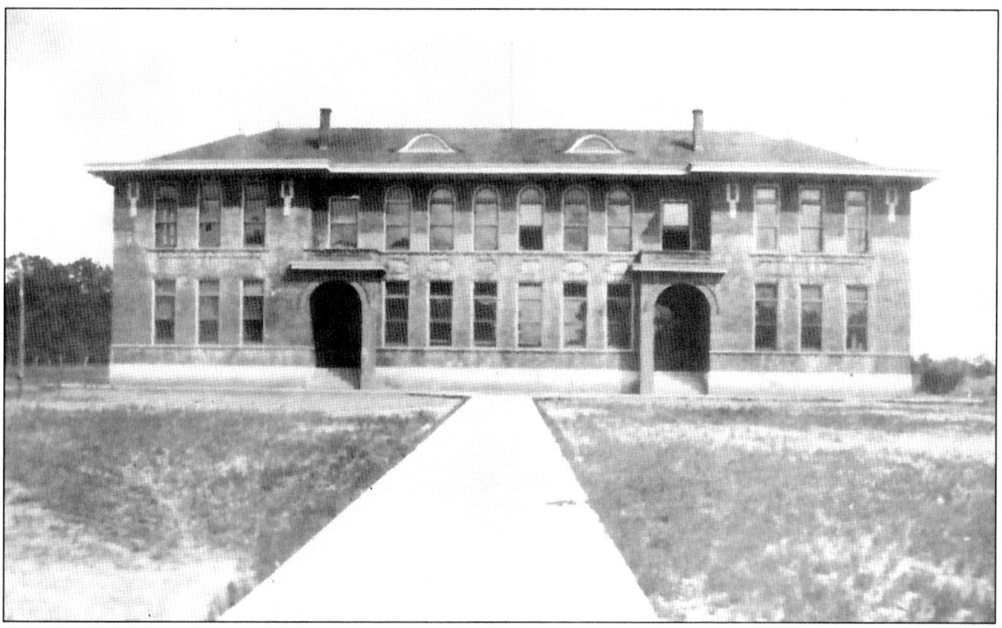

In the early 20th century, city growth and an increasing student body dictated the construction of a new school building to replace the two-story frame one constructed in 1875. In 1915, an impressive brick structure, affectionately called Old Main, was occupied by the student body. The building, which had fallen into disrepair and was condemned about 1969, was razed to make way for new construction in 1972.

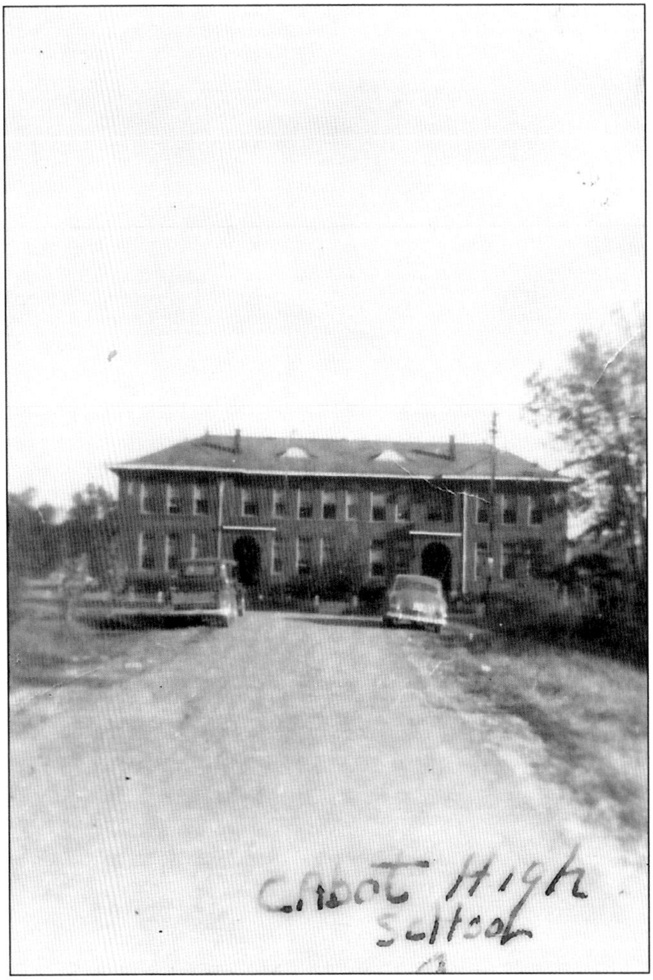

In the late 1940s, all of Cabot's approximately 500 students, grades 1–12, attended classes in Old Main. (Courtesy Jack and Betty Carrington.)

The 2011 Cabot High School graduation ceremonies held at Verizon Arena in Little Rock saw almost 600 diplomas presented to smiling faces. Less than 100 years ago, it was a much different story. During that ceremony conducted at Old Main in 1917, twelve students received their high school diplomas.

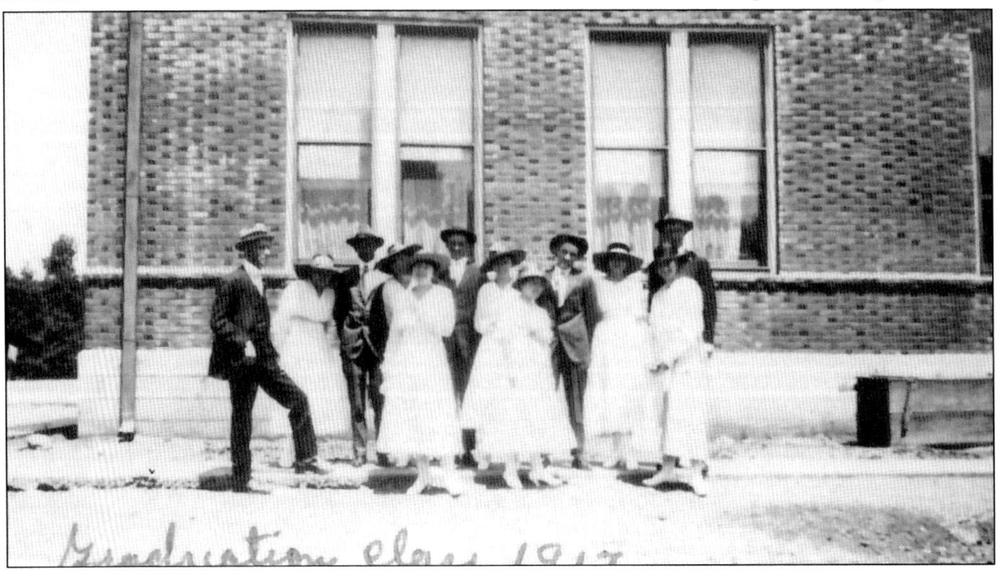

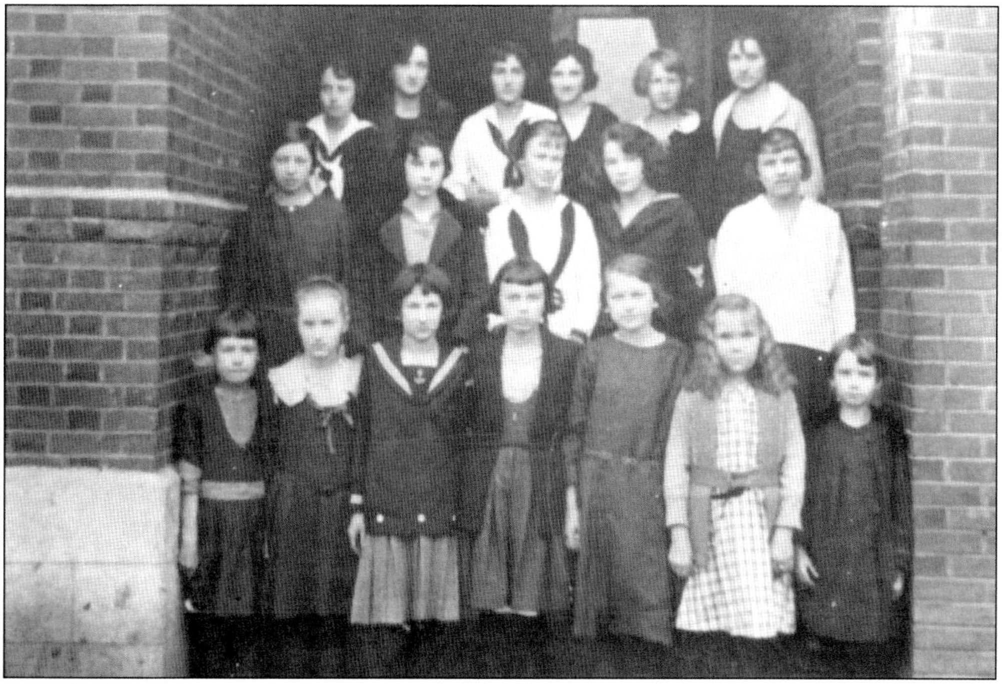

Music has been a part of the school curriculum since the early days of the school. Students of Grace Birmingham's 1922–1923 music class are shown posing in front of Old Main school building.

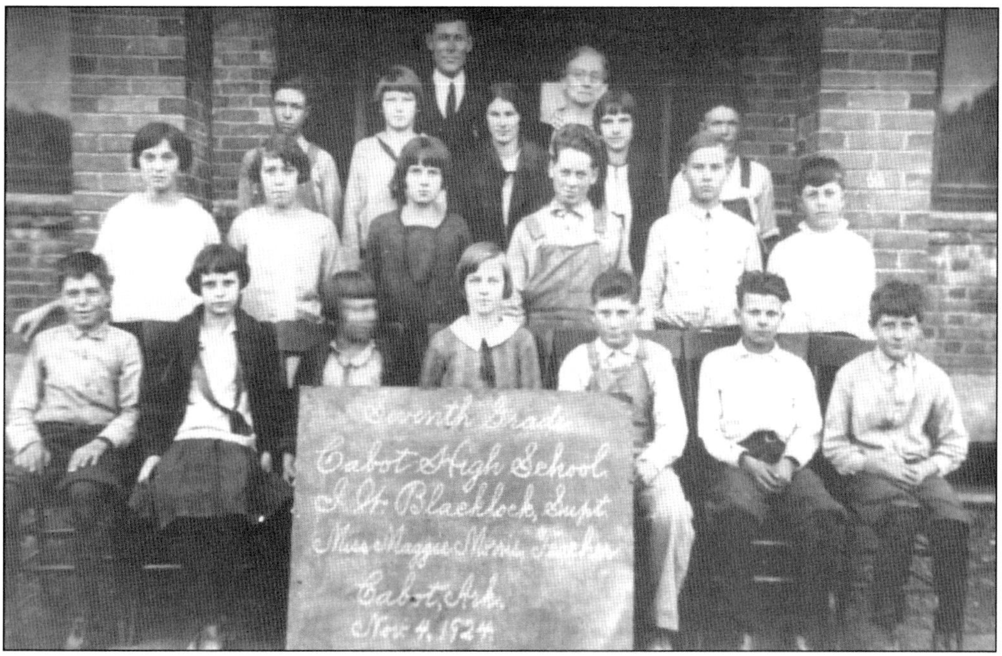

While individual photographs of students are common in modern times, years ago such school photographs were rarely taken. In years past, the class picture, which is still taken of schoolchildren today, was the norm. Classes, especially the lower grades, were often posed on the front steps of Old Main. In this photograph is the 1924 seventh grade class of Maggie Morris. Superintendent Blacklock is shown standing to her right. (Courtesy Museum of American History.)

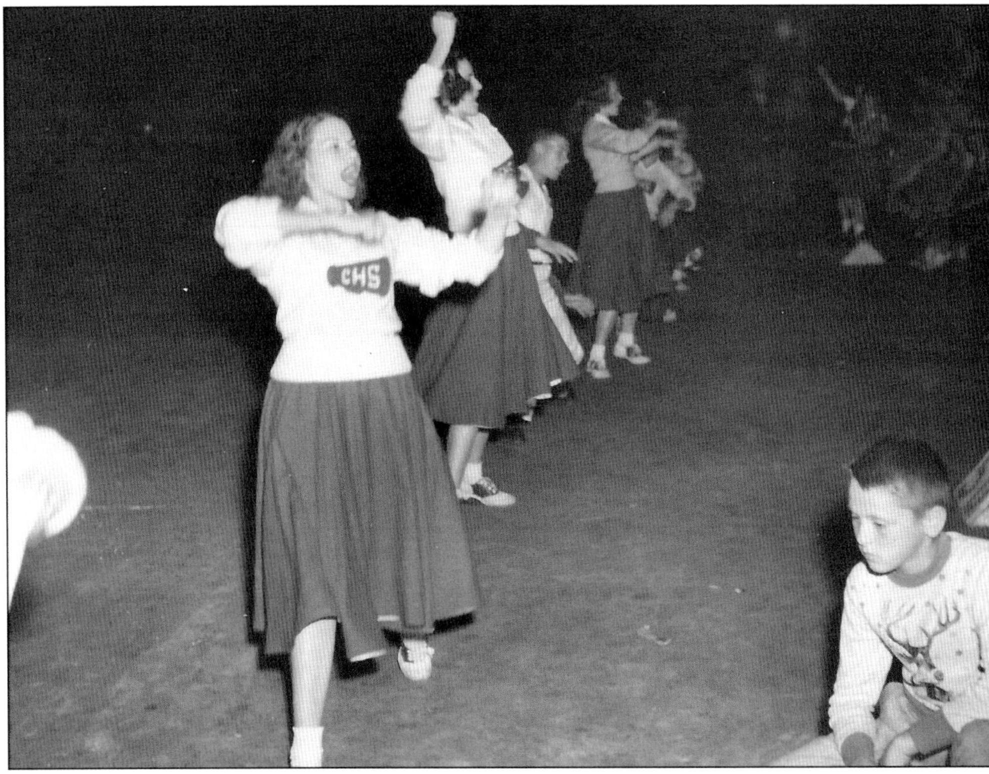

Cheerleaders have been an integral part of school spirit since the development of high school sports. The high school squad is shown here on the sidelines cheering on the 1949 Panther football team to victory. (Courtesy Judy Lowman Collection from the Museum of American History.)

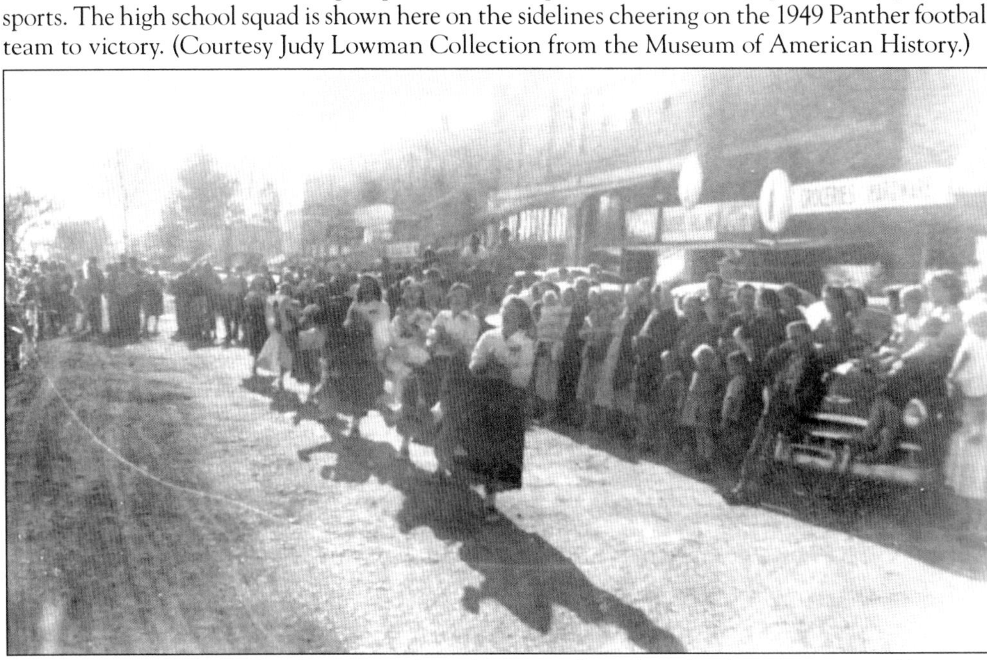

Over the years, many school activities have been conducted in the downtown area. For many years, the downtown 1930s auditorium was used for sporting and social events. Cheerleaders are shown here in one of those many downtown events held in the 1950s.

The Future Farmers of America, founded in 1928, has grown into one of the largest young people's organizations in the United States. It has long been a part of the local schools. Activities generally conclude with a yearly banquet, such as the well-attended one being enjoyed by Cabot members in 1950. (Courtesy Judy Lowman Collection from the Museum of American History.)

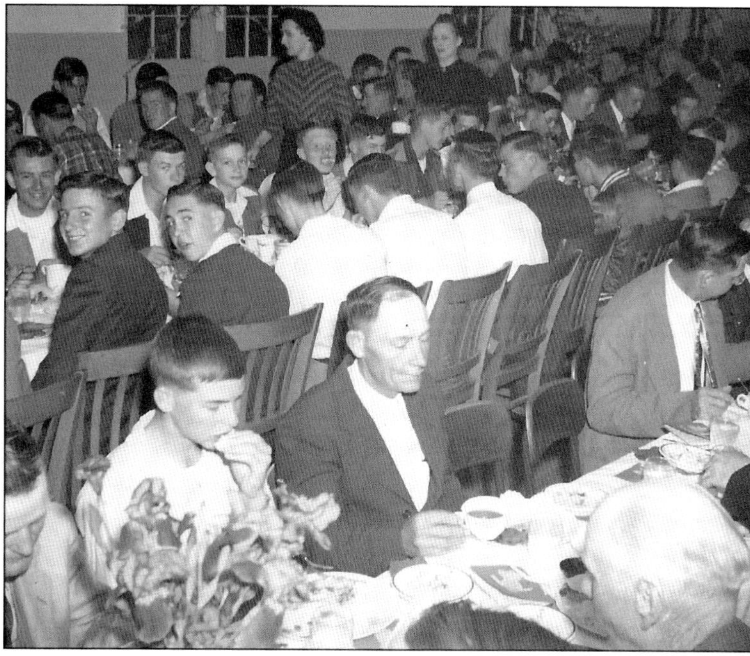

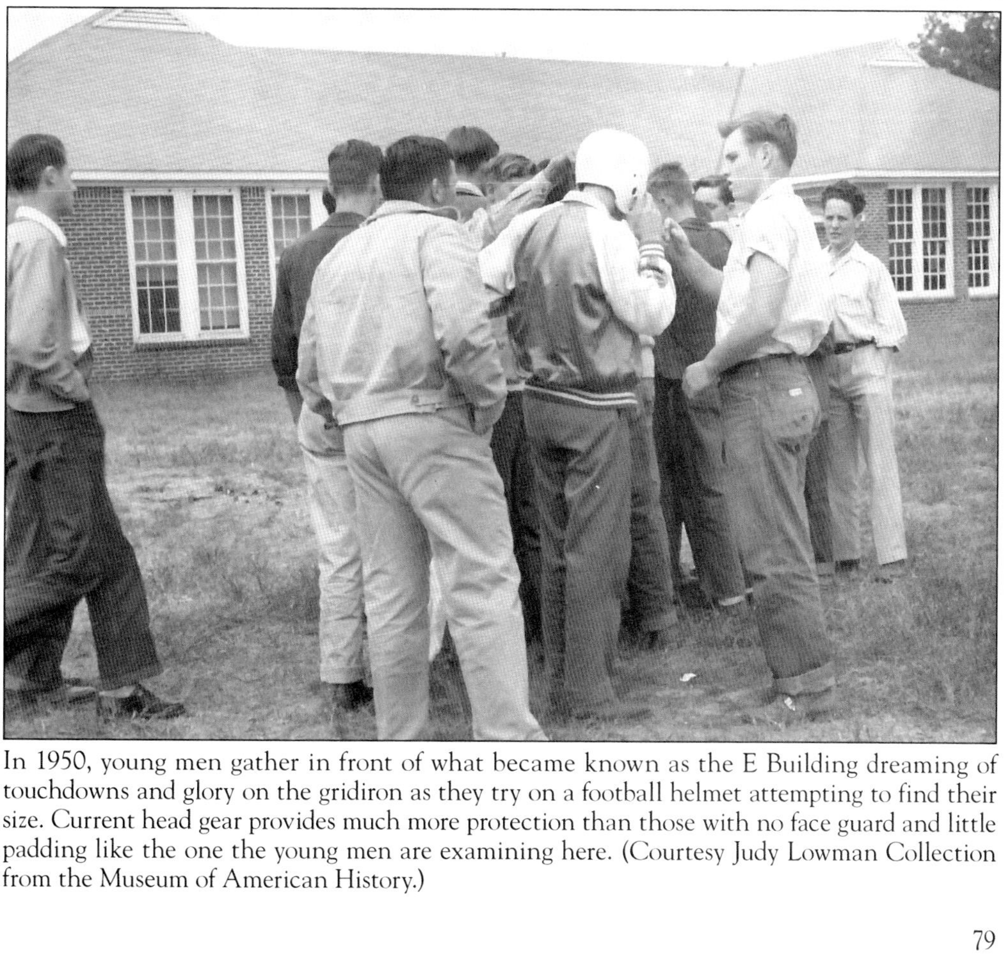

In 1950, young men gather in front of what became known as the E Building dreaming of touchdowns and glory on the gridiron as they try on a football helmet attempting to find their size. Current head gear provides much more protection than those with no face guard and little padding like the one the young men are examining here. (Courtesy Judy Lowman Collection from the Museum of American History.)

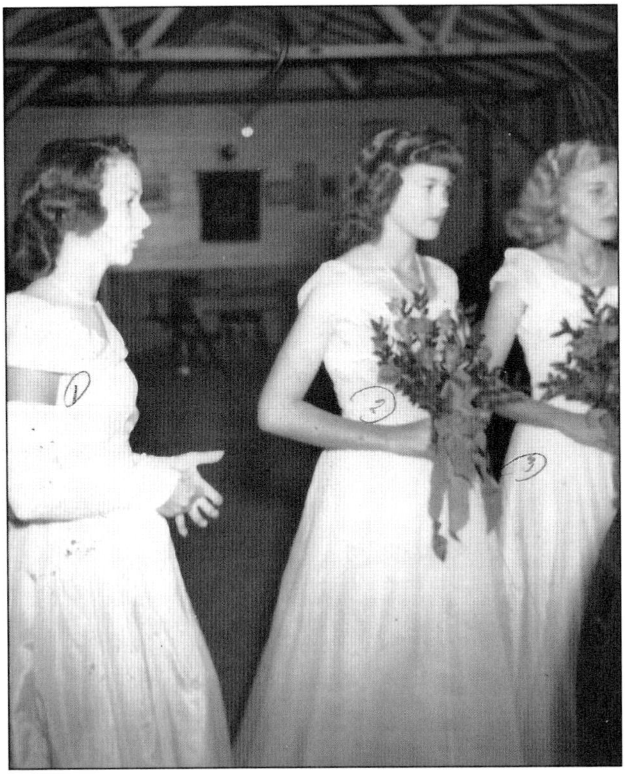

Homecoming festivities are a long-standing tradition that runs deep in public schools. Much of the 1949 activities, due to rain, were conducted in the high school agriculture building, where homecoming royalty Rose Dodd, Mary King, and Clara Dodd presided. (Courtesy Judy Lowman Collection from the Museum of American History.)

Homecoming football games traditionally draw one of the season's largest crowds. Among the typical festivities is the crowning of homecoming royalty selected by the student body. Such royalty is seen here seated upon a float in the 1940s. (Courtesy Judy Lowman Collection from the Museum of American History.)

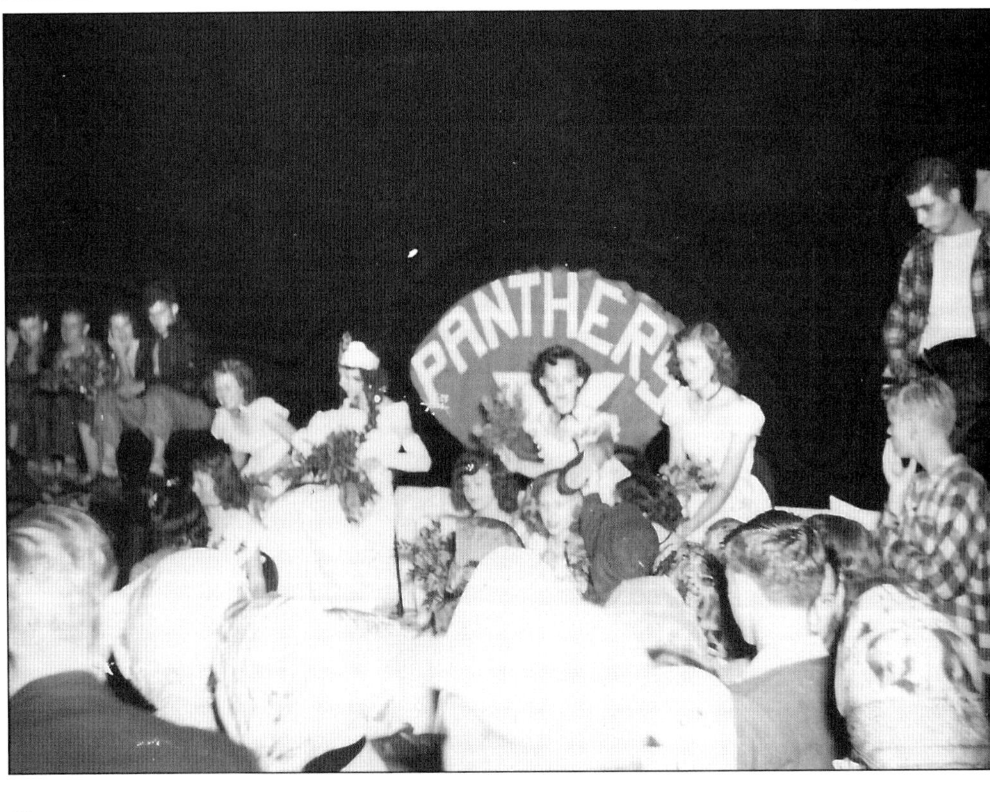

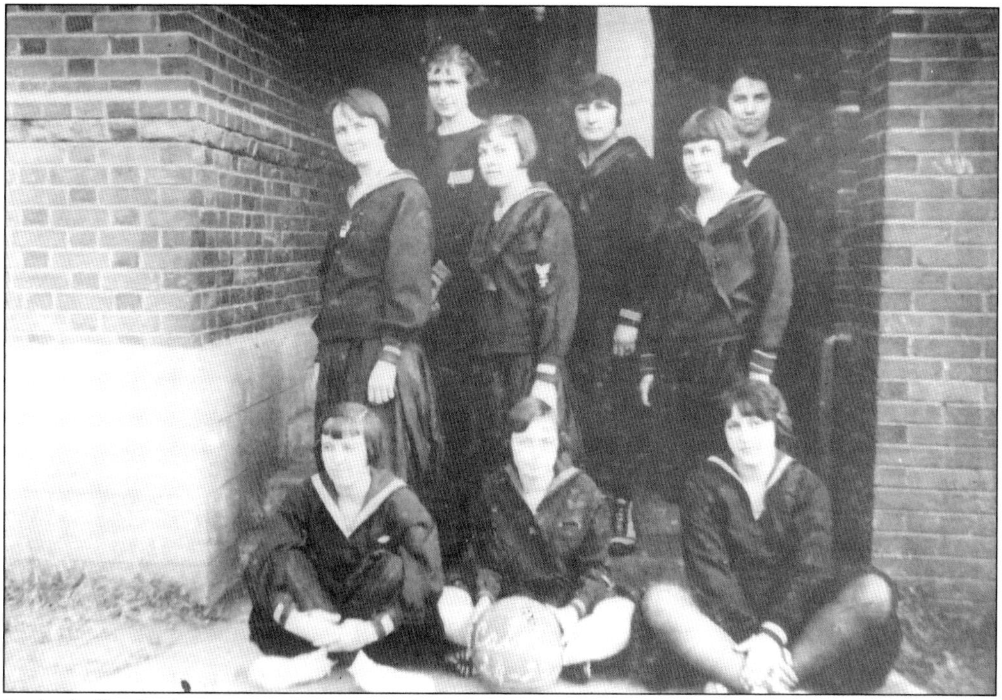

Basketball, which originated in Massachusetts in 1891, experienced rapid growth. In less than a year, the game was expanded to include the ladies. By 1895, ladies basketball was well established in many of the nation's high schools. The game was introduced at Cabot in the early 1900s, as is documented by the 1924–1925 team photograph.

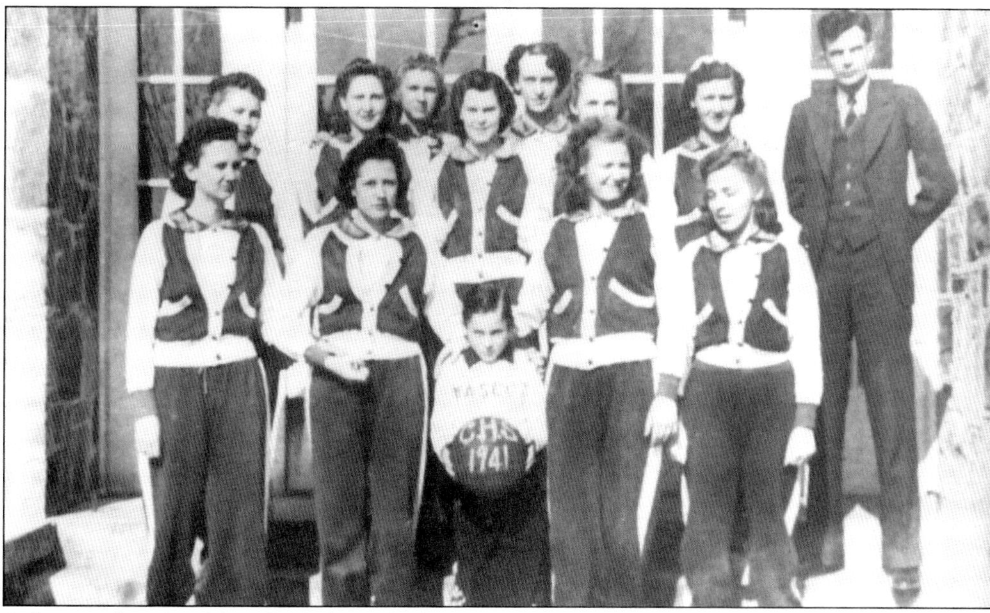

Cabot High School has fielded a girl's basketball team since the early 1900s. Over the years, the Lady Panthers have won many championships. In 1941, the Lady Panthers were crowned Lonoke County Champions by defeating Midway by a score of 49-22. Advancing to the AAU Championships, they were defeated by the eventual champion, Flippin, by a score of 38-35.

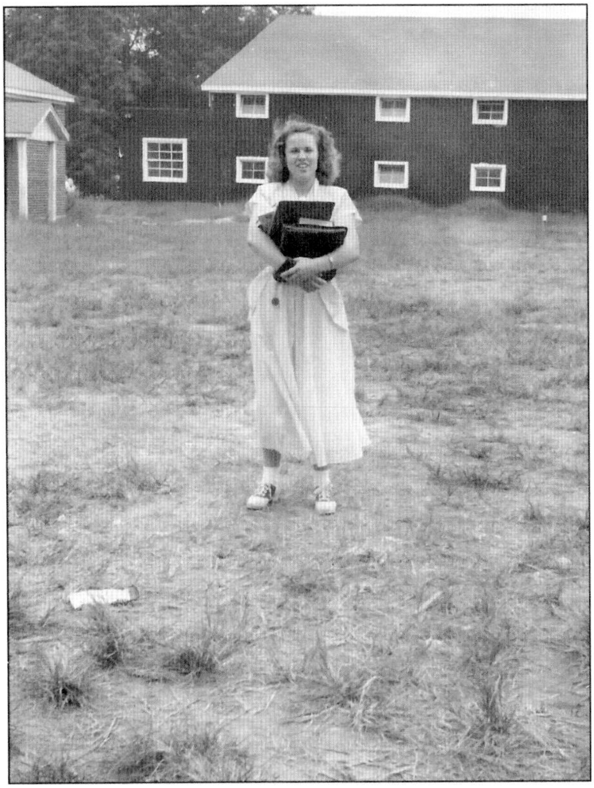

On December 20, 1960, the high school gym (in the background), which had been constructed about 10 years before, was consumed by fire, causing an approximate $40,000 loss to the school. The agriculture building at left also had smoke and water damage. A new gym was occupied in 1961 and is still in use today. (Courtesy Judy Lowman Collection from the Museum of American History.)

Today, the band is the largest nonathletic extracurricular activity offered at the high school. During its early days, it was a much smaller affair. One of the early bands provides the music for the school cheerleaders during a football game in 1949. (Courtesy Judy Lowman Collection from the Museum of American History.)

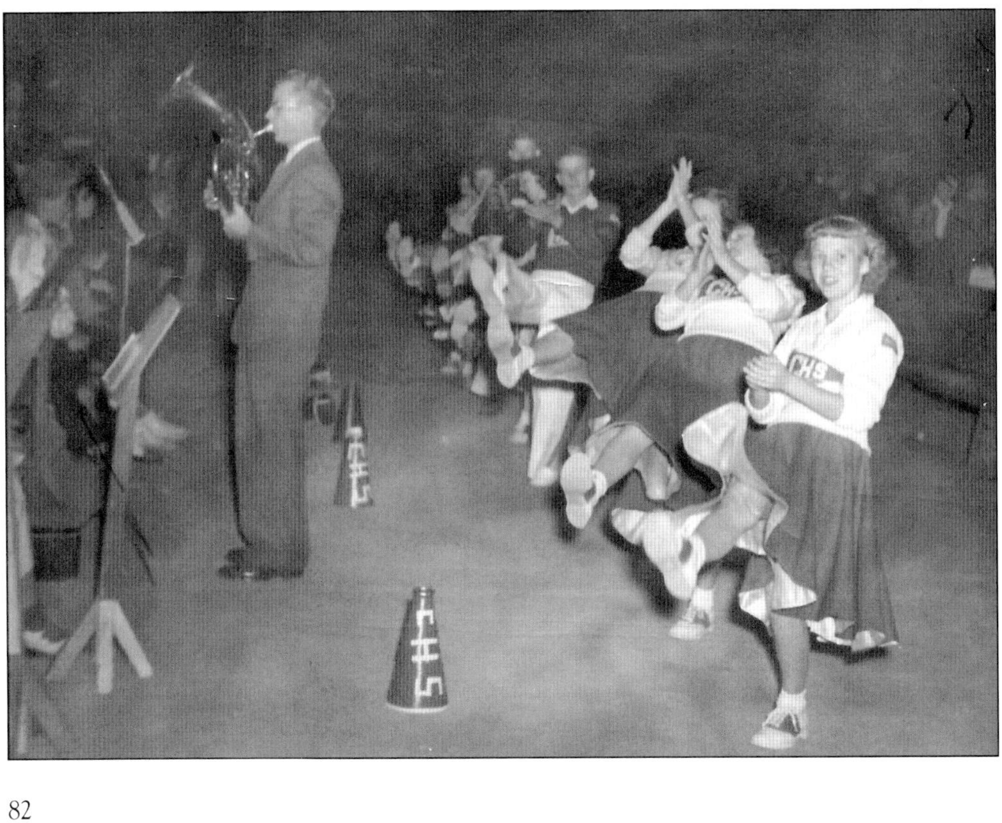

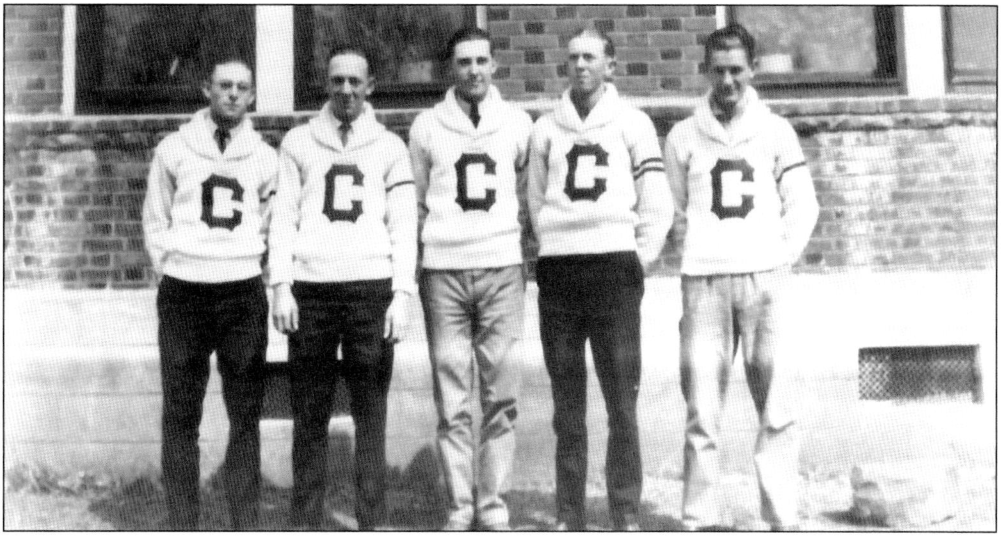

While football is the sport with the greatest following at Cabot High School, basketball is also popular. While not as successful as football, recent boy's basketball teams have been very successful. Basketball was a much different sport when the high school team had their photograph taken in the 1920s. Of special interest are the gold letter sweaters with a purple C, the school colors at that time. (Courtesy Museum of American History.)

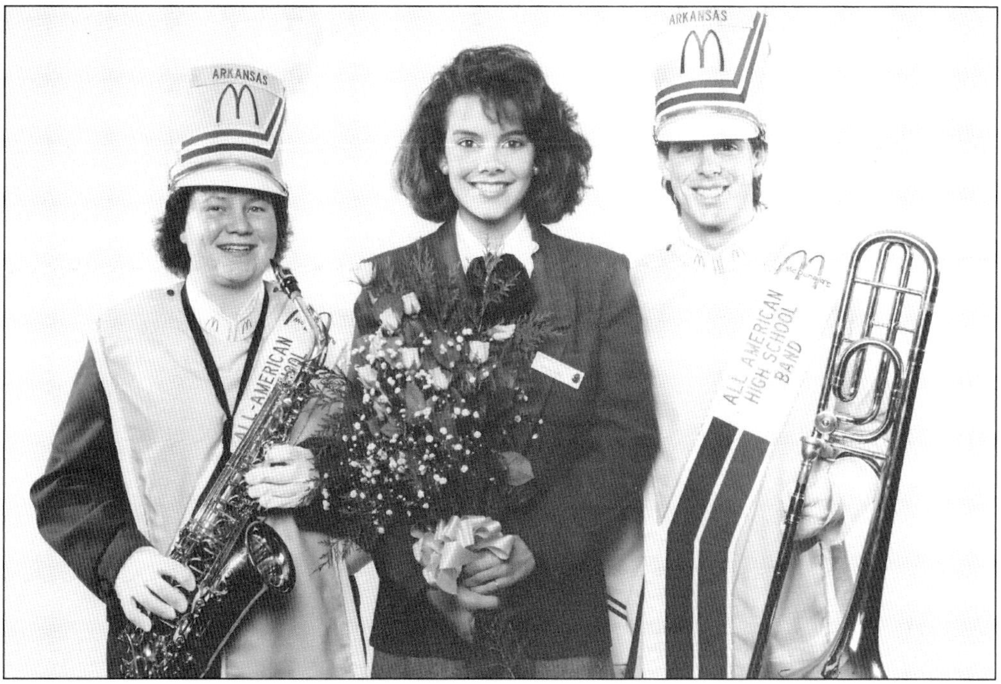

One of the most recognized school groups, both locally and nationally, is the high school band. The band regularly rates as one of the state's best. Individual honors for band members are also common. In 1986, Rhonda Eddy, left, received the honor of McDonald's All-American and had the honor of marching in the Tournament of Roses Parade. Also pictured are the Rose Bowl Queen and a fellow Arkansas band member, Thomas Huston, of North Little Rock. (Courtesy Museum of American History.)

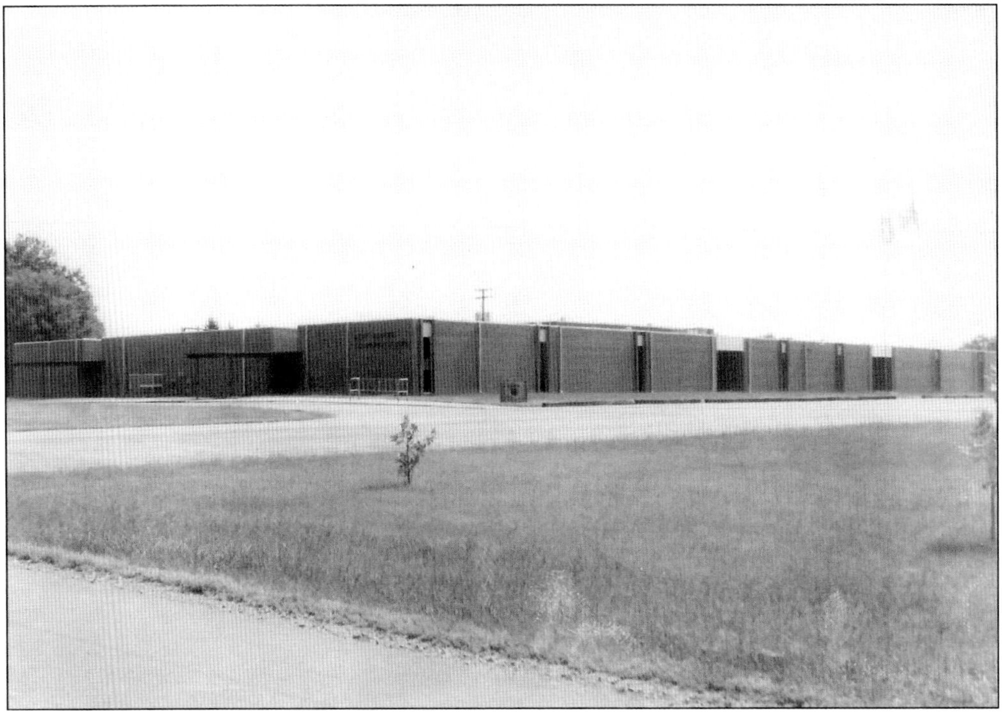

As the school district began to experience growth, the school's physical campus began to expand to other locations. The first elementary school constructed off the main campus was Eastside Elementary, completed in 1971. It is still in use today.

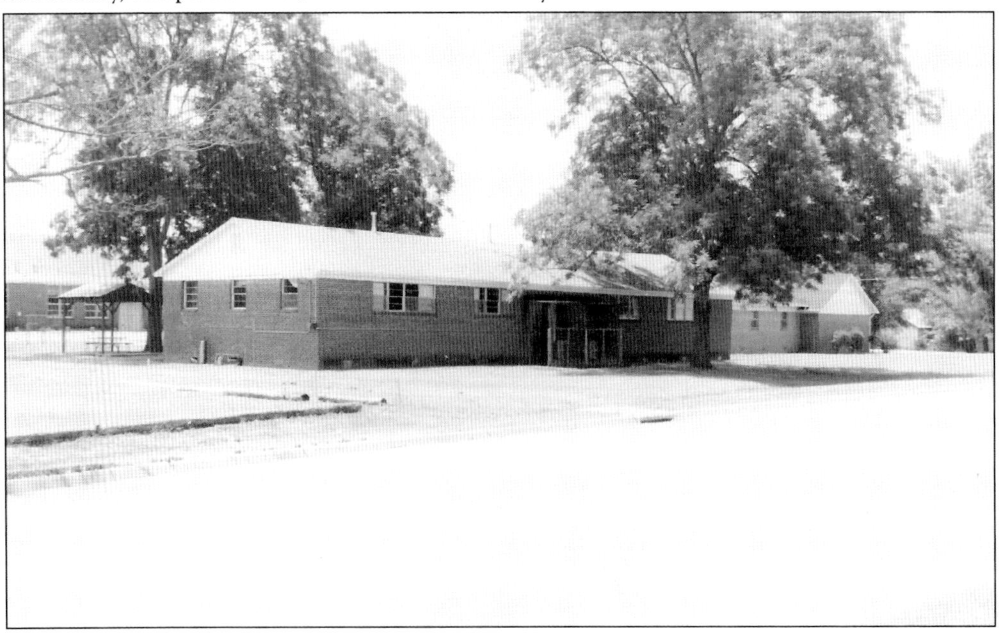

Over the last few years, many of the old buildings located on the high school campus have been removed for new construction. The building shown here was originally constructed in 1958 to house the school band program. In later years, it was converted to two classrooms and before demolition was home to the award-winning ROTC program.

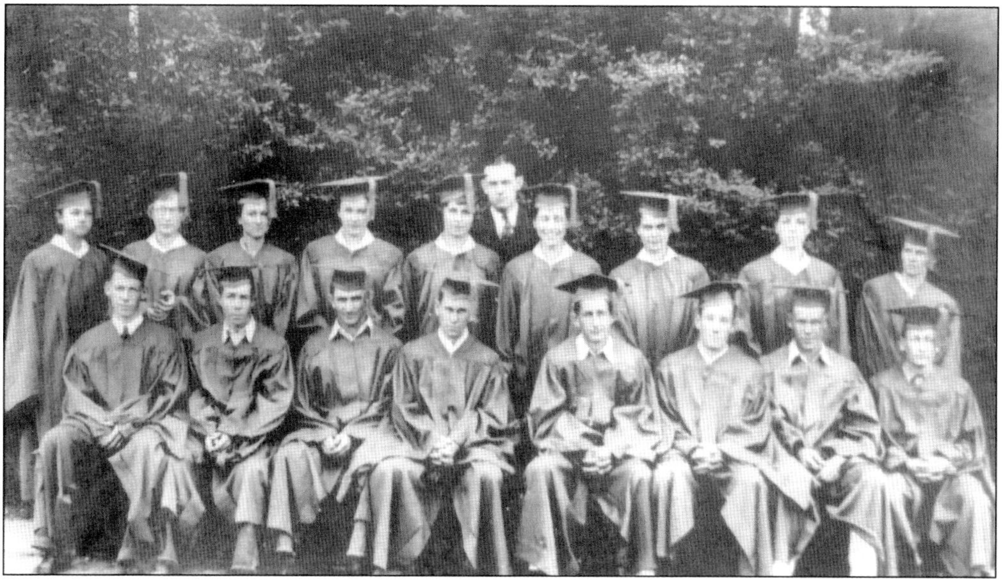

The size of the class of 1935 and its 17 members is a far cry from the graduating classes of present-day Cabot High School, which normally numbers into the hundreds.

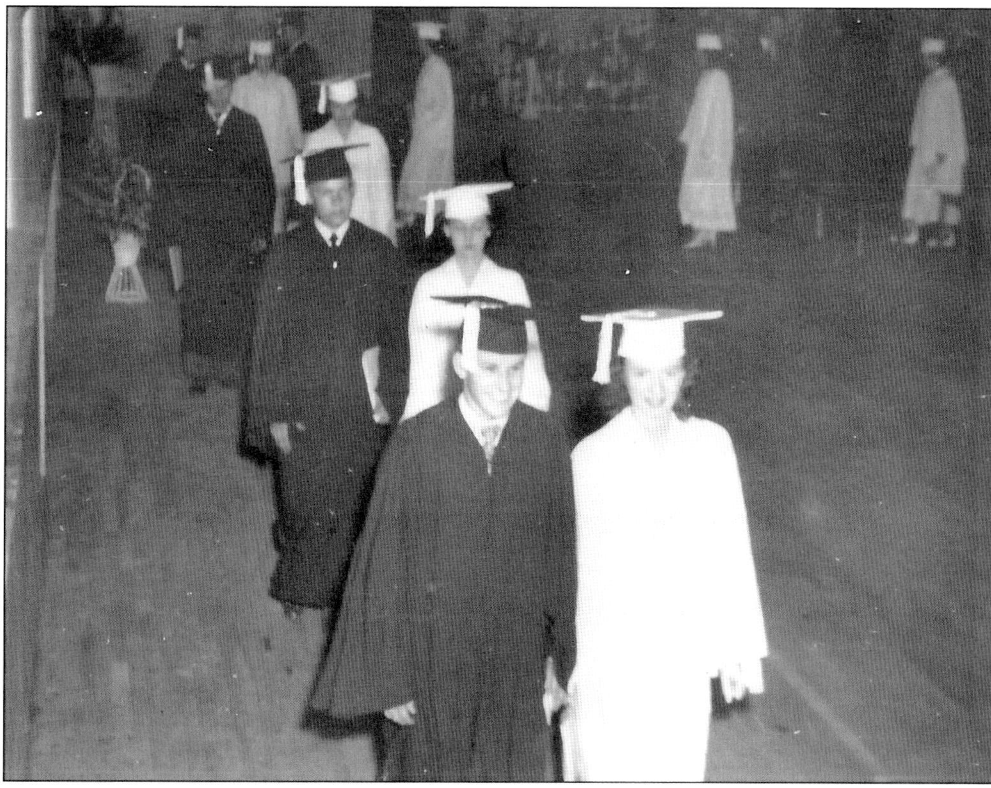

Today's senior class has grown to such a size that it is forced to travel to Little Rock to a venue large enough to seat the class and guests for graduation ceremonies. Students in the 1950s walked the line to receive their diploma in the high school gym. (Courtesy Judy Lowman Collection from the Museum of American History.)

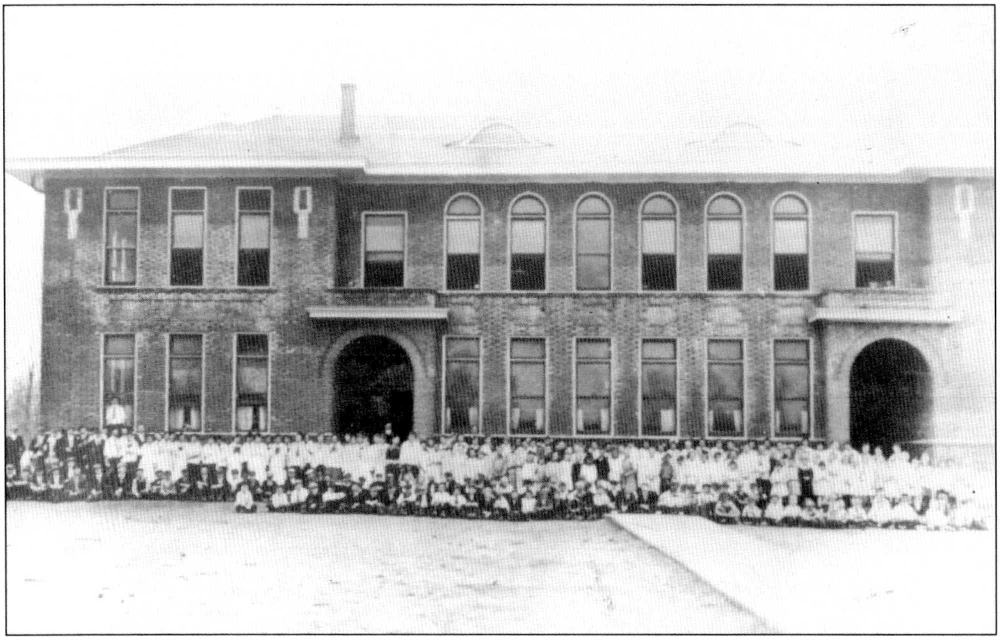

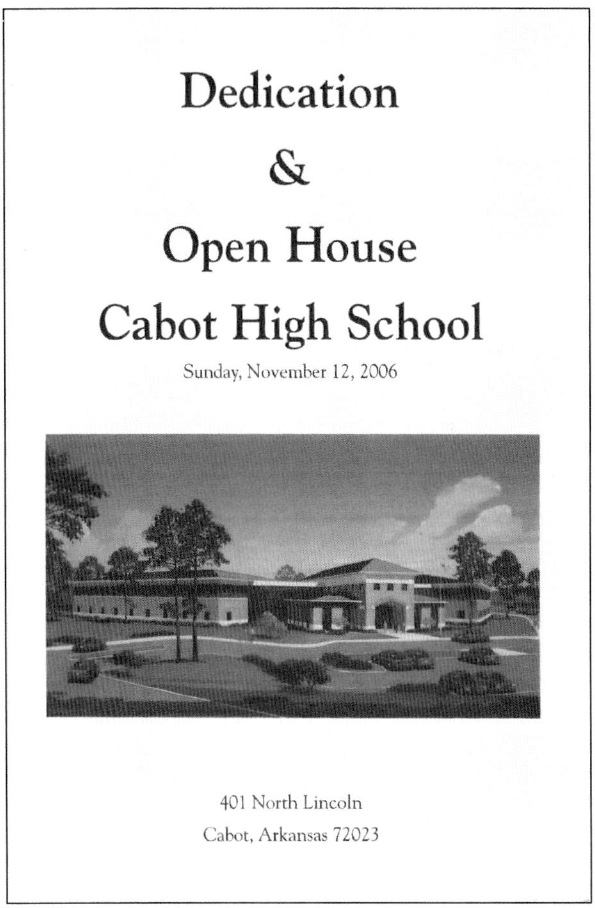

Dedication

&

Open House

Cabot High School

Sunday, November 12, 2006

401 North Lincoln

Cabot, Arkansas 72023

Long gone are the days when Cabot schools occupied one building or could assemble the entire student body for a single photograph. In this 1920s photograph, the student body numbered a little over 100 students.

In the fall of 2006, the students of Cabot High School began school in a two-story multimillion-dollar facility. Prior to the opening of the new building, the high school campus consisted of several buildings covering multiple acres. While the students still attend classes in other buildings, most of the students are now educated in this central location. The building was officially dedicated during a ceremony on November 12, 2006. (Courtesy Museum of American History.)

Seven

Football

Friday night high school football is king in Cabot. At the end of each week, football fans hit the road or settle into the seats of one of the state's finest high school football complexes to follow their Panthers through another season of hard-hitting football. The team is a perennial contender for a state championship, always finishing high in the state rankings and having been crowned champions twice in the school's history. The success in recent years is a far cry from when the school fielded its first team in 1926. In those days, the colors were purple and gold and the mascot was the Pirates. Though being defeated by England 69-0 in the school's first game, the team would finish with a respectable 4-4 record in the inaugural season.

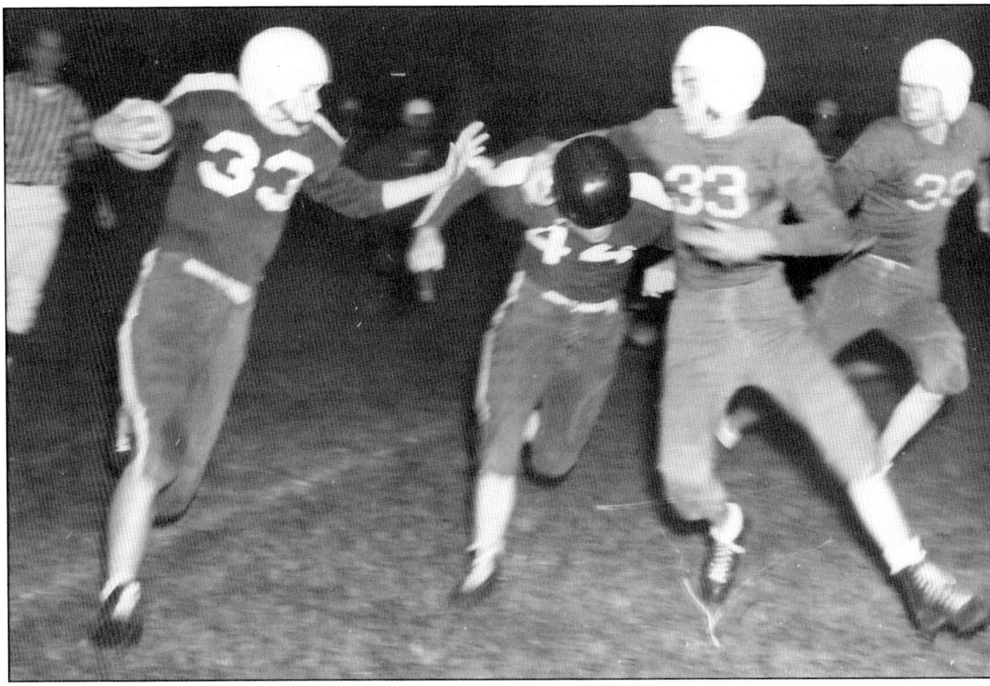

Today, high school football is king in Cabot, with crowds of over 5,000 packing the school stadium on any Friday night. Since the fielding of the first team in 1926, the Pirates, and now Panthers, have become perennial powers in Arkansas football. Cabot teams have won many conference championships and two state titles in 1983 and 2000. In one of those early games, Gene Weeks, No. 33, is seen here gaining yards against onetime county rival Lonoke. (Courtesy Jack and Betty Carrington.)

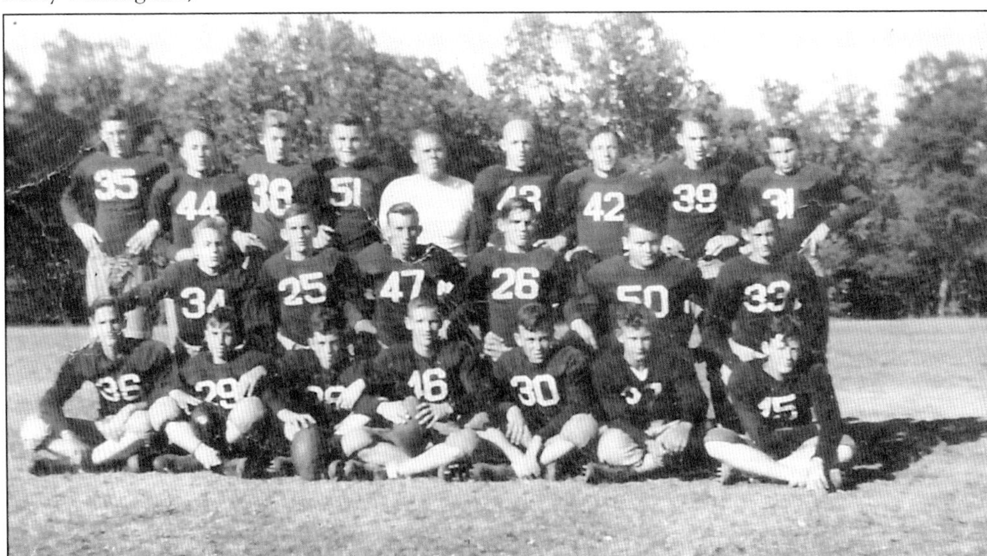

The school's popular football program was discontinued during World War II. With the war's conclusion in 1945, plans were made to restart the sport. But it was not until 1946 that the first postwar team, shown here, took the field. That first season saw the team compose a 4-7 record. (Courtesy Jack and Betty Carrington.)

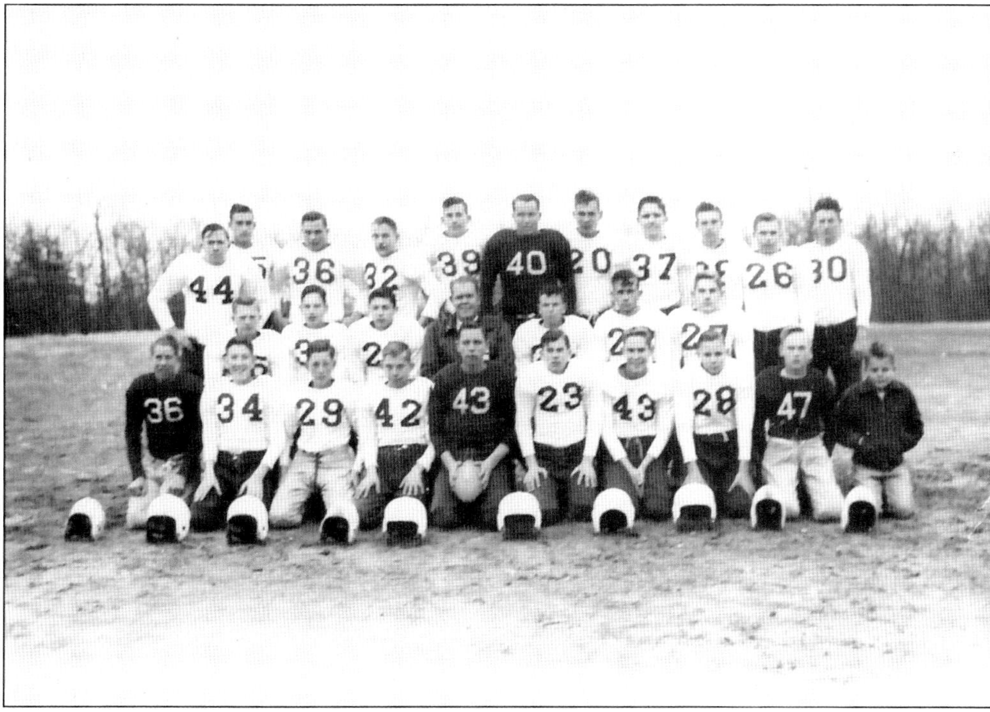

Once football was reinstated, it took some time for the program to get back on a regular winning track. The number of players on the squad increased, and the quality of players slowly improved. Still, by 1949, when this team took the field, they could only manage a 4-6-1 record. (Courtesy Jack and Betty Carrington.)

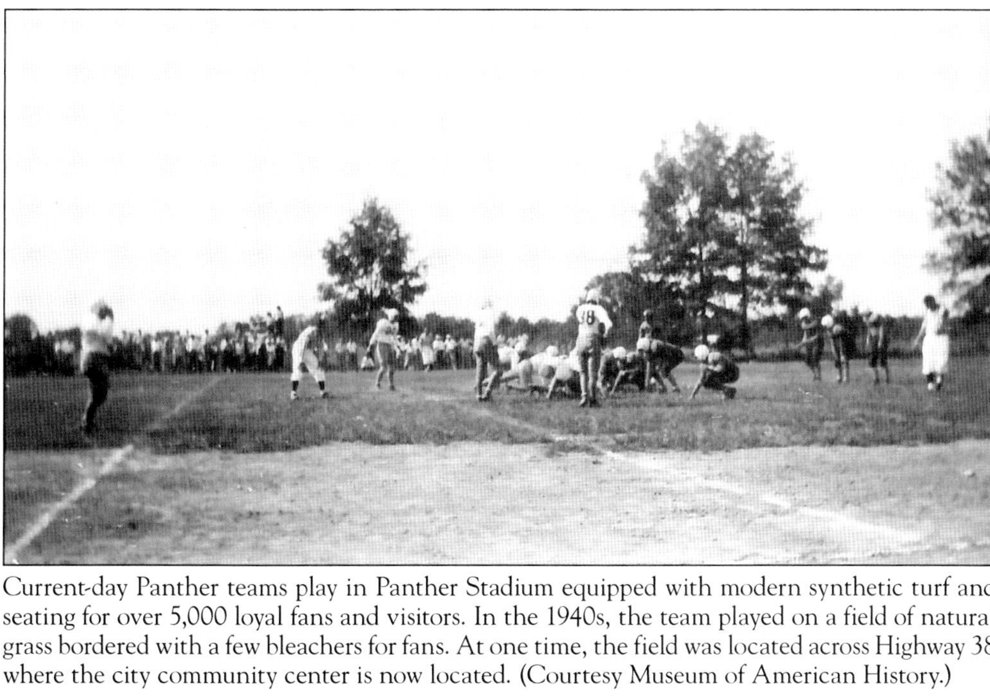

Current-day Panther teams play in Panther Stadium equipped with modern synthetic turf and seating for over 5,000 loyal fans and visitors. In the 1940s, the team played on a field of natural grass bordered with a few bleachers for fans. At one time, the field was located across Highway 38 where the city community center is now located. (Courtesy Museum of American History.)

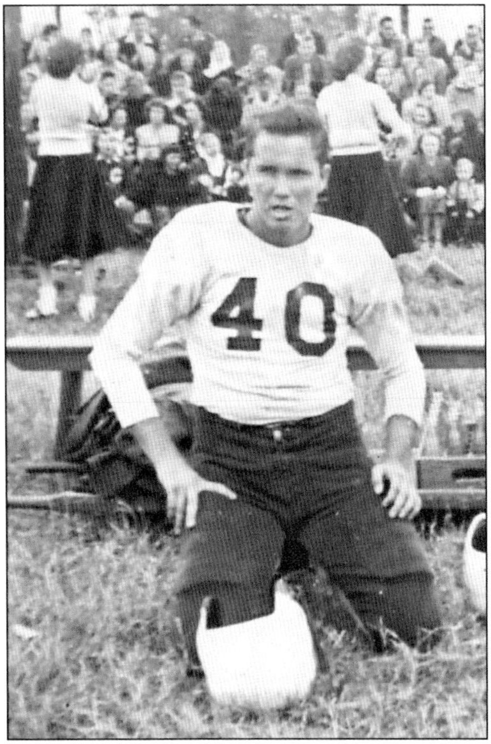

In 1949, L.C. "Jack" Carrington (No. 40) became the first Cabot High School football player to be selected to the Arkansas All State Team. Recruited by the University of Arkansas, Carrington went on to complete his playing days at Arkansas State Teacher's College in Conway, now the University of Central Arkansas. He later became a respected coach at Jacksonville, Dewitt, and Cabot, where he coached for 10 years during the late 1960s and early 1970s. He also served as Cabot High School principal from 1977 to 1990 and 1992 to 1996. (Courtesy Jack and Betty Carrington.)

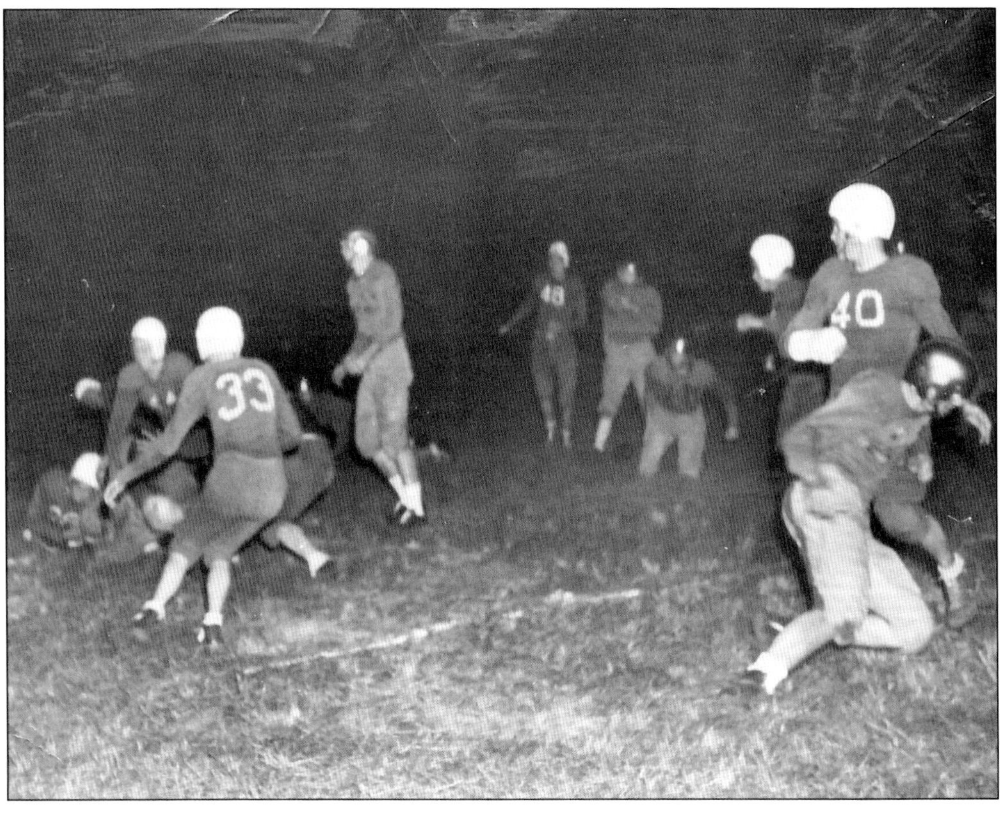

The annual homecoming is an eagerly awaited school event. While there are many activities surrounding the busy weekend, the one most anticipated is the Friday night football game with the crowning of homecoming royalty. In this 1946 photograph, Junior Maid Betty Murphy is escorted by senior football player, and later prominent community businessman, Jack Lowman. (Courtesy Jack and Betty Carrington.)

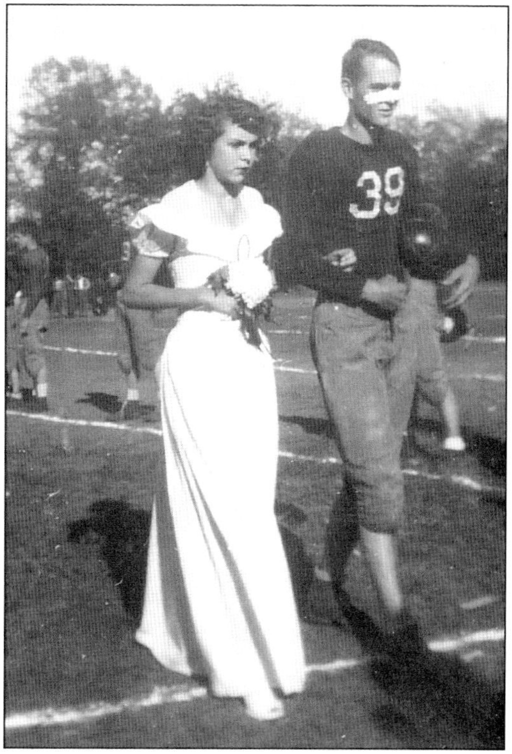

The Cabot Panthers and Lonoke Jackrabbits were longtime rivals on the football field. The rapid growth of Cabot schools necessitating the move to an upper division resulted in the discontinuing of the series in the 1980s. A Cabot player, in white helmet, is shown in this photograph during the 1949 contest between the two arch rivals. (Courtesy Jack and Betty Carrington.)

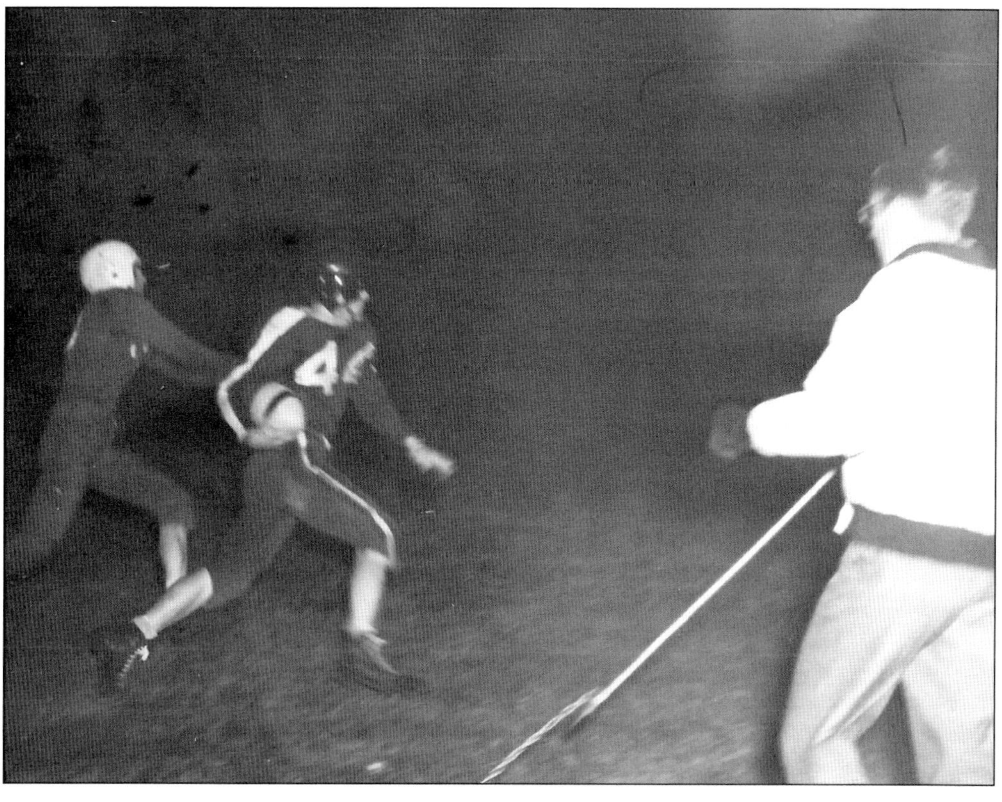

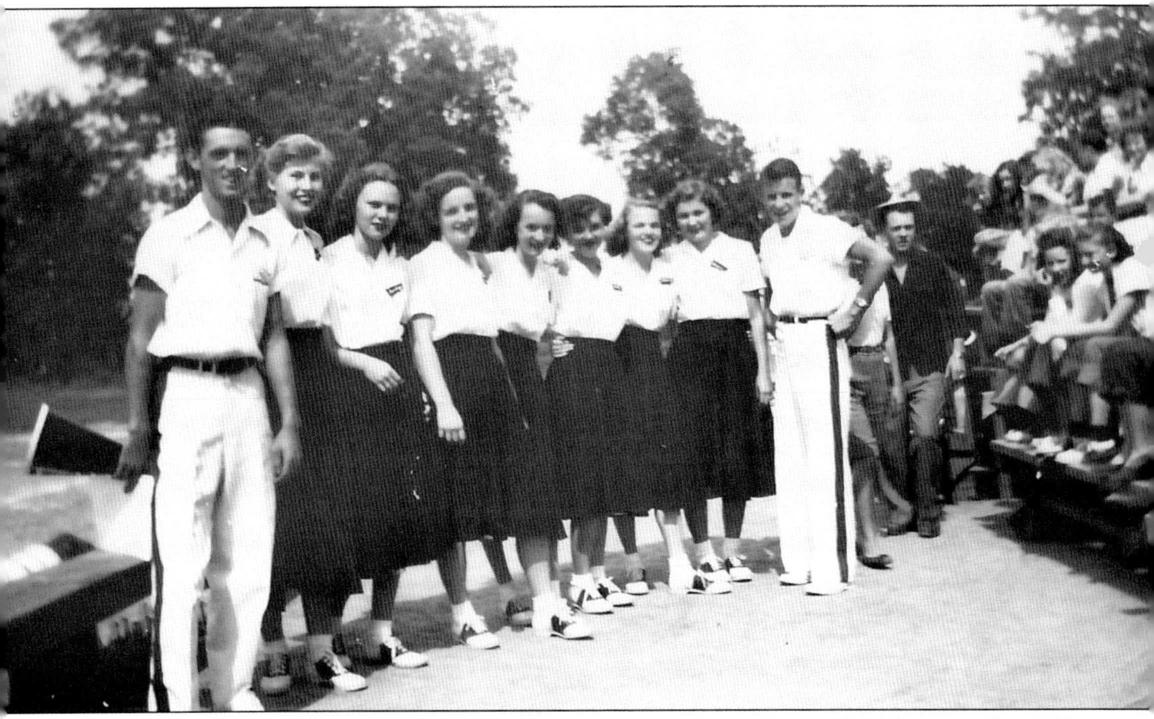

While the uniform of the high school cheerleader has changed considerably since the 1950s, the spirit has not. Cabot cheerleaders, standing along the football sidelines, cheer the Panthers to another victory. Today, the cheerleaders are joined in cheering on the Panthers at each game by the Panther Dance Team. (Courtesy Judy Lowman Collection from the Museum of American History.)

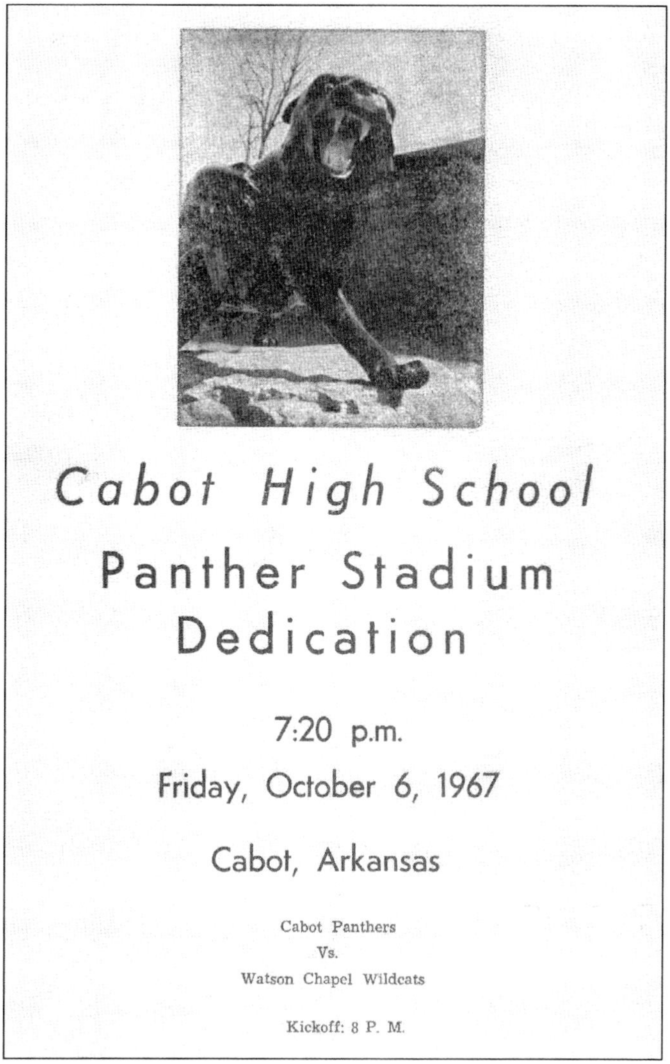
Cabot High School

Panther Stadium Dedication

7:20 p.m.

Friday, October 6, 1967

Cabot, Arkansas

Cabot Panthers
Vs.
Watson Chapel Wildcats

Kickoff: 8 P. M.

Panther Stadium, the home field for the Cabot team, is located on the high school campus. Constructed in 1967, the stadium was dedicated on October 6, 1967, with victory over Watson Chapel and the honoring of the 1926 team, the school's first. Over the years, the stadium has gone through many improvements, making it one of the best high school facilities in the state. (Courtesy Museum of American History.)

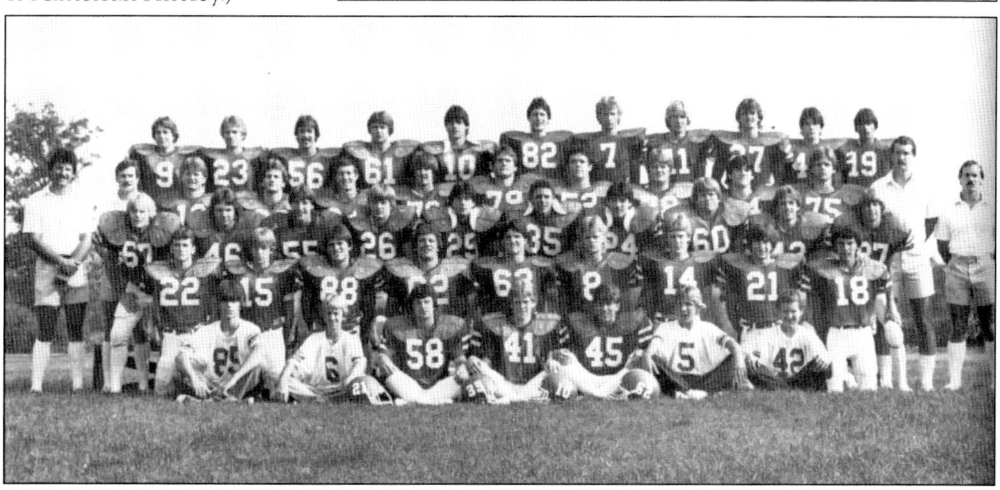

Until the 1983 season, the best that any Panther team had finished in the state playoffs was the semifinals in 1976. Though finishing second in the 1983 conference race, the Panthers finished the season with only one loss. Running through the playoffs, the school secured its first state championship by defeating the Rivercrest Colts in a rain plagued championship game at War Memorial Stadium by a score of 20-6. (Courtesy Museum of American History.)

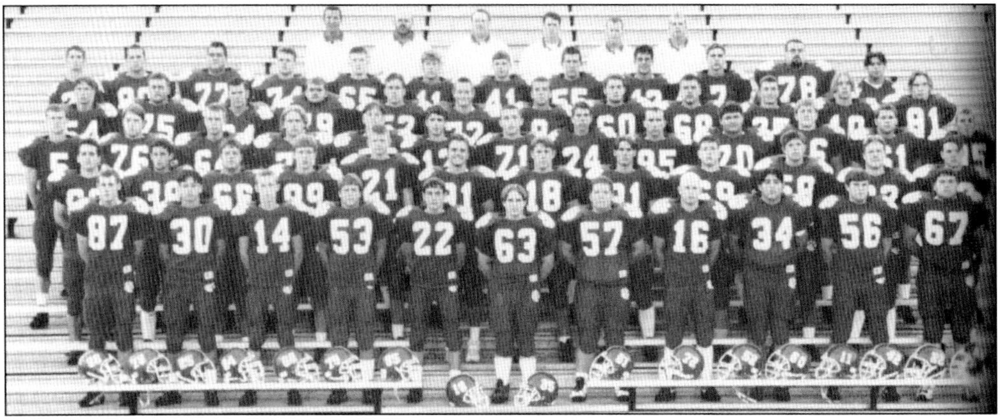

One of the most disappointing endings of a football season in school history came during the 1997 season. After a stellar regular season, the conference champions, in the state's largest classification, were ready to bring home a second state title. Making it to the championship game with a 13-0 record, the Panthers were defeated by Fort Smith Southside 38-21. (Courtesy Museum of American History.)

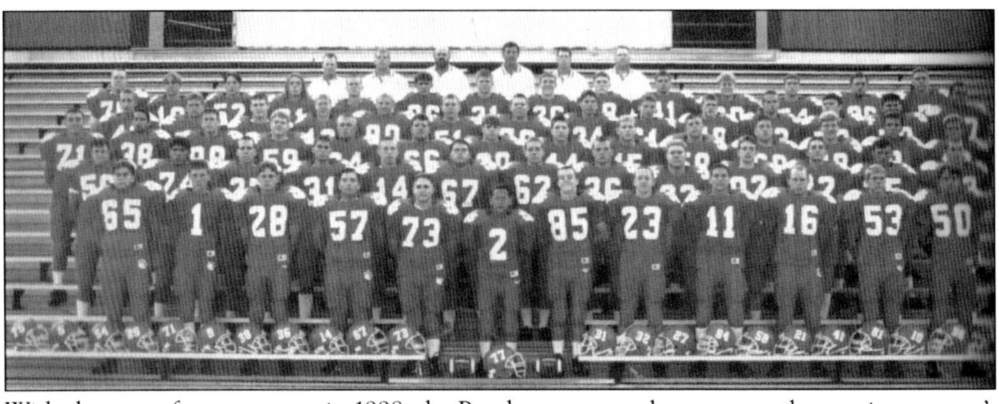

With the start of a new season in 1998, the Panthers were ready to avenge the previous season's loss in the state championship game. The two-time defending conference champions once again marched through the playoffs, reaching the championship game against Little Rock Fair. The Panthers suffered a devastating second-year-in-a-row loss, losing by a score of 7-6. It was only the Panthers second loss of the season, both to Fair. (Courtesy Museum of American History.)

Over the years, a number of respected men have served as the Panther head football coach. One of these leaders was Don Meador, the first coach after the sport was revived following World War II. Meador, a graduate of Ouachita Baptist University, coached at the school for four seasons. (Courtesy Jack and Betty Carrington.)

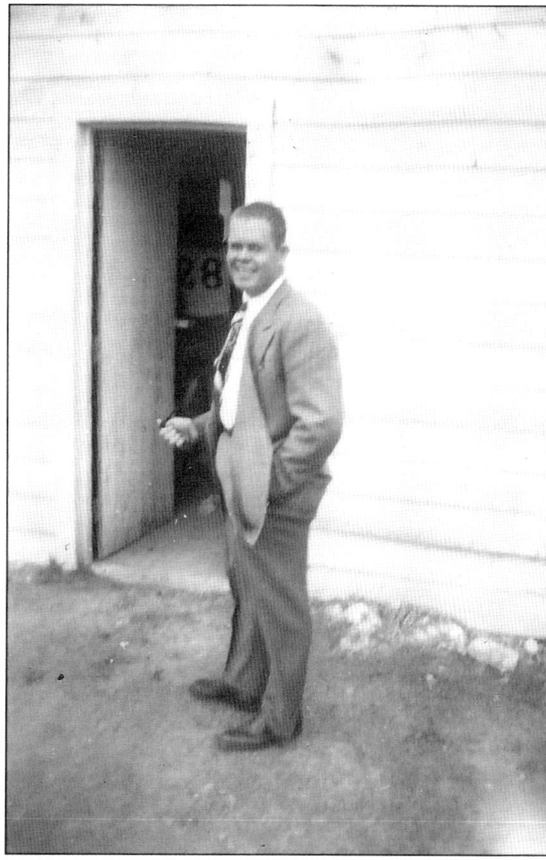

Since being hired as the head football coach in 1982, Mike Malham has become the schools longest tenured coach, amassing a record of over 200 victories. During his time coaching the Panthers, the team has won two state championships and finished ranked in the state's top 10 almost every season. Before beginning his career as a coach, Malham was a star defensive player at Arkansas State University with a brief career with the NFL's Chicago Bears. Pictured after winning the 2000 state championship are Coach Malham, with, from left to right, his wife, Alexis; daughter Lexi; and son Matt. (Courtesy Mike Malham.)

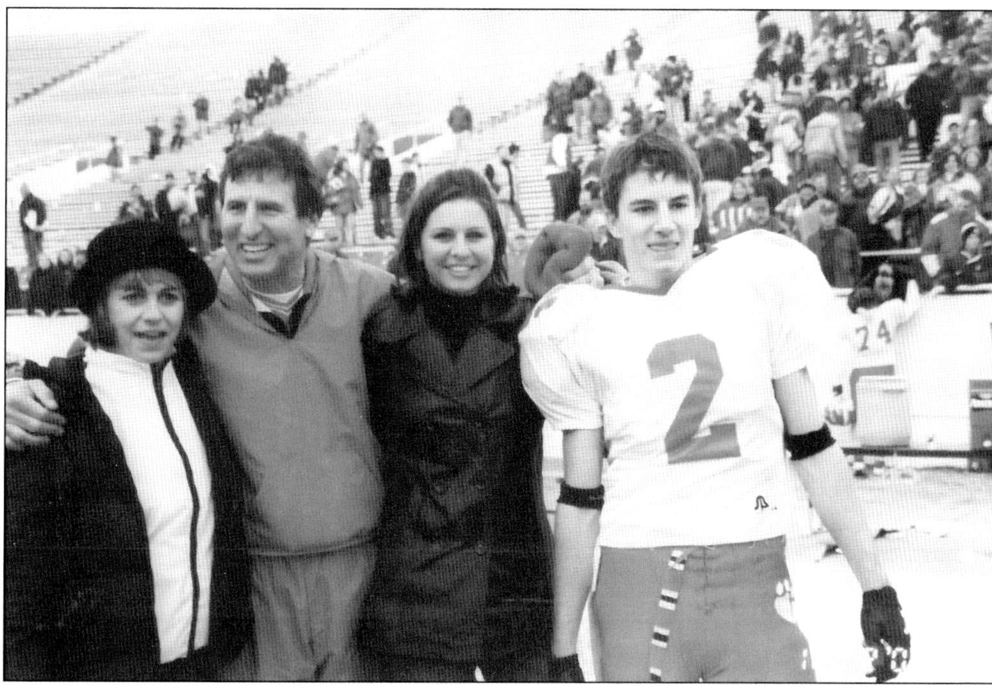

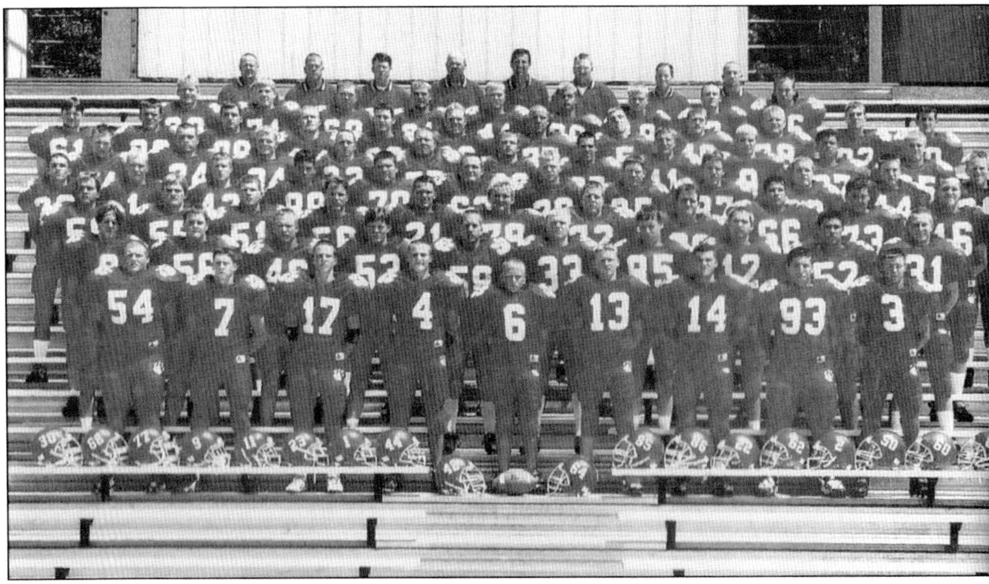

With the conclusion of the 2000 postseason, the Panthers had advanced to the state championship game three out of four years. The two appearances prior to the 2000 game resulted in a second place finish. There was much anticipation as the Panthers advanced once again to the championship game. Anticipation ended in jubilant celebration as the Panthers defeated Fort Smith Southside by a score of 28-21, securing the school's second state football crown. (Courtesy Museum of American History.)

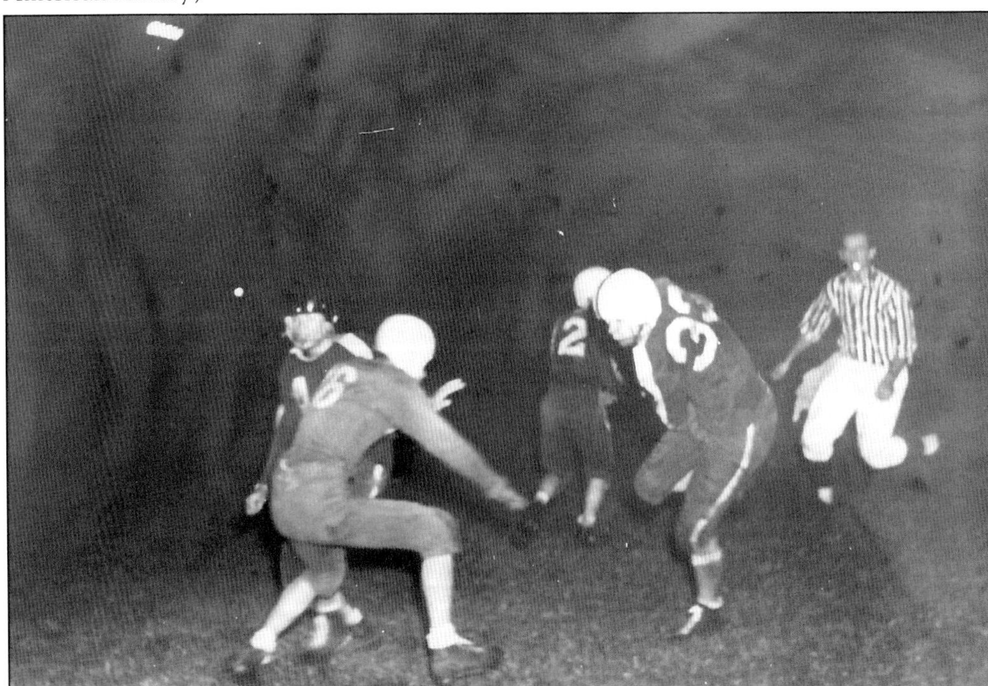

Traditionally, Panther football teams have been run oriented. Today, Cabot teams are always one of the leading rushing teams in the state of Arkansas. It is not uncommon for a Panther running back to be the state's leading rusher during the season. (Courtesy Museum of American History.)

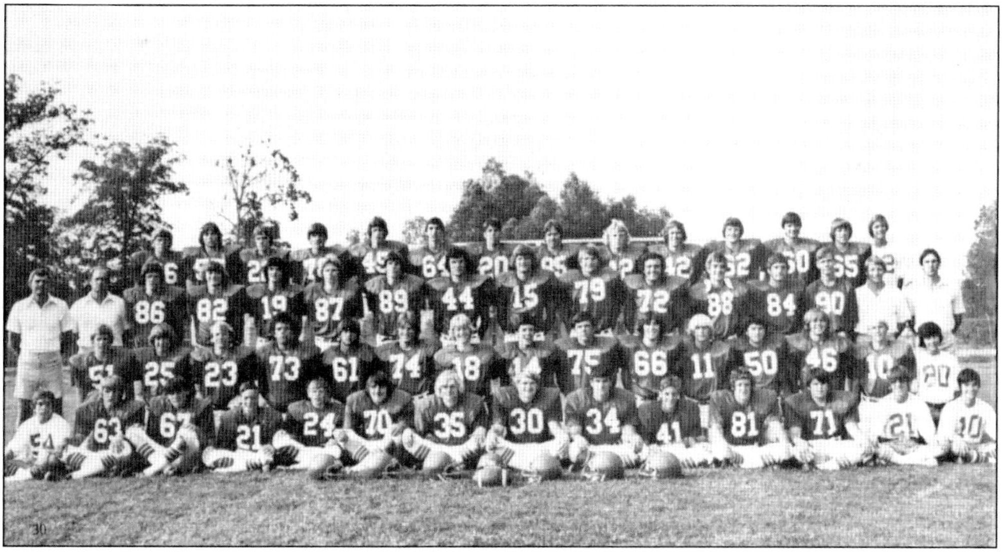

Perhaps one of the best teams to ever play in Panther Stadium was in 1976. The Panthers missed completing a perfect season by just one game, that one being the last. Cabot entered their second-round state playoff game in Little Rock with a perfect 12-0 record. When the last horn sounded, the Arkadelphia Badgers had escaped with a 7-6 victory. It would be another seven years before the Panthers would have a chance at the title. (Courtesy Museum of American History.)

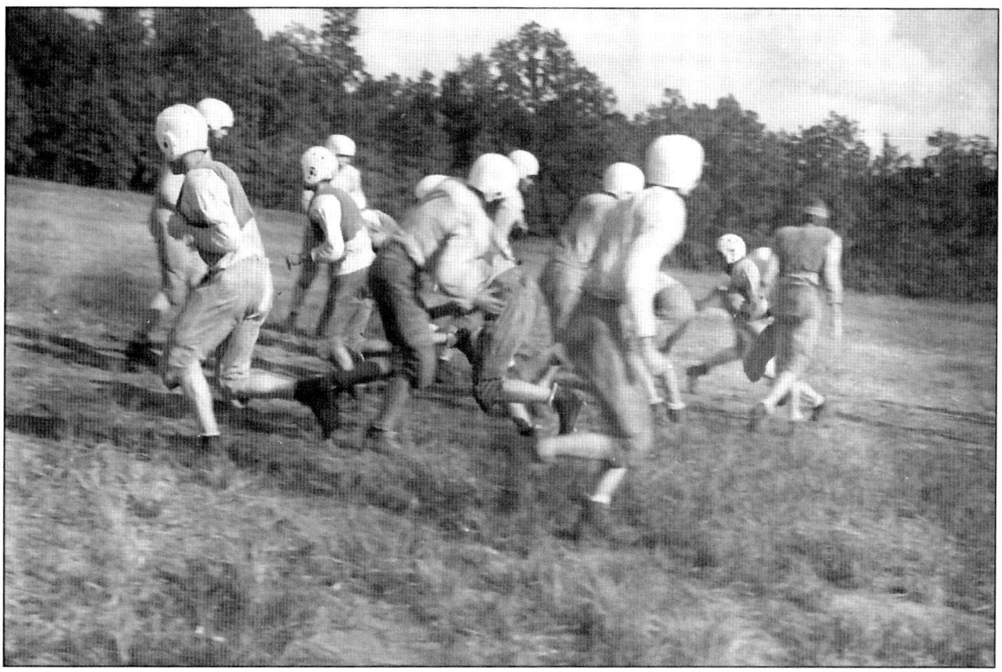

As the old saying goes, "Practice makes perfect." Visit the practice fields of the Cabot football team on any afternoon during football season, and many times in the off season, and this principle can be seen in action. Long numerous hours are spent on the practice field before the team hits the playing field on Friday nights. It seems that this routine has always been true, as these Cabot players in the 1950s can attest. (Courtesy Judy Lowman Collection from the Museum of American History.)

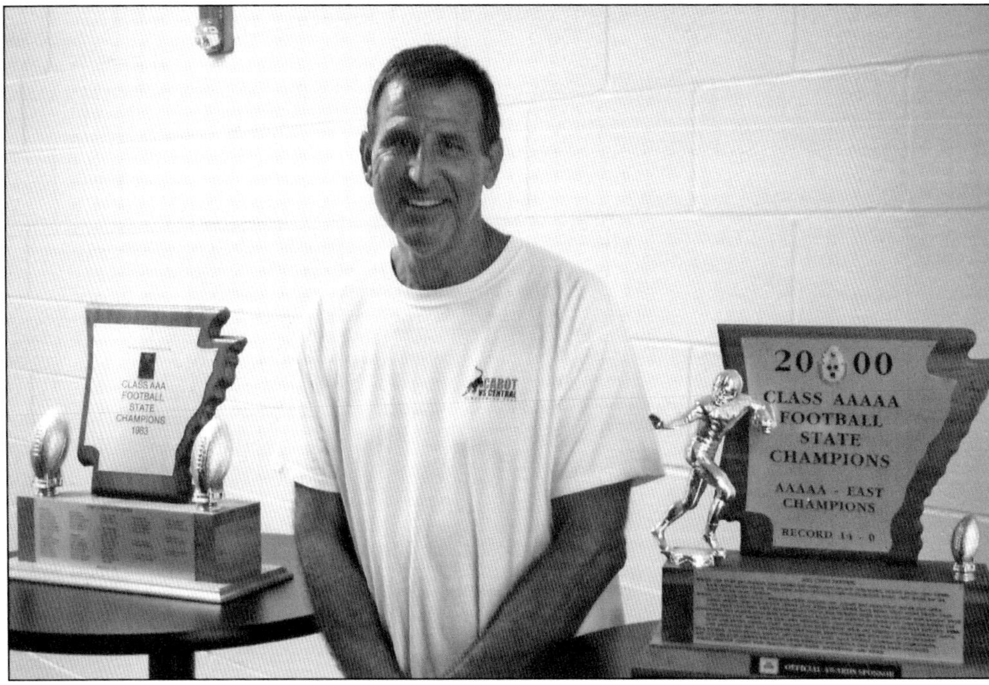

Longtime coach Mike Malham, with 246 victories under his belt, proudly displays the 1983 and 2000 state championship trophies. Coach Malham, as of 2011, has coached his teams to more victories than any active coach in the Arkansas high school ranks. (Courtesy Museum of American History.)

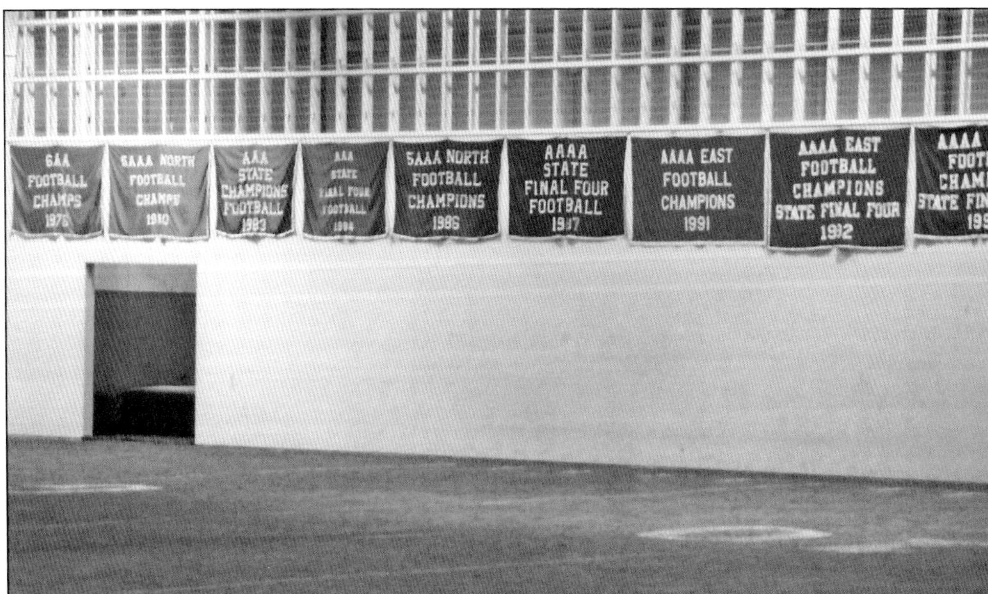

The banners displayed in the football field house document the storied history of Cabot football. Dating from the 1950s, the Panthers have won 13 conference championships and two state titles. The Panthers have participated in 10 state semifinal playoffs and have had 10 seasons with 10 or more victories. (Courtesy Museum of American History.)

Eight

Some Gave All

During Cabot's more than 120 years of existence as an incorporated city, the United States has been engaged in a number of conflicts fought to defend the nation. In each of those wars, large numbers of Americans have served in the armed forces, at home and abroad. Like many other communities throughout the United States, a significant number of Cabot citizens have served their country, dating from the mid-1800s to modern times. Many of those local soldiers did not survive the war, while others returned home as veterans making contributions to their local community. Today, those veterans are honored by a veteran's monument, Camp Nelson Confederate Cemetery, a yearly Veteran's Day service, and a local American Legion Post.

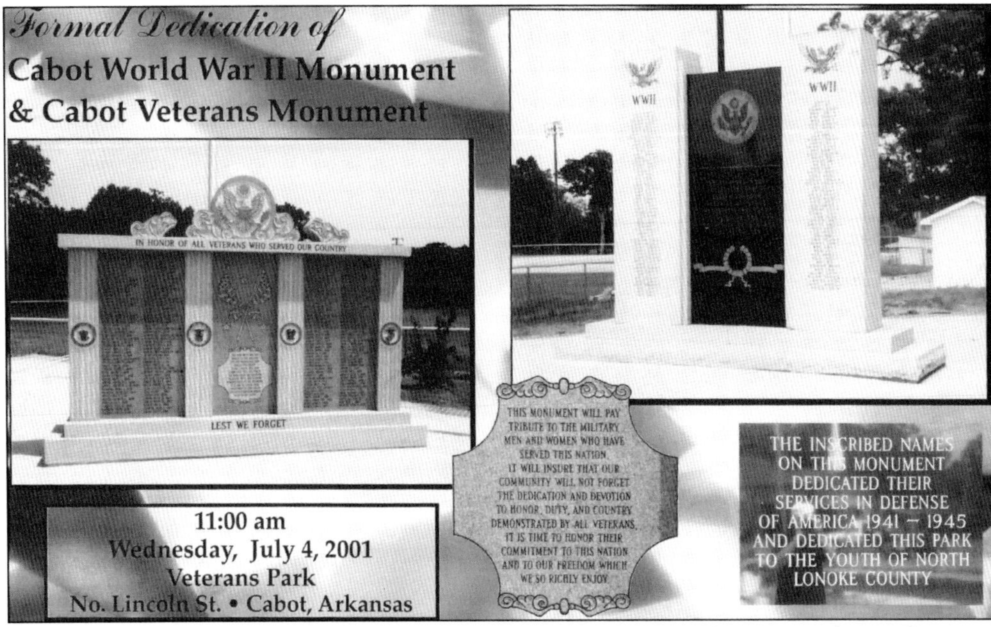

On July 4, 2001, the newly erected Cabot World War II Monument and Cabot Veterans Monument was dedicated in the presence of a large crowd gathered at Veterans Park. The monument pays tribute to all veterans, male and female, who have served the nation. (Courtesy Museum of American History.)

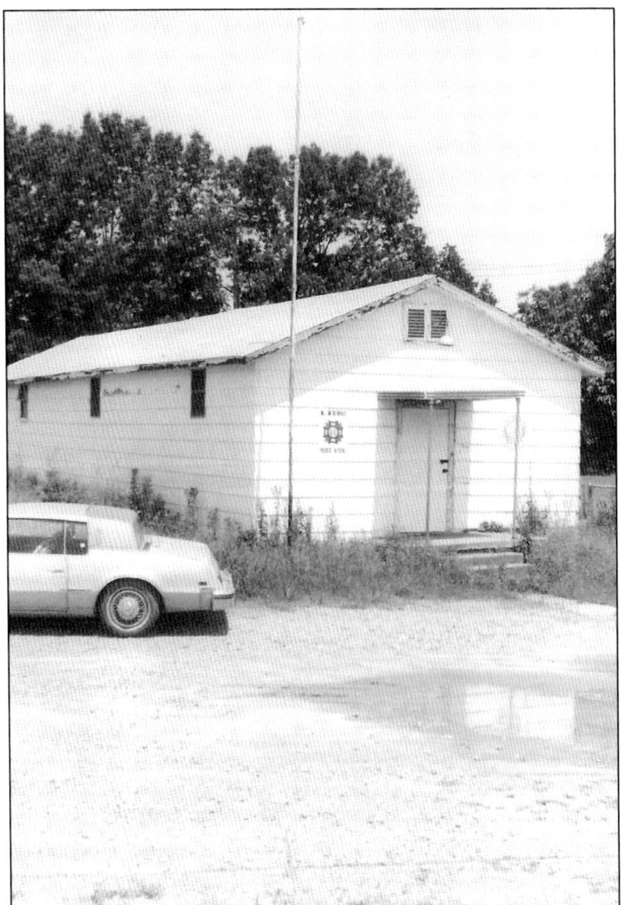

The American Legion, a national veteran's organization, was founded in 1919 by US servicemen on duty in France during World War I. With the conclusion of the war, its popularity grew rapidly throughout the nation. Cabot veterans formed the William M. Burks Post No. 4770 and used this building located at Veterans Park on Highway 38 as a meeting hall for many years. It was razed to make way for a veteran's monument in the late 1990s.

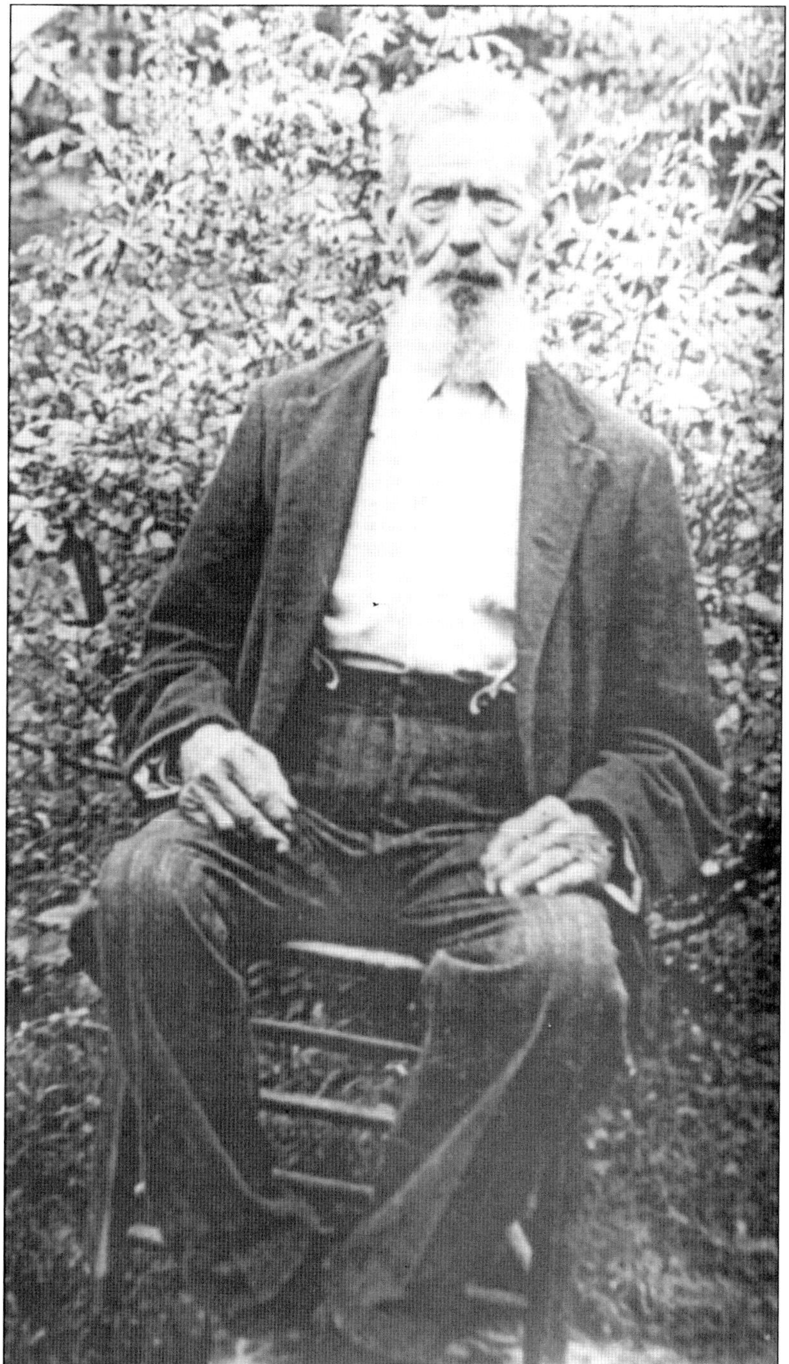

Nicholas A. Brewer moved from Alabama to present-day Lonoke County in the 1850s. During the Civil War, he served in the 37th Arkansas Infantry and was captured at the Battle of Helena, Arkansas, on July 3, 1863. He spent the duration of the war in prison. After the war, he returned to Arkansas, living on a farm about five miles south of Cabot. He died there on January 27, 1919. (Above, courtesy Jerry Sue Brewer Floyd.)

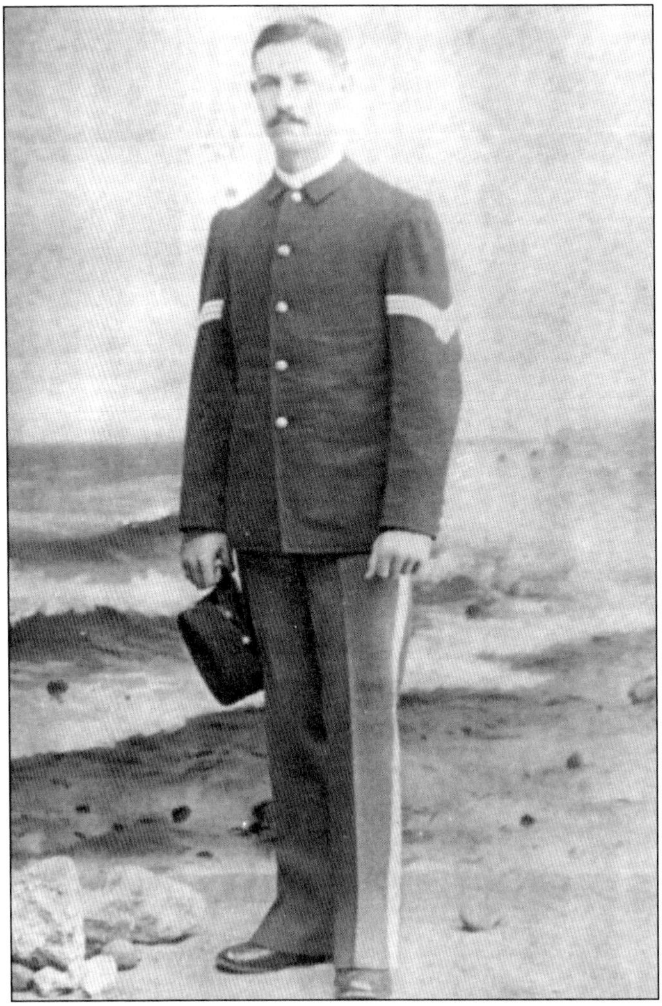

Jerry Brewer was one of over 2,000 Arkansas men who served in the military during the start of the late-19th-century Spanish-American War. Brewer, who later became a postman, served in Puerto Rico as a sergeant in the 11th US Cavalry. He died on July 17, 1963, and is buried in Mount Carmel Cemetery. (Courtesy Jerry Sue Brewer Floyd.)

This government headstone marks the grave of Jefferson Brewer at Mount Carmel Cemetery.

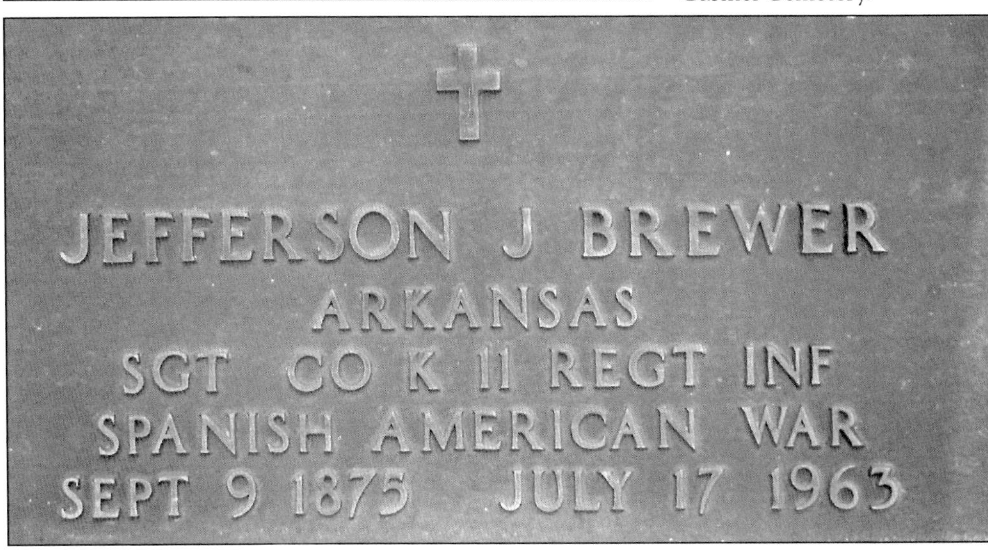

Tallie Harrell, a self-employed farmer living at nearby Austin, was just 26 years old when he registered for the draft in 1917. Before war's end in 1918, he was one of 10 Cabot area men killed in the war. (Courtesy Museum of American History.)

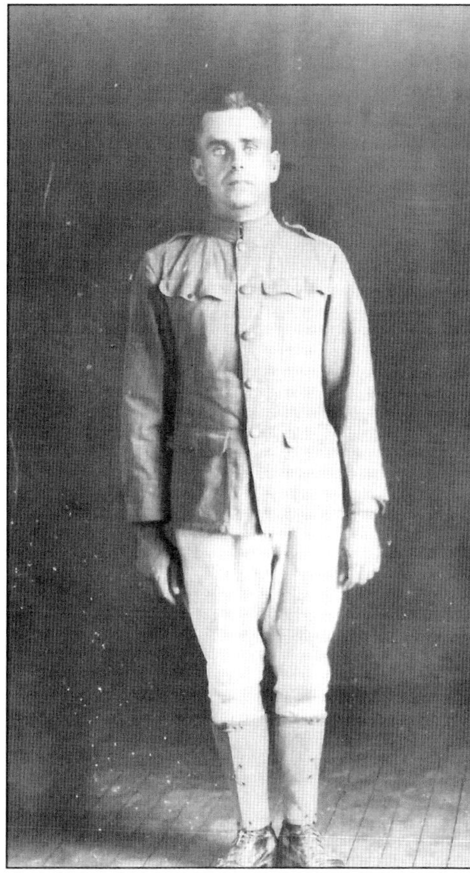

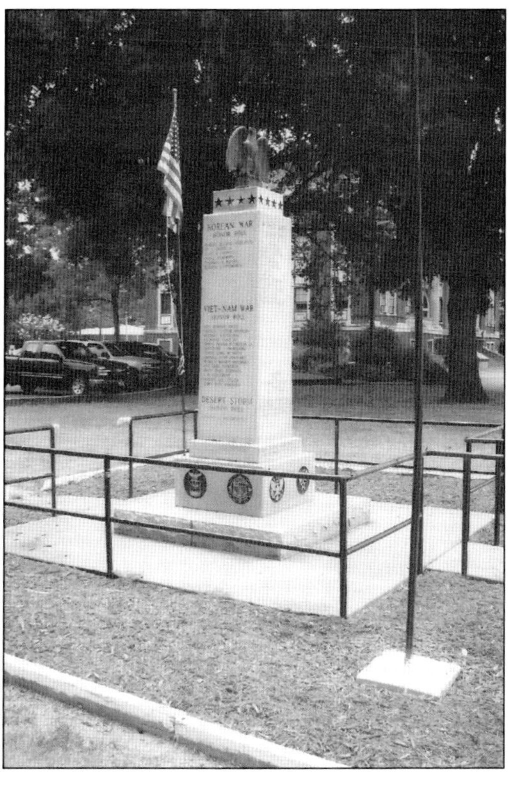

Lonoke County men, including those from Cabot, who died in the service of their country are remembered with an impressive granite monument erected on the county courthouse lawn in Lonoke. Dedicated on November 12, 1988, the monument is dedicated to over 100 veterans who gave their lives in conflicts from World War I through Desert Storm.

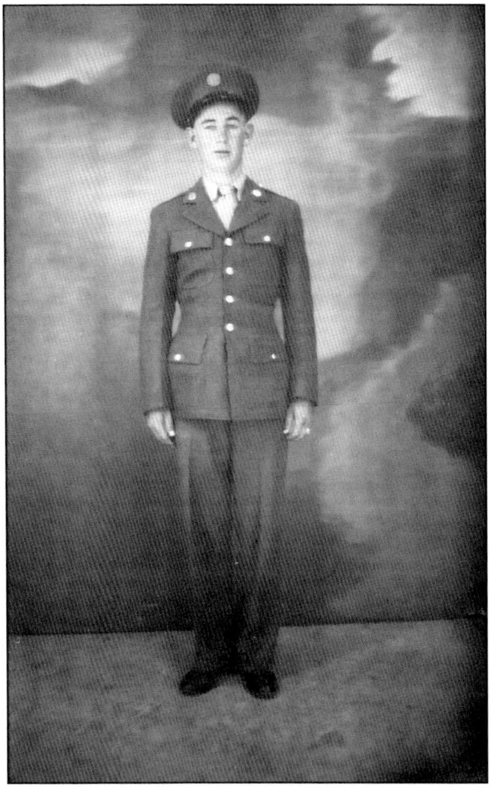

On April 15, 1945, John Hampton Collier, a private in the 27th Infantry US Army, died of wounds incurred while engaged with Japanese forces at Luzon, Philippine Islands, during World War II. Collier was awarded the Purple Heart. His remains were never returned to his family; instead, they were interred with honor at Manila American Cemetery. (Courtesy Museum of American History.)

Some of the most dreaded news anticipated by a family during World War II was a report of a loved one in the military being wounded in action. Even worse was a report of that soldier's death. On May 3, 1945, the Collier family received a telegram informing them of the death of their son John while he was engaged in combat at Luzon in the Philippine Islands. (Courtesy Museum of American History.)

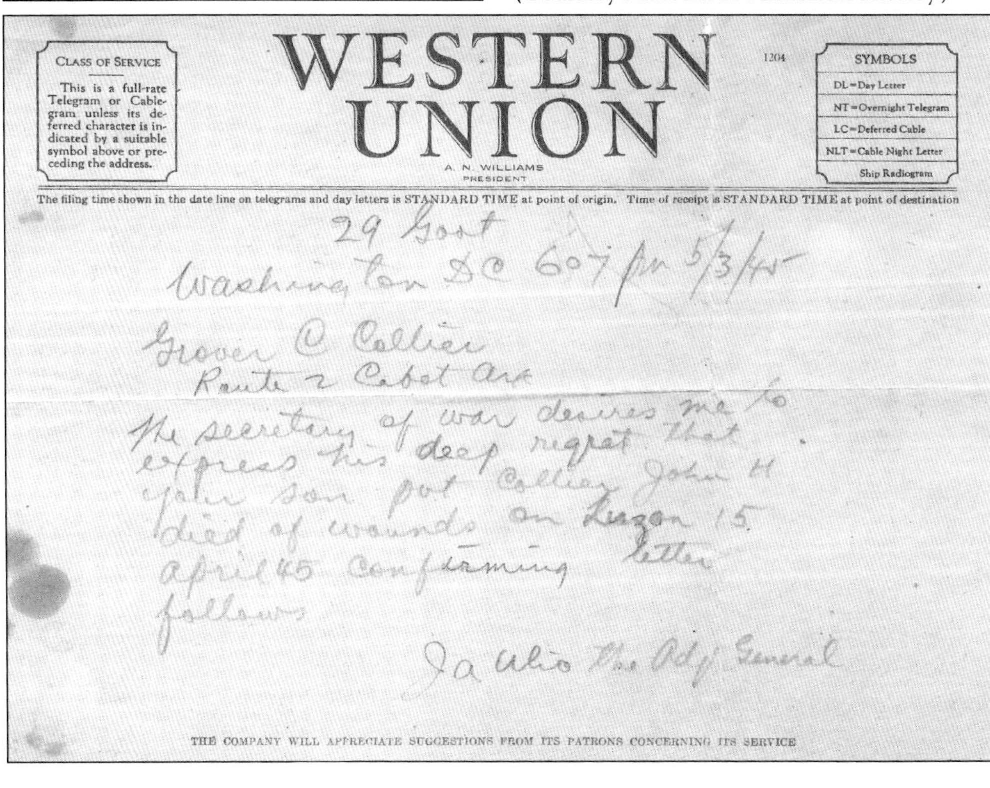

CLASS OF SERVICE

This is a full-rate Telegram or Cablegram unless its deferred character is indicated by a suitable symbol above or preceding the address.

WESTERN UNION

A. N. WILLIAMS
PRESIDENT

1204

SYMBOLS
DL=Day Letter
NT=Overnight Telegram
LC=Deferred Cable
NLT=Cable Night Letter
Ship Radiogram

The filing time shown in the date line on telegrams and day letters is STANDARD TIME at point of origin. Time of receipt is STANDARD TIME at point of destination

29 Govt
Washington DC 607 pm 5/3/45
Grover C Collier
Route 2 Cabot Ark
The secretary of war desires me to express his deep regret that your son pvt Collier John H died of wounds on Luzon 15 april 45 confirming letter follows
J A Ulio The Adj General

THE COMPANY WILL APPRECIATE SUGGESTIONS FROM ITS PATRONS CONCERNING ITS SERVICE

Prior to World War II, Grover Payton Collier, brother of John H., served in the Civilian Conservation Corps. He was inducted into military service in 1941 and was assigned to New Guinea where he was severely wounded in the hip. He spent the remainder of his military service in Australia before returning home to Arkansas. He died on January 9, 1998. (Courtesy of Museum of American History.)

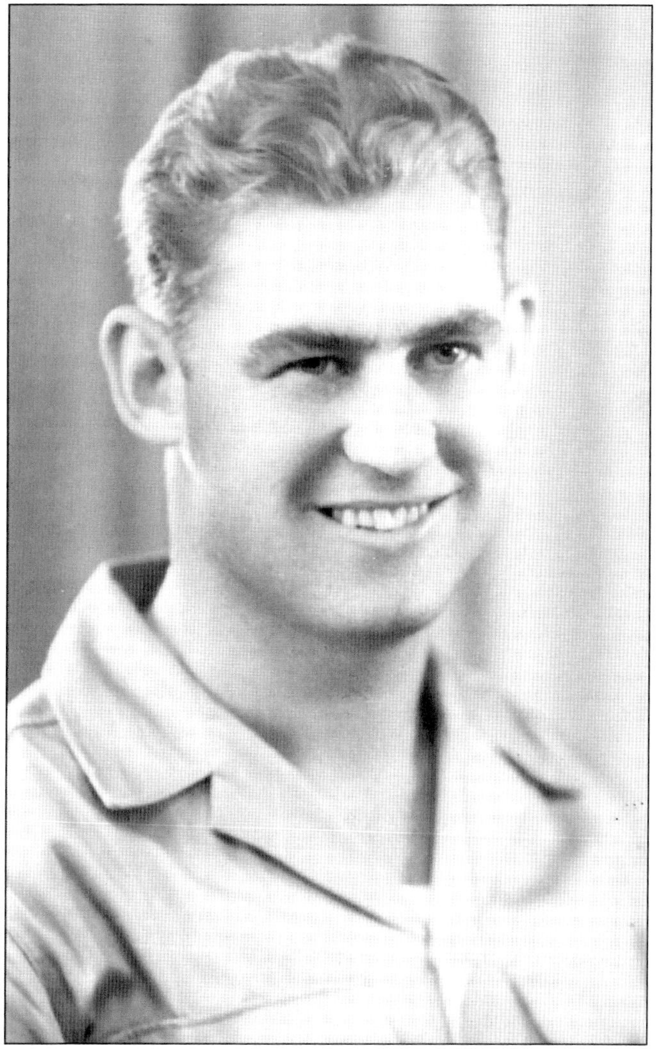

This headstone marks the burial site of Grover Payton Collier at Mount Springs Cemetery. (Courtesy Museum of American History.)

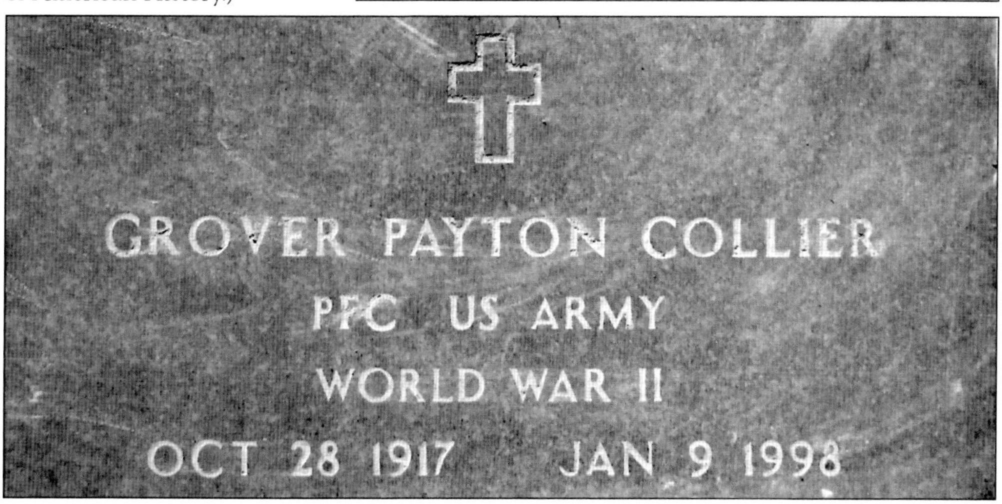

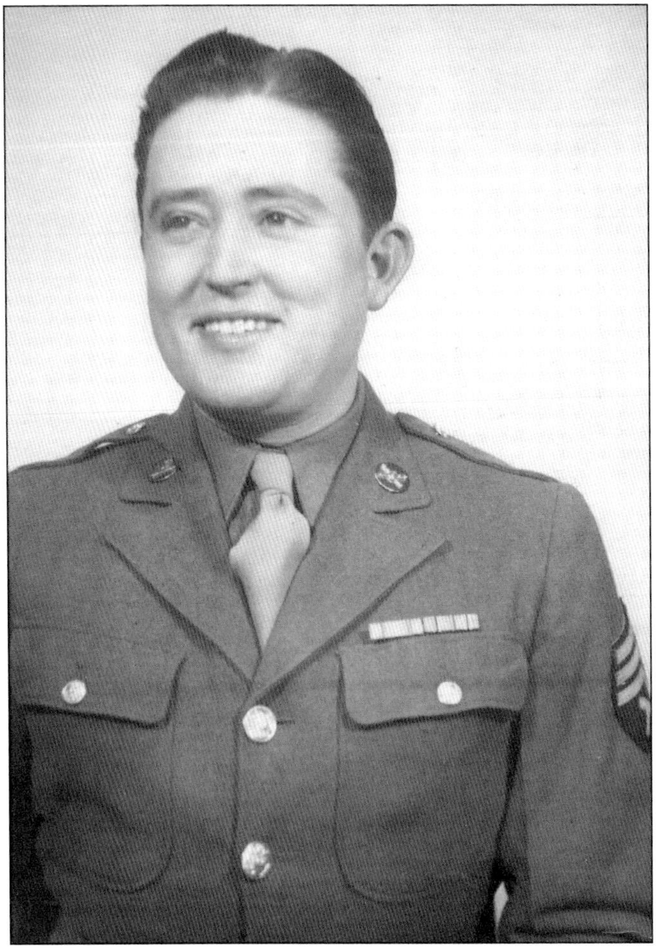

Future mayor Willie Ray was serving in the Arkansas National Guard just prior to America's entry into World War II. Holding the rank of tech sergeant in the 206th Coastal Artillery Headquarters Battery, he was stationed at Dutch Harbor, Alaska, for approximately two years. (Courtesy Gene Ray.)

Military life was difficult in wartime Alaska. Attack by enemy forces was always a threat, as was extreme cold. However, there was still time for entertainment, even in such an isolated area. Sergeant Ray is shown in this photograph with fellow soldiers and movie star Joe E. Brown, who had traveled the great distance to entertain the troops. (Courtesy Gene Ray.)

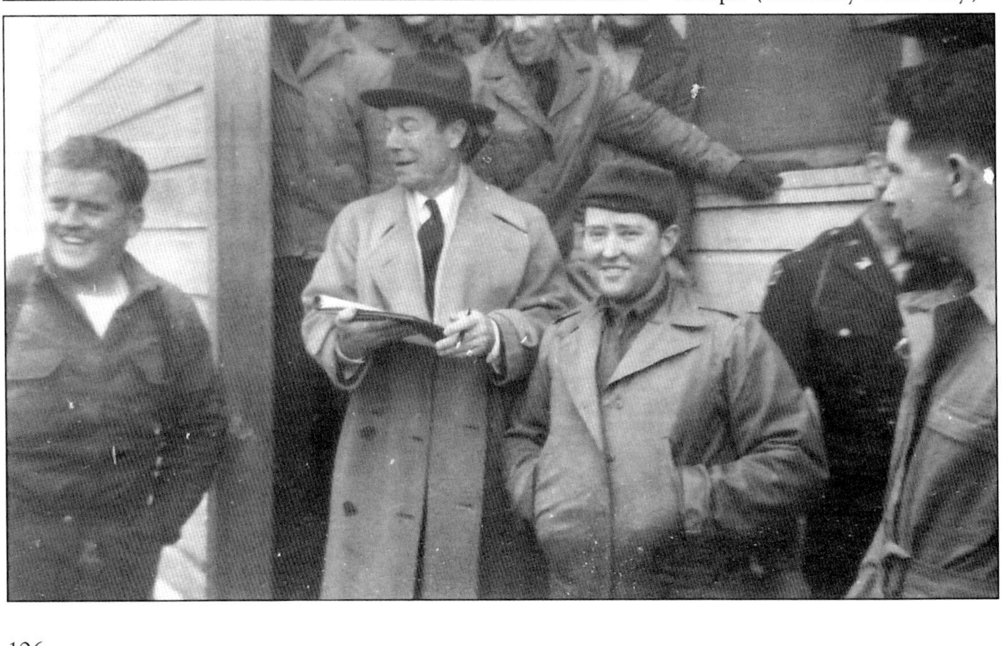

Longtime resident Jack Carrington served his country during the Korean War. He was inducted into the US Air Force on January 3, 1951, completing his basic training at Lackland Air Force Base. He is shown here pulling duty as a security officer while stationed at Lowry Air Force Base in Denver, Colorado. He was discharged in 1954. (Courtesy Jack and Betty Carrington.)

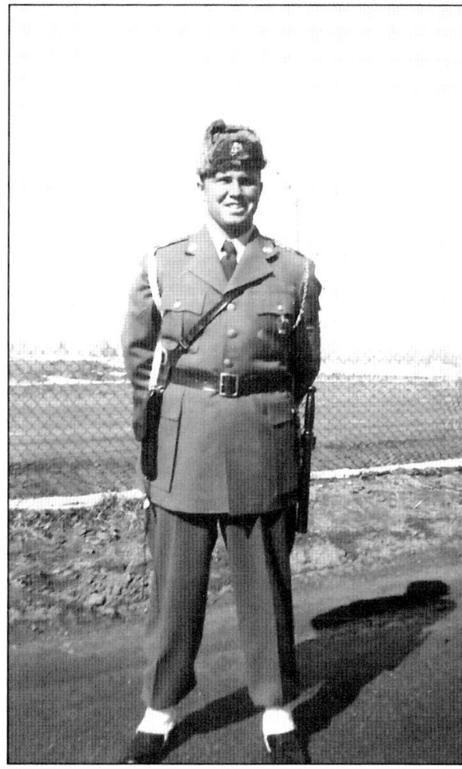

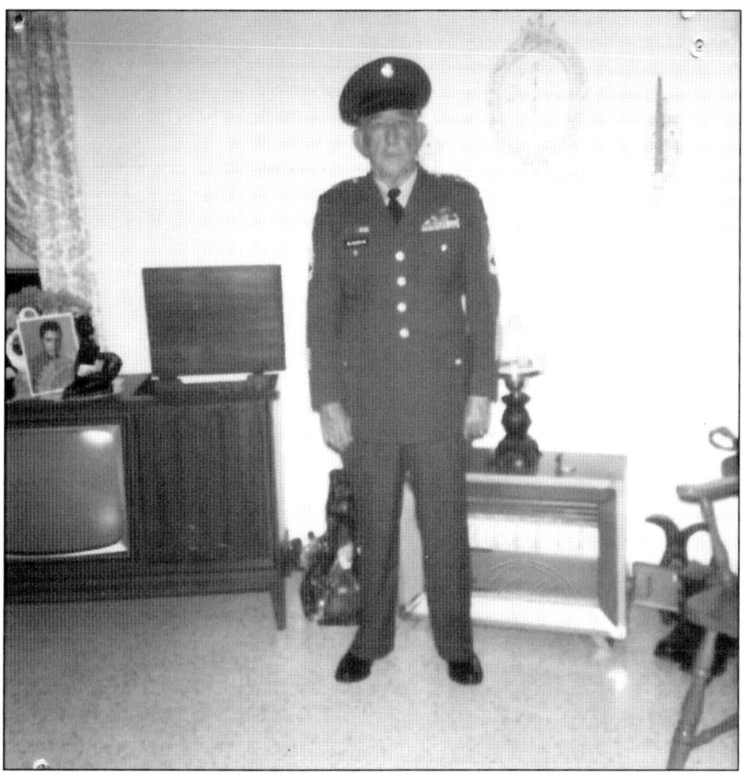

Samuel B. McGloflin, whose son later served in Vietnam, was a member of the 35th Infantry Division during the Korean War in the 1950s. The longtime resident of Cabot was also a member of the first Cabot High School football team in 1926. (Courtesy Joe McGloflin.)

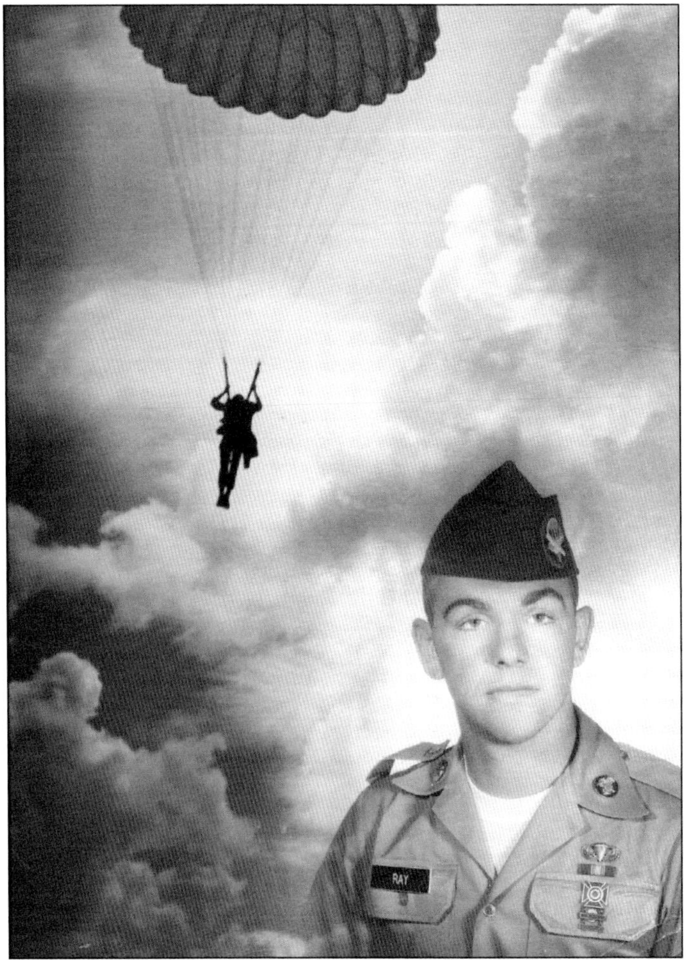

On May 12, 1970, Michael Wayne Ray, 21 years old, was mortally wounded by enemy fire while serving as a member of Company C 173rd Combat Support Battalion (Airborne) in Vietnam. For his "meritorious achievement in ground operations against hostile forces," he was awarded the Bronze Star with 2 Oak Leaf Cluster and a Purple Heart. (Courtesy Museum of American History.)

This headstone marks Ray's burial site at Mountain Springs Cemetery. (Courtesy Museum of American History.)

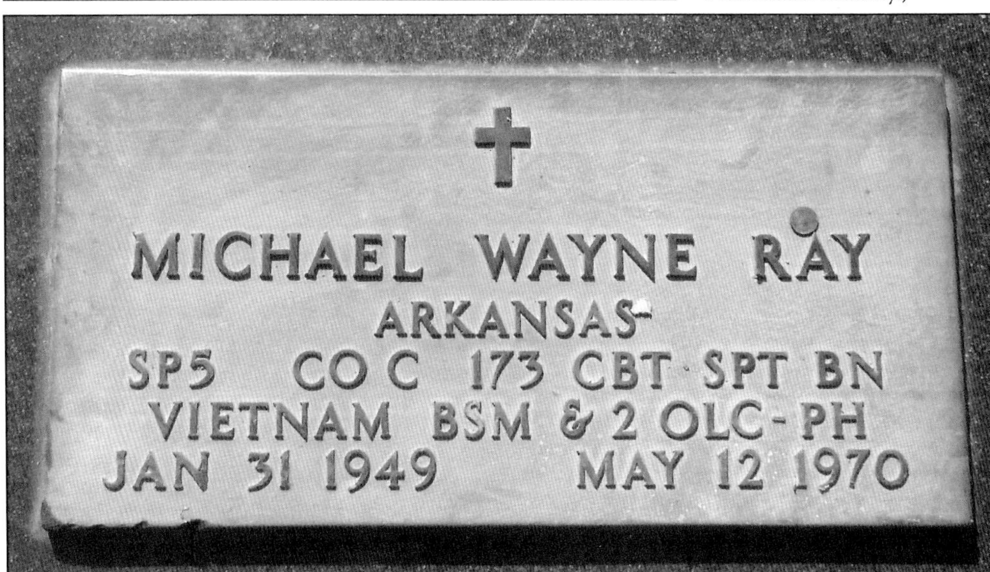

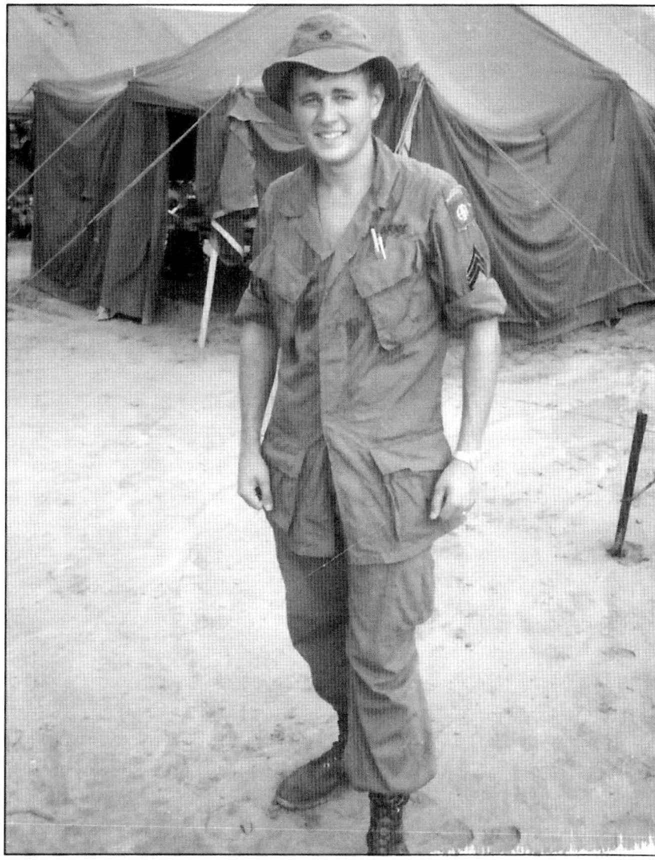

S.Sgt. James Fred Campbell spent approximately one year in Vietnam as a member of the All American 81st Division. For his service in combat, Campbell was awarded the Bronze Medal on two occasions. After returning to Cabot, he became a well-respected community leader and businessman. (Courtesy Museum of American History.)

Of the many photographs that Sergeant Campbell sent home to his family, perhaps the strangest was this one of him draped with a huge snake. Helping him hold up the reptile is his South Vietnamese interpreter, Trung Kim Qui. (Courtesy Museum of American History.)

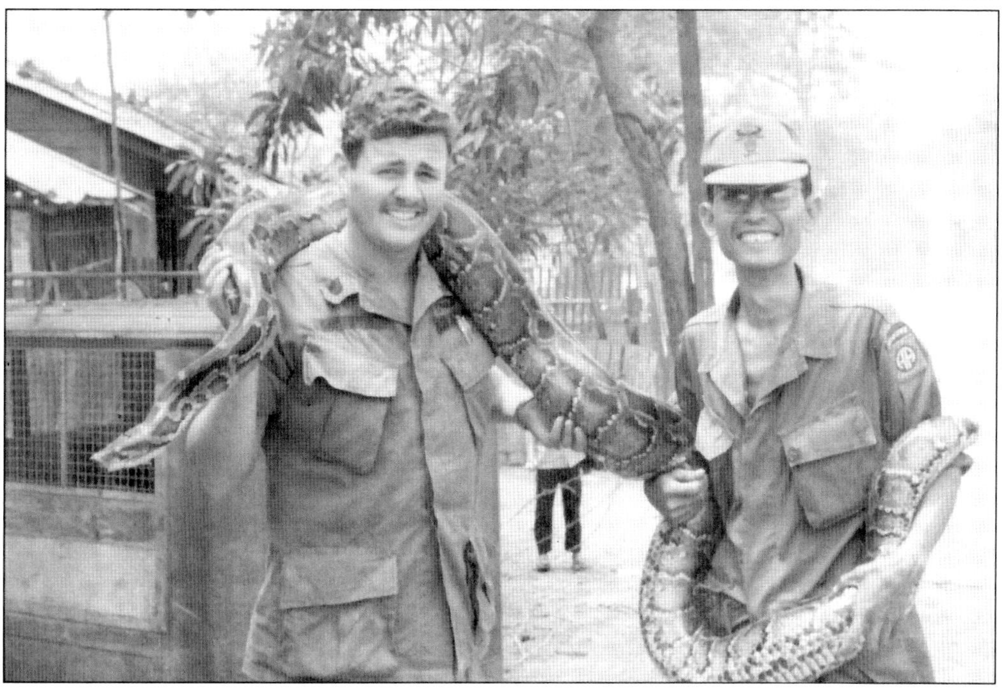

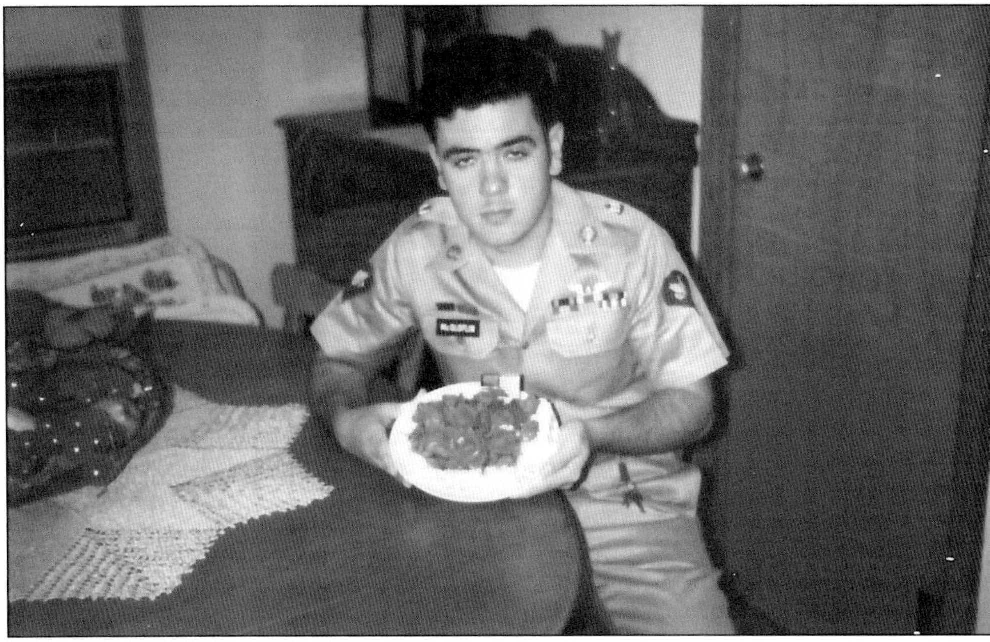

A number of Cabot's young men served their country during the war in Vietnam. One such local boy was Joe McGloflin, who served as a sergeant in the First Air Cavalry Headquarters Company. McGloflin spent approximately four years, 1969–1973, in the service. After returning home, he was employed by the local school district for many years. Today, he is retired but spends much of his time working with local veterans' organizations. (Courtesy Museum of American History.)

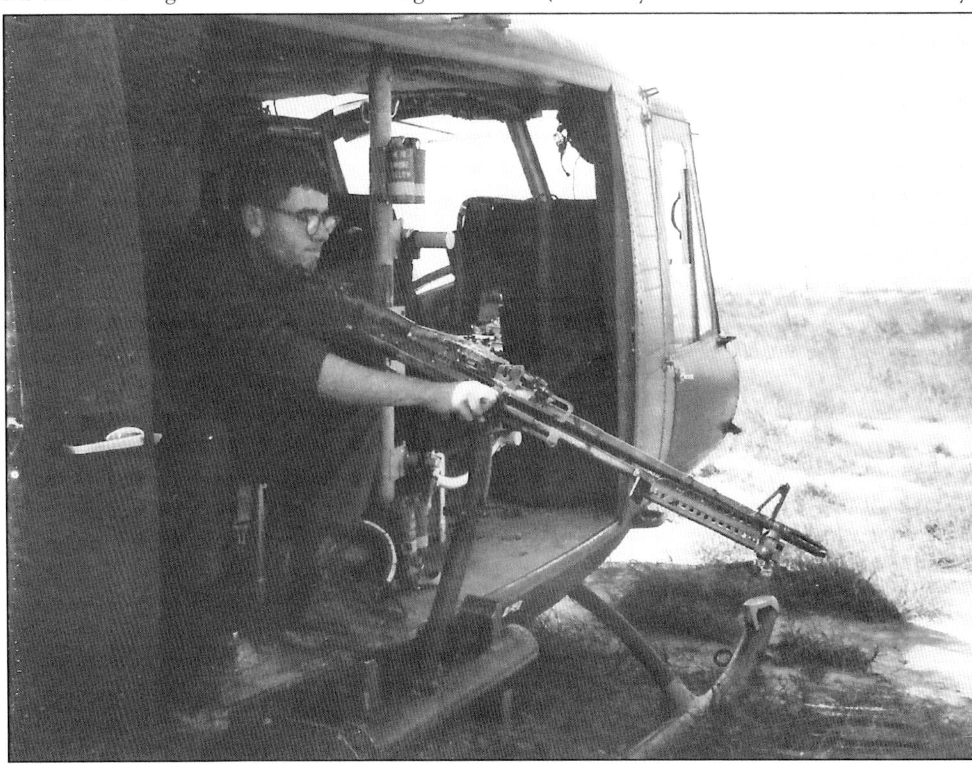

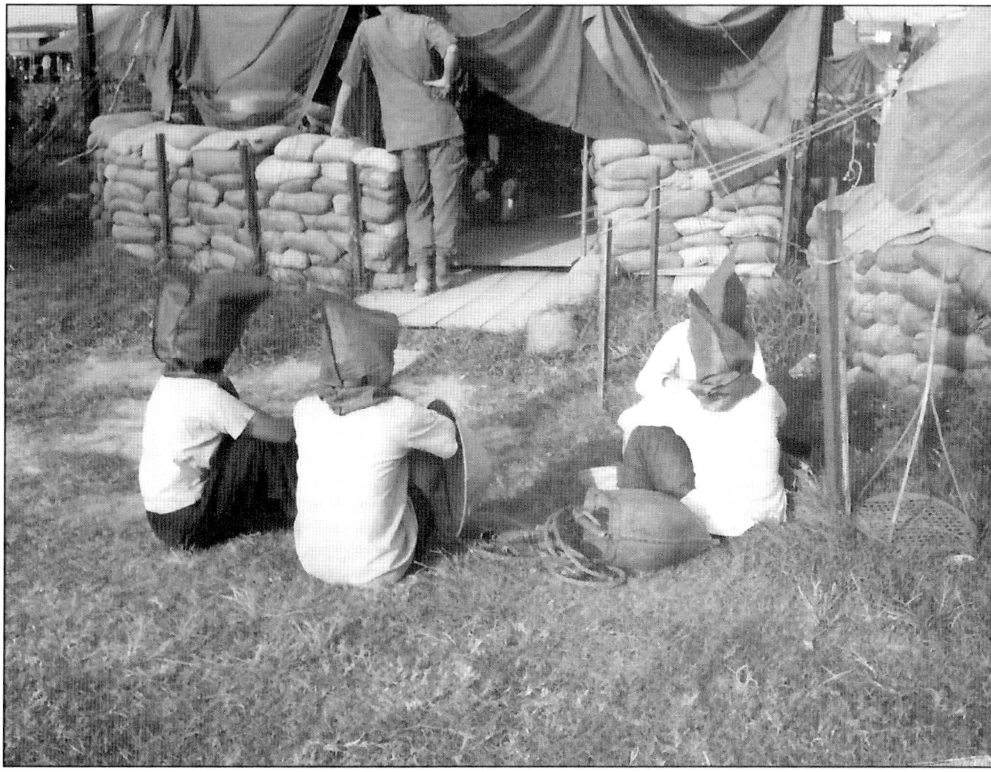

Censorship during a time of war has always limited the information that a soldier can share with family members back home. It is somewhat surprising that this photograph of Viet Cong prisoners, sent home by Freddie Campbell, was able to make it through the stringent military censorship procedures. (Courtesy Museum of American History.)

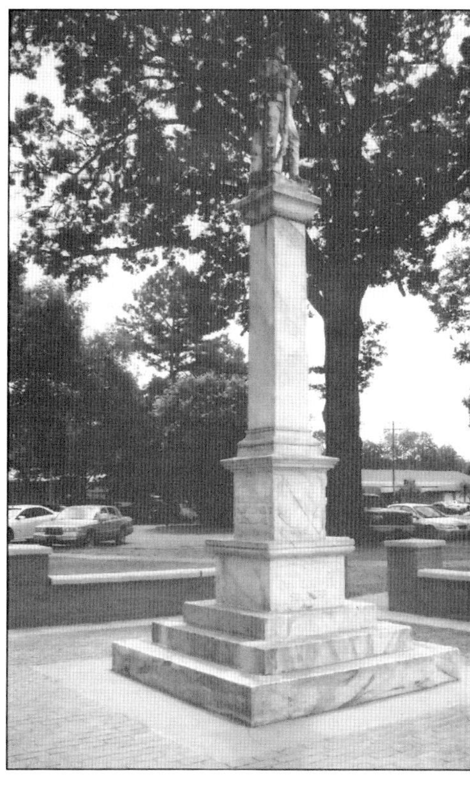

The Confederate Soldiers Monument, located on the grounds of the Lonoke County Courthouse, is the second monument dedicated to the memory of county veterans. The impressive stone monument, topped with a Confederate soldier, was dedicated by a local United Daughters of the Confederacy chapter in 1910. (Courtesy Museum of American History.)

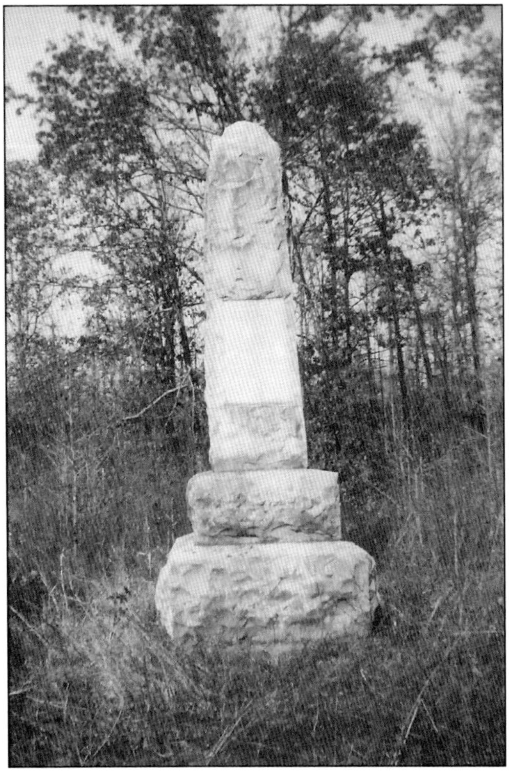

During the Civil War, a camp of Confederate Arkansas and Texas soldiers was established east of present-day Cabot. Many soldiers died from disease and were buried in unmarked graves near their camp, called Camp Hope. It was later renamed Camp Nelson. In 1906, a group of local Confederate veterans established a memorial cemetery and dedicated this 12-foot-tall Batesville marble monument to their fallen comrades. (Courtesy J.O. Isaac Collection from the Museum of American History.)

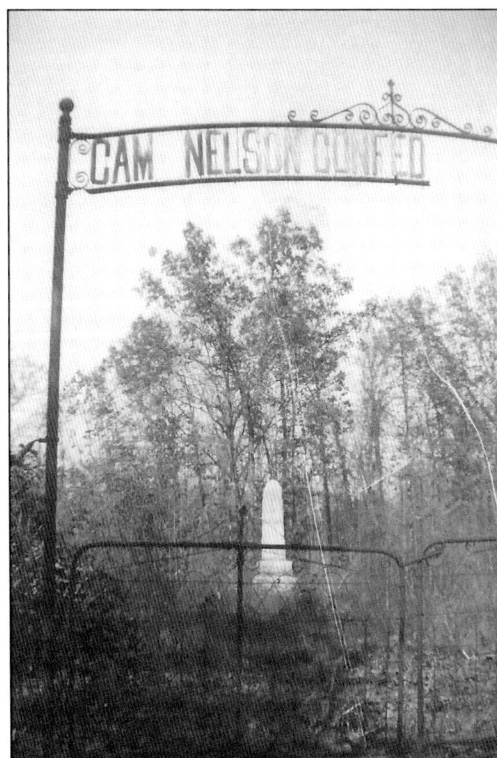

The arched gate is part of the original fence, constructed in 1906, surrounding the graveyard. The overgrown condition of the area can clearly be seen in this 1961 photograph. (Courtesy J.O. Isaac Collection from the Museum of American History.)

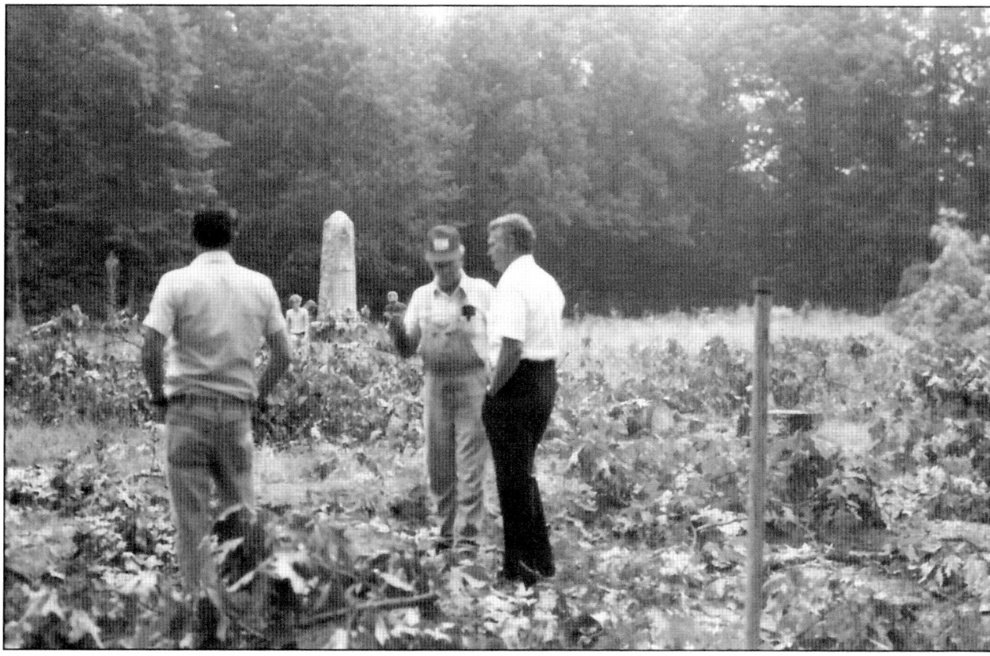

By the mid-20th century, Camp Nelson Confederate Cemetery had fallen into disrepair, as can be seen in this photograph. In 1980, high school ROTC director J.O. Isaac organized an effort to fully restore the cemetery. Isaac, in hat, is seen here speaking to county judge Dud Spence. (Courtesy J.O. Isaac Collection from the Museum of American History.)

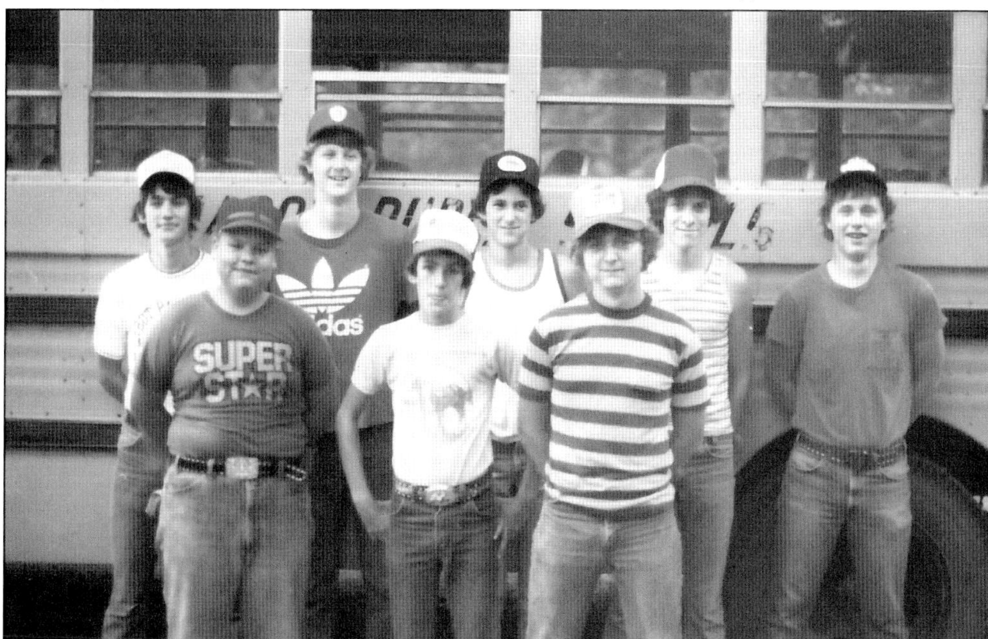

Much of the restoration work was completed by Cabot students in the Future Farmers of America and ROTC programs. A group of FFA members pose for a photograph before beginning a long day of hot work at the cemetery in the summer of 1981. (Courtesy J.O. Isaac Collection from the Museum of American History.)

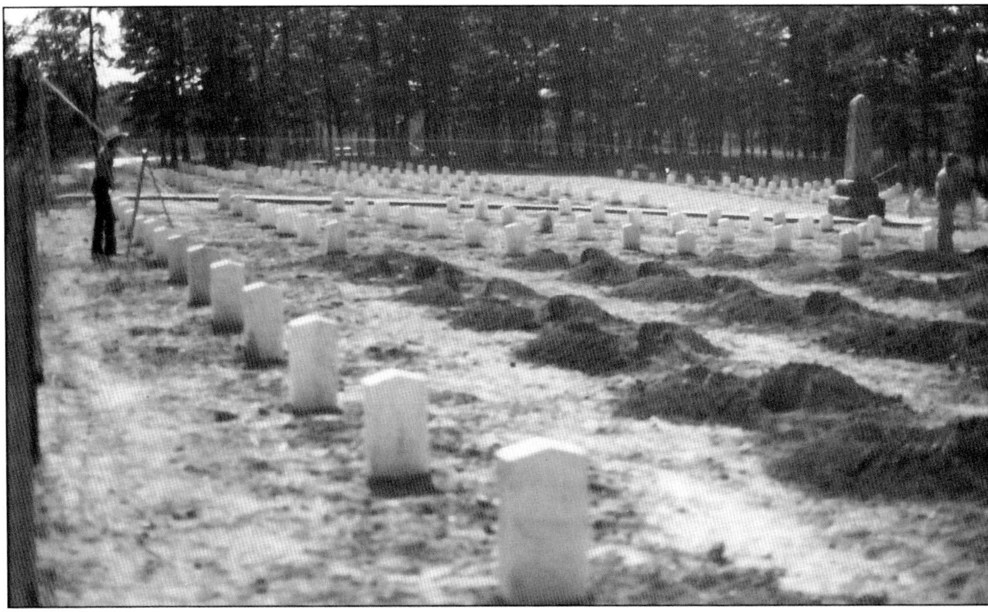

During the restoration, the surface of the cemetery was completely cleared of trees and brush. Many truck loads of earth were brought in to level the area. Once leveled, old headstones were removed and replaced by new marble ones supplied by the US government. (Courtesy J.O. Isaac Collection from the Museum of American History.)

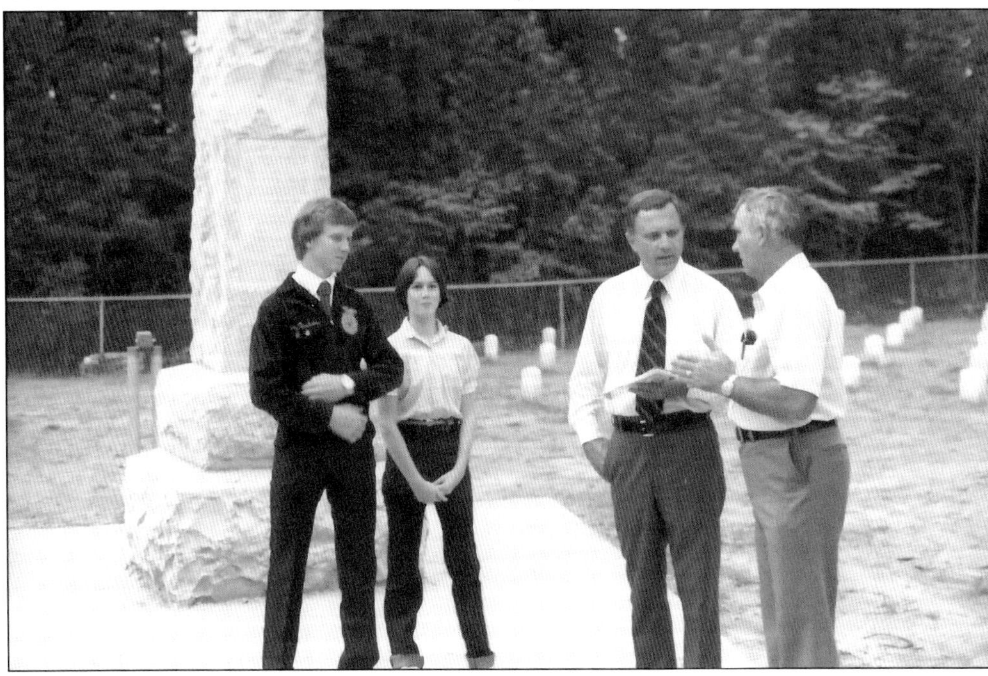

Once work was completed, a rededication was held on April 25, 1982. Among the many dignitaries in attendance were Congressional Medal of Honor recipient Maurice Britt, former governor Orval Faubus, and Gov. David Pryor. Pryor is seen here with J.O. Isaac and Future Farmers of America chapter president Steve Dixon. (Courtesy J.O. Isaac Collection from the Museum of American History.)

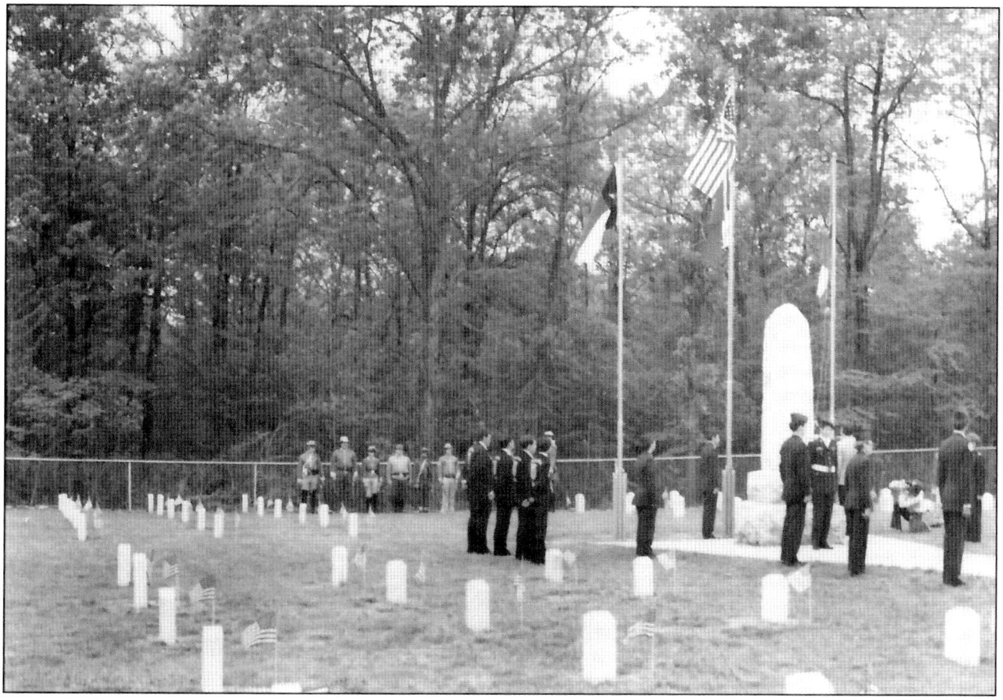

During the 1982 rededication ceremonies, Civil War reenactors prepare to fire a volley in salute while FFA members stand at attention. The raised flags were of special significance, having been flown over the capitols of Arkansas, Texas, Virginia, and the United States. (Courtesy J.O. Isaac Collection from the Museum of American History.)

The five men shown here at the rededication ceremony in 1982 were the driving force in the restoration of the cemetery. They are, from left to right, (first row) ROTC instructor J.O. Isaac and history teacher Mike Polston; (second row) Future Farmers of America teachers Arnold Kaylor, Lynn White, and Larry Robertson. (Courtesy Museum of American History.)

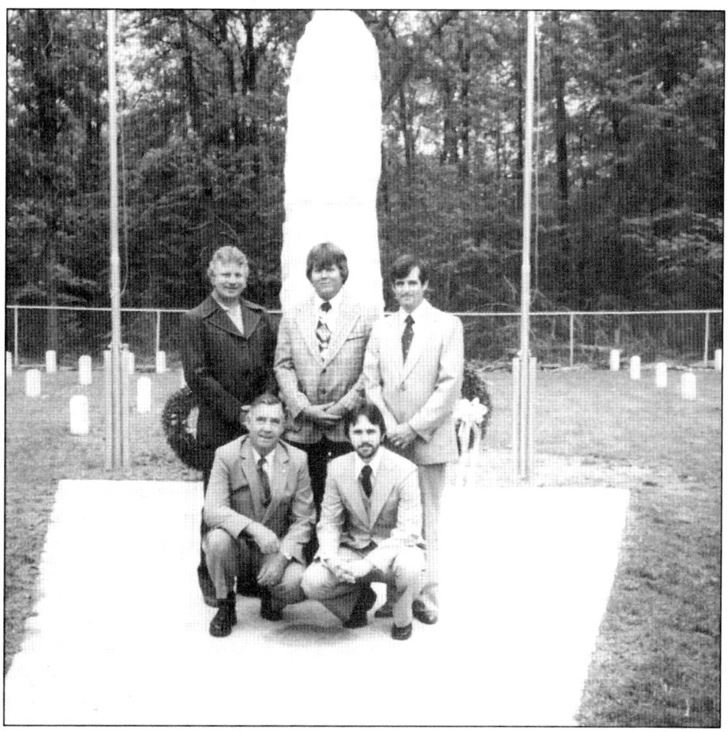

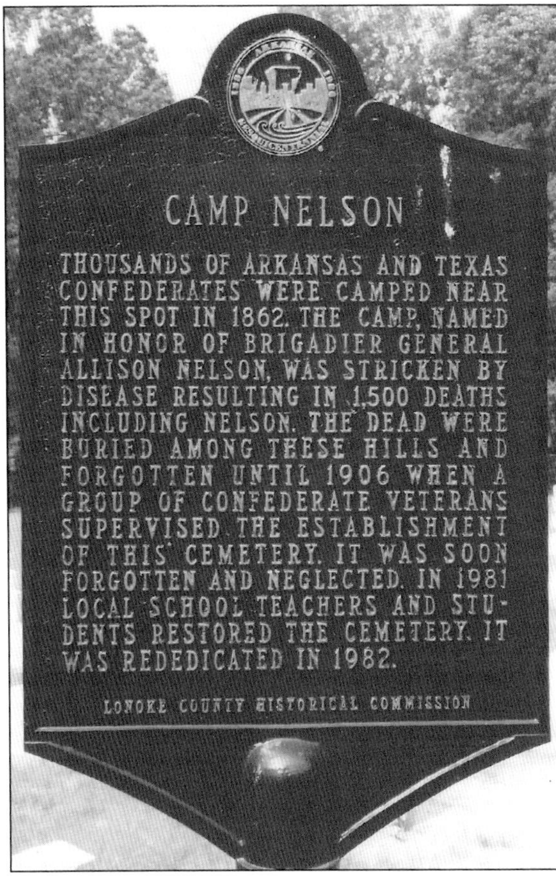

Since the restoration of the cemetery in 1981, activities continue that recognize the historical importance of the site. The cemetery is regularly cleaned, flags are placed on individual graves each year, and the historical marker seen here was placed in 1986. Recently, the original 1906 gate, which was in poor condition, was removed and a new one installed. (Courtesy J.O. Isaac Collection from the Museum of American History.)

As of today, Camp Nelson Confederate Cemetery, which is surrounded by residential neighborhoods, is a well-kept area visited by many people each year who wish to honor their ancestors who fought in the Civil War and may be buried in one of the graves marked Unknown CSA Soldier. (Courtesy Museum of American History.)

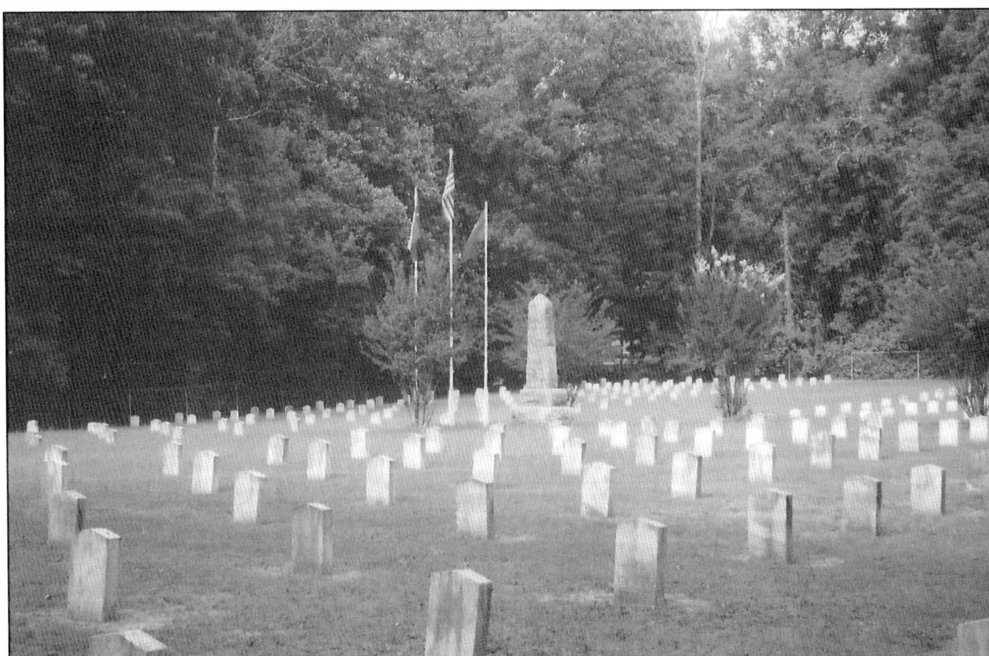

Nine

FACES

People are what make a community. The history of any city is created by numerous persons, who through the years, have contributed to the advancement of their home. Cabot is no different. Many times, communities are home to famous people who are familiar to most everyone. More often, the people of a community who make a difference are the ones that remain anonymous and behind the scenes, never seeing their photographs in the newspaper or on television. The history of Cabot, during its almost 140 years, has been made by all these people.

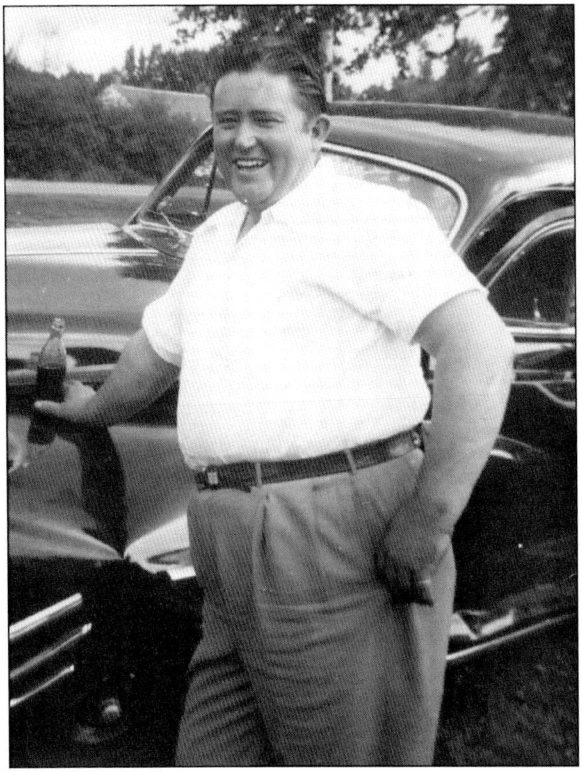

Longtime mayor Willie Ray is credited by many local residents as being the leading force in the recovery of the town after the destructive tornado. He became a leading businessman after moving to Cabot in the 1950s. He served on the city council and as mayor for many years. (Courtesy Gene Ray.)

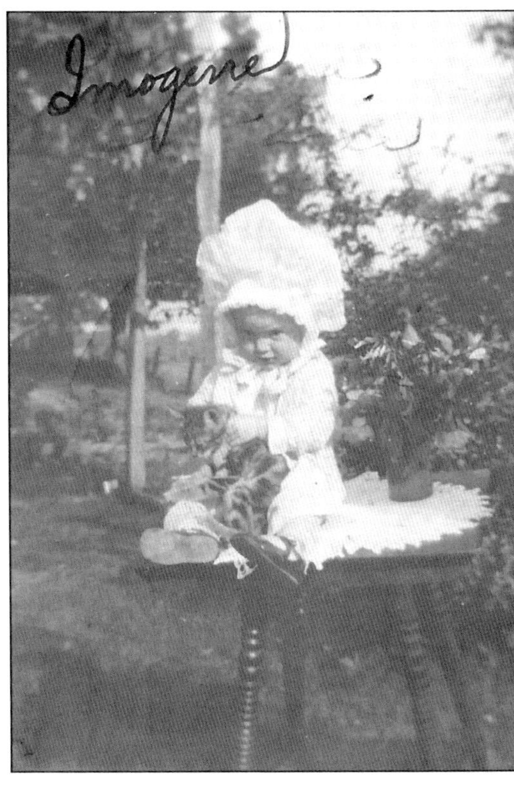

Imogene Ray, while not receiving as much attention as her husband, the mayor, has always actively promoted the city. For many years, she has operated several properties, including a popular beauty parlor. She is shown here as a young child. She still remains a popular local personality. (Courtesy Gene Ray.)

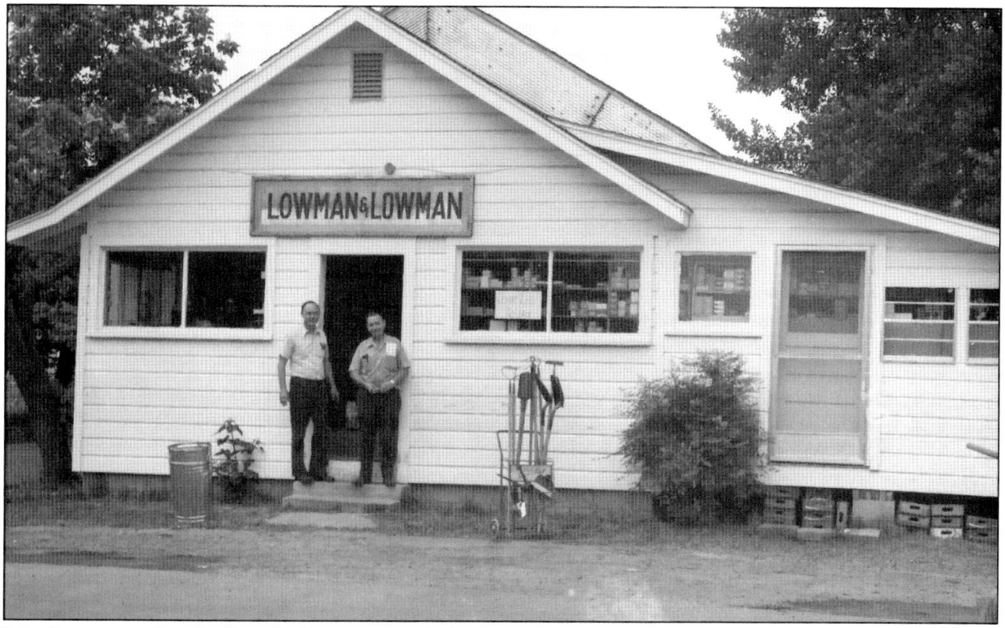

The Lowman family founded a mercantile business during the town's early development. By the mid-20th century, the store was owned by brothers Jack and Jake. The popular store was located in downtown, except for a brief time after the tornado, when it was housed in this building on West Olive Street.

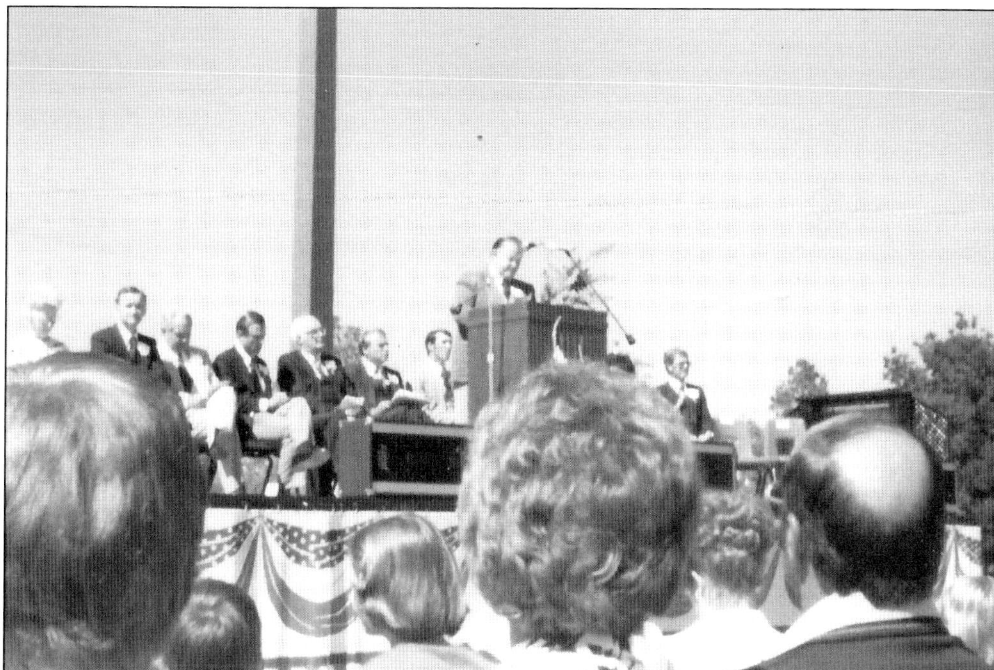

On October 1, 1978, as a part of the first CabotFest, a new community center was dedicated in an afternoon ceremony. A number of local dignitaries were present on the speakers' platform. Among them was Mayor Willie Ray, shown delivering a speech. Also shown are Supt. Don Elliot, fifth from left, and city leader Dearl Dixon, seventh from left. (Courtesy Gene Ray.)

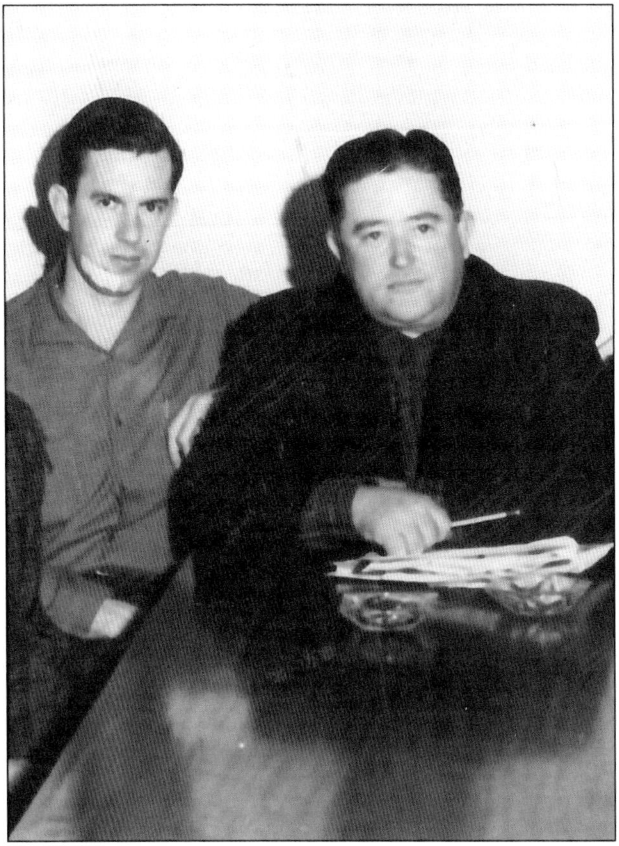

J.M. Park (left) was an important city business leader in the 20th century. An active promoter of the city, Park was a member of a prominent financial family and was president of the Bank of Cabot for a number of years. He served as chairman of the city's centennial committee in 1991 and was a leading force in the establishment of a scholarship program for local students. He is seen here with Mayor Willie Ray.

After the bombing of Pearl Harbor on December 7, 1941, Americans across the United States lived in a paranoid world, expecting an attack at any moment on the mainland. Ernest L. Bailey, local businessman and Cabot mayor in the 1940s, caused considerable panic when he flew his airplane over the town dropping advertising leaflets to promote his business.

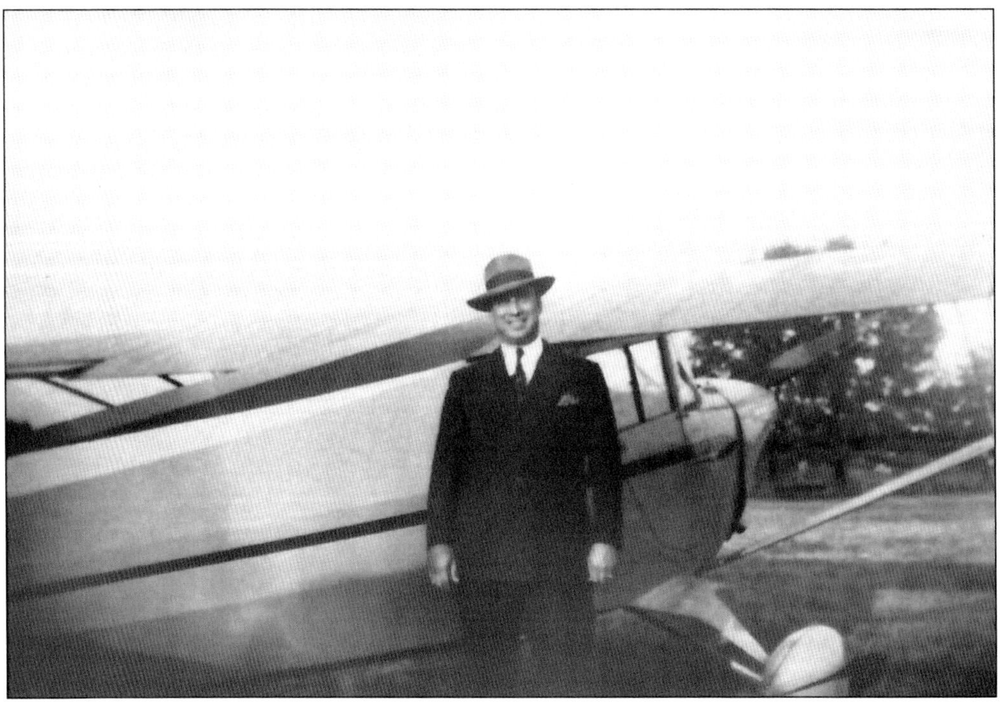

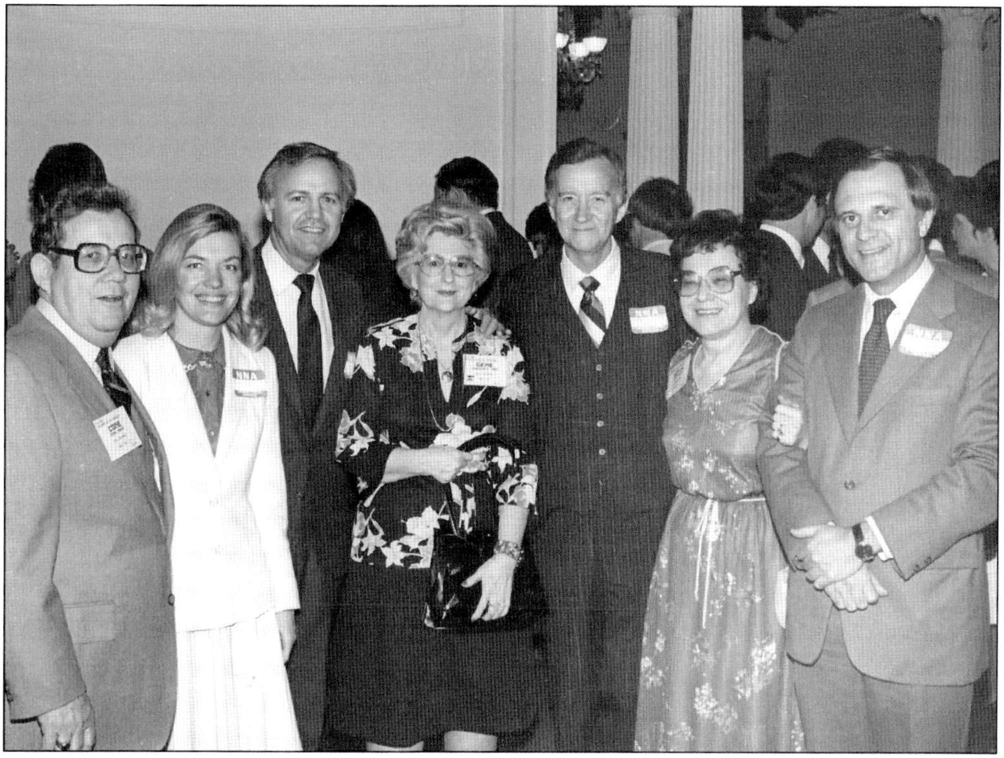

In 1955, Cone and Betty Magie founded the *Cabot Star* newspaper. Within a short time, they had purchased the competing *Cabot Herald* and merged the papers into the *Cabot Star Herald*. Over the years, the Magie family became the major publishers of newspapers in Lonoke County and the surrounding area. The *Star Herald* remains in publication, though under different ownership. They are, from left to right, Cone Magie, Lana Bethune, Congressman Ed Bethune, Gene Ray, Congressman John Paul Hammerschmidt, Betty Magie, and Sen. David Pryor. (Courtesy Gene Ray.)

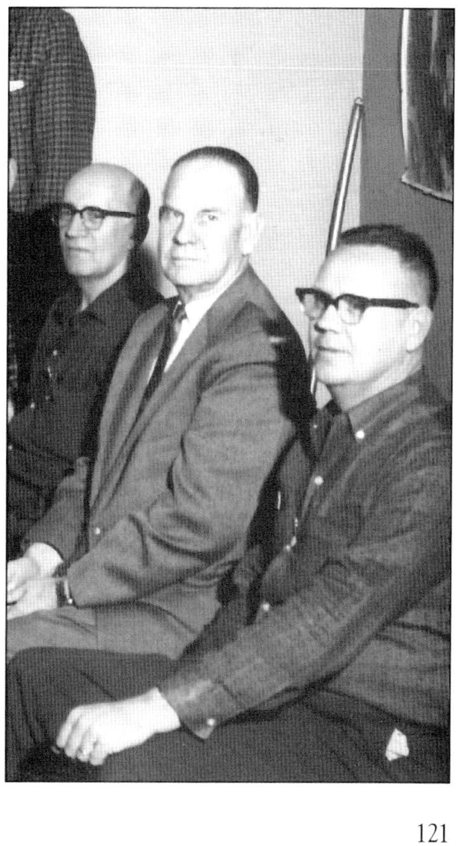

Charlie Templeton, a graduate of Cabot High School, was one of the most respected citizens of the area. An active promoter of the development of the city and owner of a well-known grocery store, Templeton was also a loyal supporter of the school system. He is shown here as a member of the Cabot City Council. From left to right are Bernard Ray, unidentified, and Charlie Templeton.

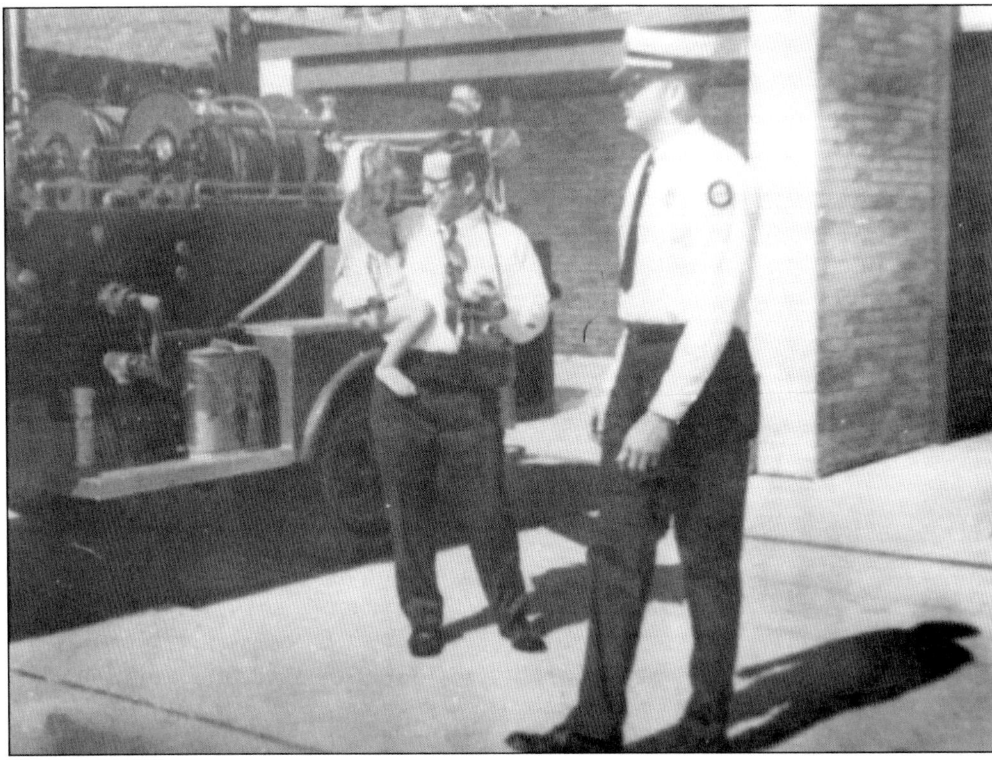

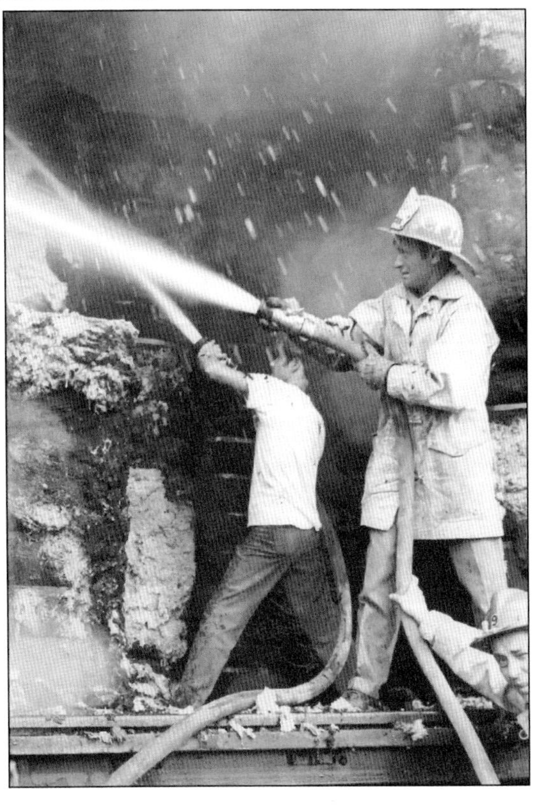

Many years have passed since a single downtown fire station was sufficient to protect Cabot residents in the event of fire. Today, several stations are located throughout the area to protect the city. For many years in the 1970s and 1980s, respected fire chief Carl Pickard directed the efforts of the fire department. Pickard is shown here at a station open house sometime in the 1970s. Newspaper publisher Cone Magie is standing to his right.

The firefighter has always been an important and admired figure in local communities. On each call, these public servants risk life and limb to protect others. A Cabot fireman during the 1970s demonstrates to a young boy the safe technique necessary to extinguish a fire.

Wood's Feed Store has been a mainstay of downtown Cabot since at least the mid-20th century. The store, which has been at the same location on Highway 89 for many years and is one of the last surviving "old" city businesses, remains an important supplier for local farmers. Former owner Fred Wood is shown here attending an early-1960s meeting. From left to right are (first row) Wood Bodie, Wood, and Bernard Ray; (second row) unidentified.

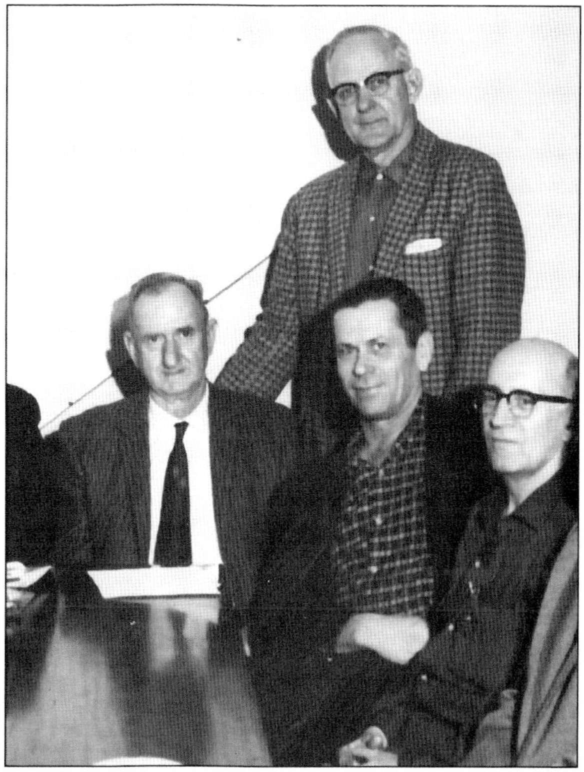

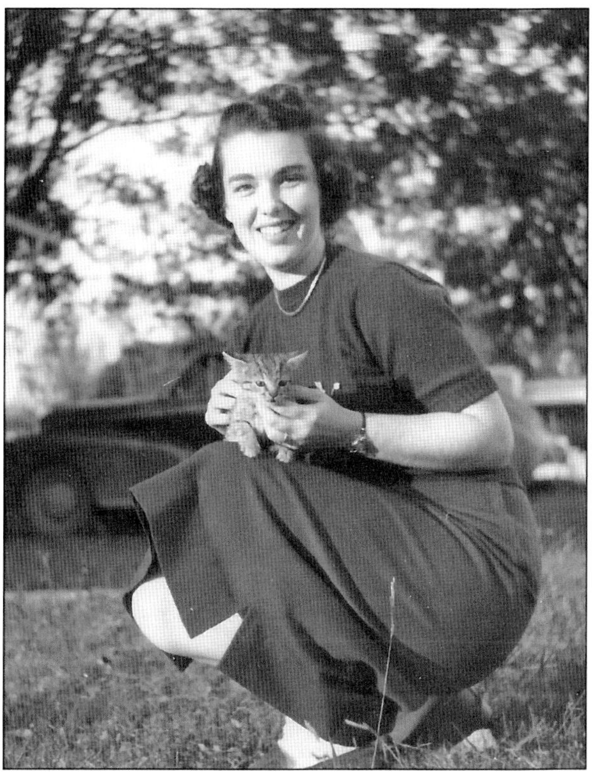

Judy Lowman, wife of the late Jake Lowman, has been one of the most active supporters for the preservation of Cabot history. She was a leading force in the planning of the very successful city centennial celebration in 1991 and has been very supportive of the local museum with her many donations. (Courtesy Museum of American History.)

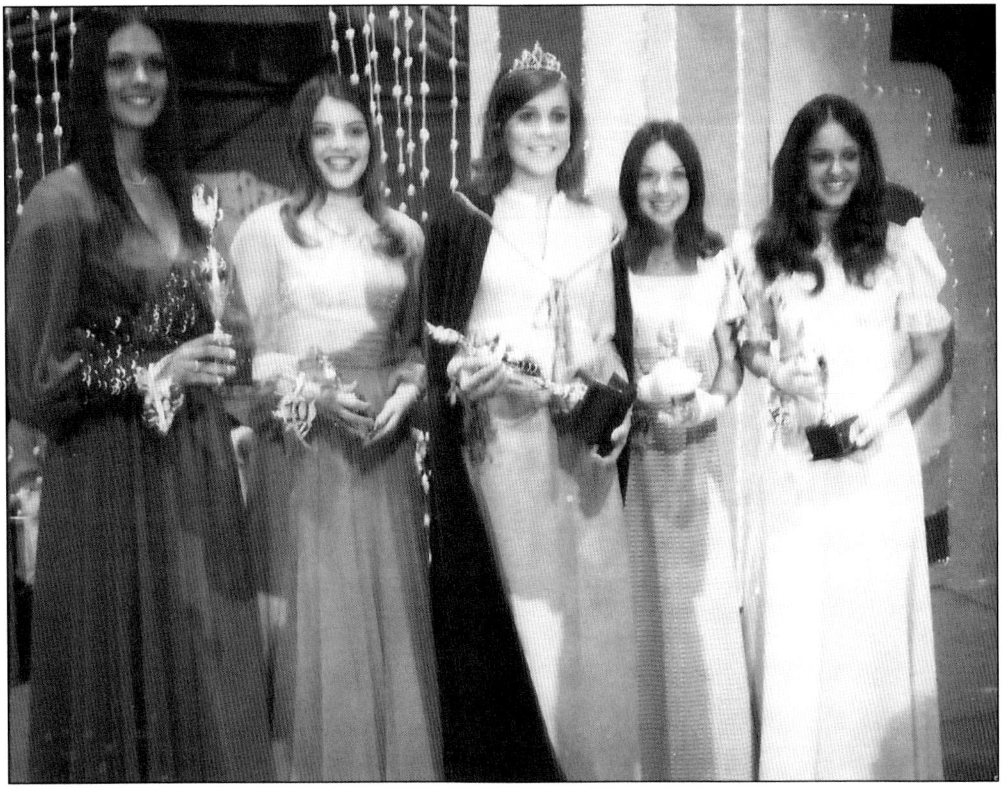

Miss Cabot, a beauty pageant for high school girls, was first held in 1953. The tradition continues today, as each spring a new Miss Cabot is crowned. A newly crowned Miss Cabot is shown here with other contestants in the early 1970s. (Courtesy Museum of American History.)

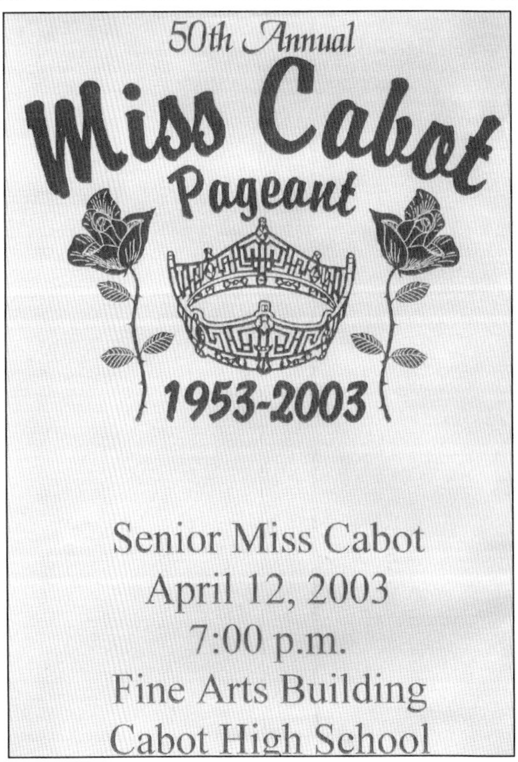

In 2003, the Miss Cabot beauty pageant celebrated 50 years. The local beauty queen, who participates in a variety of city activities, continues to be crowned annually. (Courtesy Museum of American History.)

In 1982, twenty-year-old Terri Utley became the only Arkansas contestant to be crowned Miss USA. The Cabot High School graduate went on to finish as fourth runner-up in the Miss Universe competition. She later embarked upon a career as a journalist and motivational speaker.

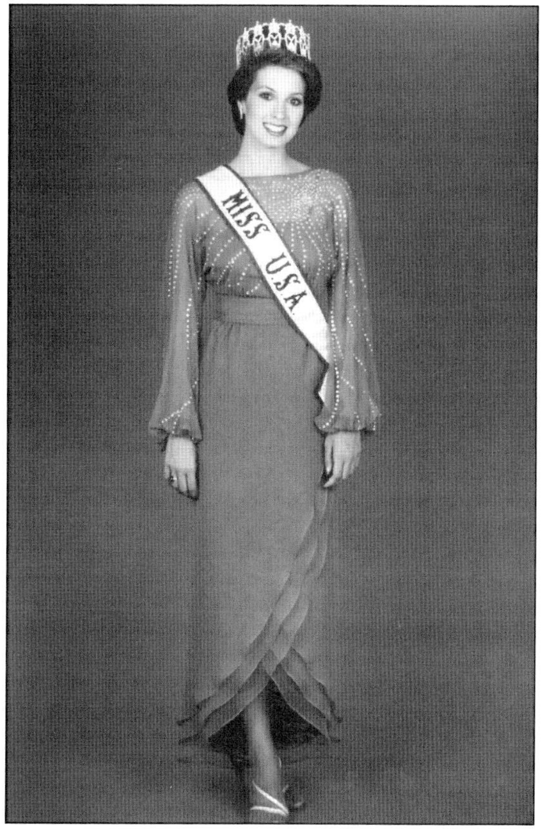

Not long after Terri Utley was crowned Miss USA in 1982, a celebration was organized to welcome the beauty queen home. Among the many activities was a parade through the city streets, in which Miss Utley was the honored quest.

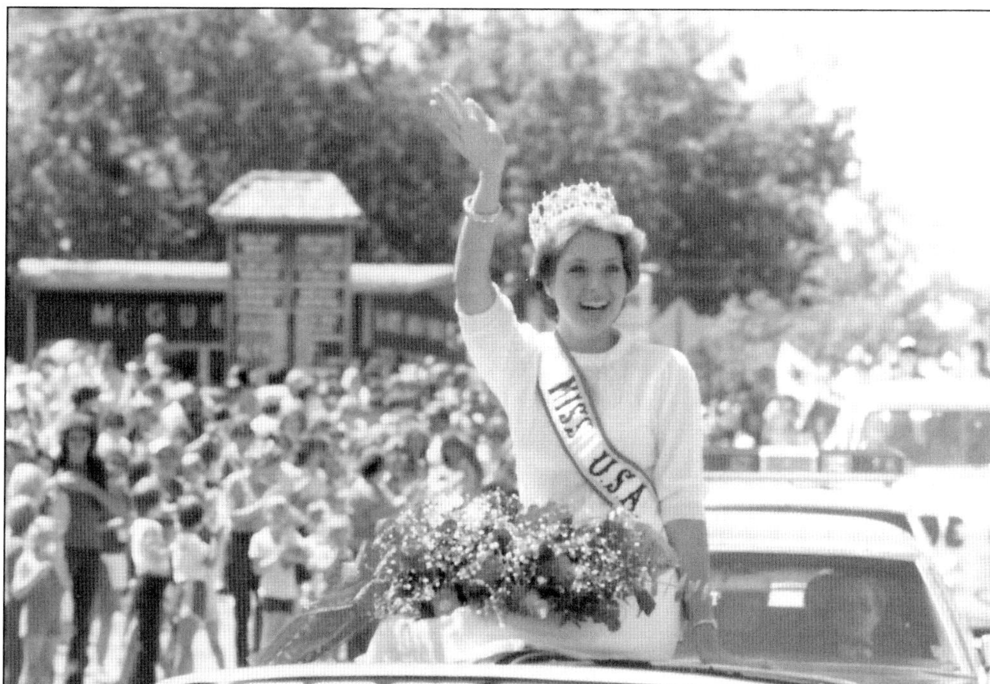

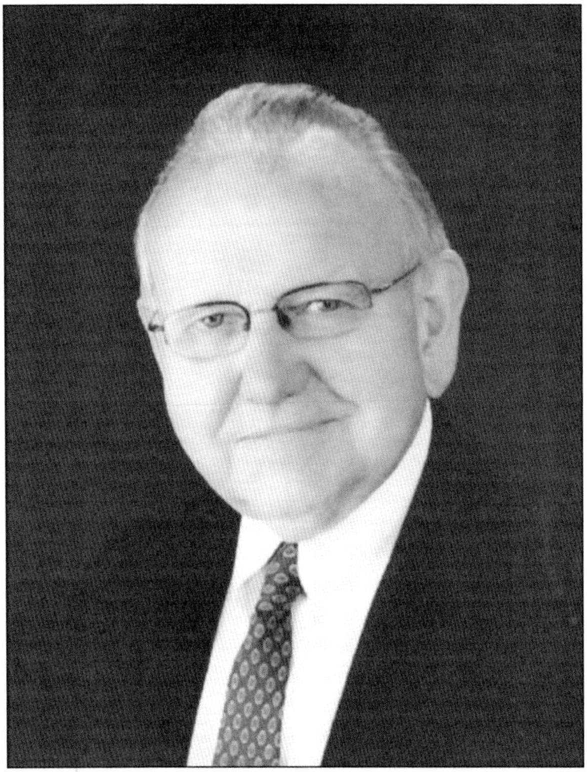

Elected in the fall of 2010, longtime resident Bill Cypert is the current mayor of the city of Cabot. The responsibility of directing the development of one of the state's fastest growing cities rest on his shoulders. (Courtesy Museum of American History.)

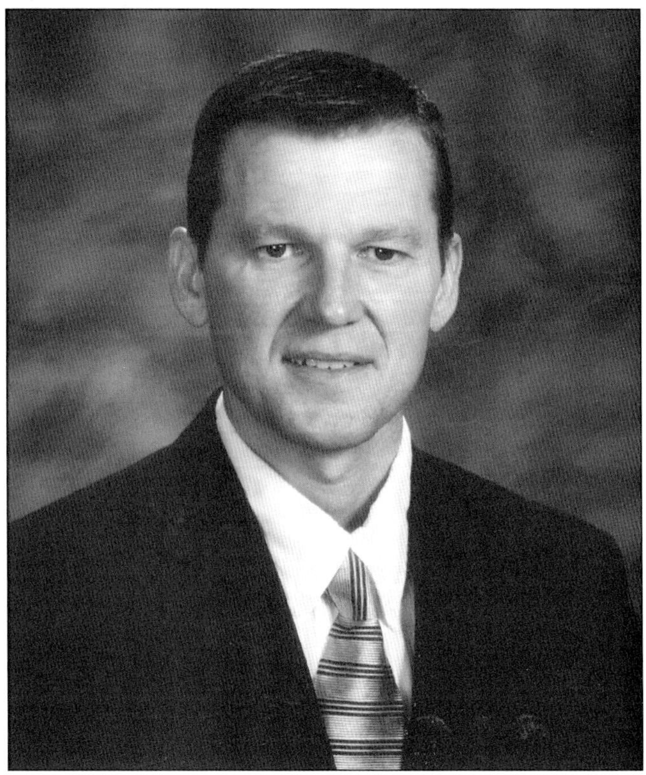

Perhaps as important as the responsibilities of the mayor are those of the school superintendent. Since 2007, the school, which is one of the state's largest and fastest growing, has been lead by Dr. Tony Thurman. Prior to his present position, Dr. Thurman held the position as principal at Middle School South and then as principal of the high school. (Courtesy Museum of American History.)

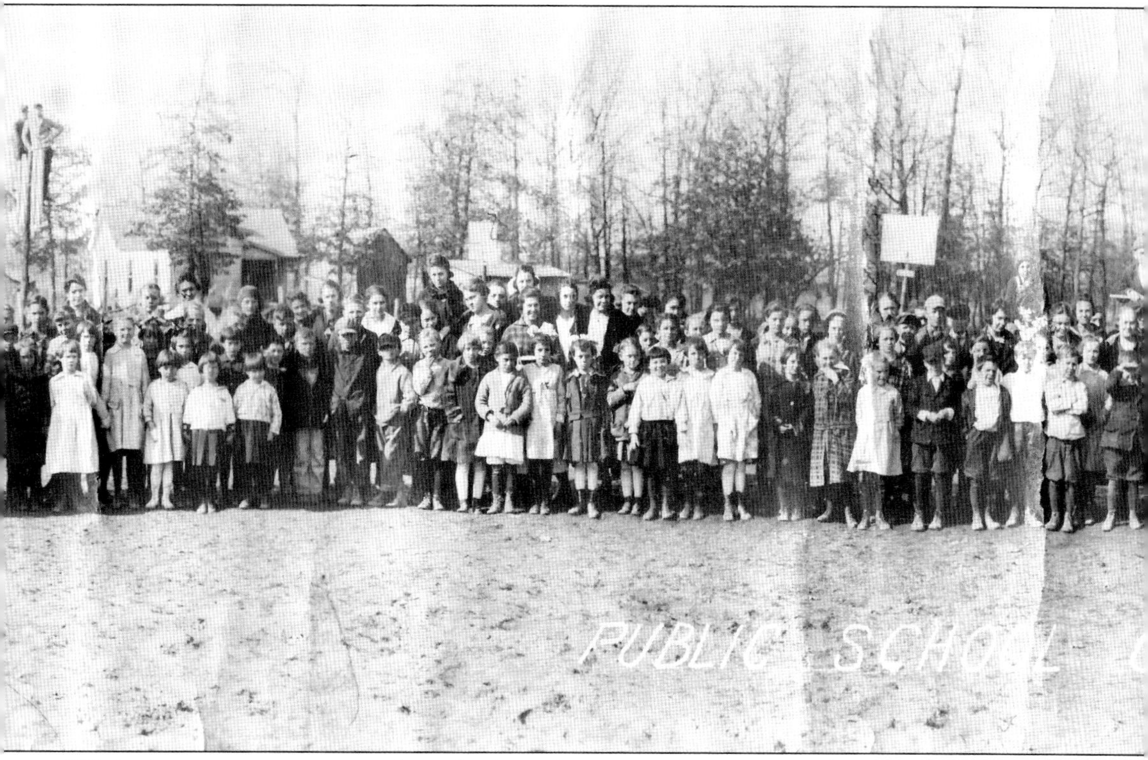

While there are many personalities both in the past and present who have made important contributions to the history of Cabot, most locals would agree that it is the school system and its students who define the community. Today's students, just like those shown here in the 1920s, will lead the city into the future.